The Hippocrene U.S.A. Guide to

BLACK FLORIDA

The Hippocrene U.S.A. Guide to

BLACK FLORIDA

Kevin M. McCarthy

Hippocrene Books
New York

Acknowledgments

The author wishes to thank the following for help with this book: Elizabeth Alexander, Carolyn Allen, Russel Belous, E.W. Carswell, Bruce S. Chappell, Weona Cleveland, Joan Crawford, Sarah Crawford, Paul S. George, Gary Goodwin, Jim Haskins, Leland Hawes, Bob Hudson, George Keyes, Eugene Monroe, David Nolan, Harold Nugent, Marsha Dean Phelts, C. Spencer Pompey, Dorothy Thompson, James L. Wattenbarger, Brent R. Weisman, Sharon Wells, and Arline Westfahl. I finally wish to thank my patient children (Katie, Brendan, Erin, and Matthew) and my devoted wife, Karelisa Hartigan, for her guidance and companionship.

For information, address:
HIPPOCRENE BOOKS, INC.
171 Madison Avenue
New York, NY 10016

Library of Congress Cataloging-in-Publication Data
McCarthy, Kevin
The Hippocrene U.S.A. guide to Black Florida / Kevin M. McCarthy.
p. cm.
Includes bibliographical references and index.
ISBN 0-7818-0291-1
1. Afro-Americans—Florida—History. 2. Historic sites—Florida—Guidebooks. 3. Florida—Guidebooks. I. Title. II. Title: Hippocrene USA guide to Black Florida.
E185.93.F5M38 1995
975.9'00496073—dc20 94-45345
CIP

Printed in the United States of America.

Contents

Foreword

According to the 1990 census, which I will be using throughout this book, African-Americans make up 14% (1,759,534) of Florida's total population (12,937,926). Despite being such a sizable minority in the state, they have often been slighted in history books and travel literature. To help rectify that situation, the 1990 Florida Legislature established a Study Commission to document the many contributions that blacks have made to the history and culture of Florida. One result of that Commission's work was the publication of the *Florida Black Heritage Trail,* a listing and short description of 141 sites throughout the state that were important in that history.

The purpose of this book is to describe those sites in more detail, placing them in historical and geographical context and adding more places that might have been included in that original list. The Florida sites are testimony to the rich contributions blacks have made to the state's art, music, and drama, as well as religion, education, and political leadership. But those sites also include evidence of the bigotry, persecution, and slaughter inflicted by the Ku Klux Klan and other hate groups; that mistreatment permeated the past and continues overtly and subtly to the present.

Here then is a description of several hundred sites throughout the state that have been important in the black history of Florida. The author hopes that residents and visitors alike will use this book as a guide to a part of our history and heritage that has too often been neglected in the past.

Introduction

African-Americans have come a long way from the time in the 1700s, when slave catchers scoured the territory's swamps looking for runaway slaves, to the 1990s, when a black became Chief Justice of the state's Supreme Court; from 1816, when American gunboats killed dozens of blacks hiding in the Negro Fort on the Apalachicola River, to 1976, when Pensacolian Daniel "Chappie" James, Jr., became the nation's first black four-star general; from the days of slavery, when Florida's plantation owners would not allow their slaves to read or write, to the 20th century, when Florida writers like James Weldon Johnson and Zora Neale Hurston produced great works of literature.

This is the story of many of those Floridians, those who prospered and those whom whites killed, those who immigrated here looking for an opportunity to raise their families and those who were born and lived here their whole lives. Florida owes much to the blacks who have lived and worked here. They toiled hard in building Henry Flagler's railroad to Key West; they brought much prosperity to north Florida towns by turpentining and logging; and they have provided its schools and churches and legislatures with outstanding examples of great people.

This book describes the many Florida sites associated with blacks over the last 466 years, when a black man came ashore with the early Spanish explorers in the Tampa area to the

1990s, when distinguished leaders were elected to the U.S. House of Representatives. One can visit most of these sites, many of which are open to the public as museums or memorials, and appreciate how much the African-American has contributed to Florida's progress.

In addition to the positive achievements of blacks in Florida, the history of this land/territory/state is also full of tragedies inflicted on them: the many lynchings by hooded terrorists, the burning of black towns like Rosewood, and the decades-long practice of separate and unequal facilities for non-whites. Fortunately, that history does have many bright spots: the site of the first free community of ex-slaves in North America (Fort Mose near St. Augustine), the establishment of the country's oldest black incorporated municipality (Eatonville), major league baseball's modern integration (Daytona Beach), and the longtime home of America's oldest man (Bartow).

No one can really deny that Florida has a long way to go to achieve racial harmony, that in fact racial discrimination still exists in Florida today. The Tallahassee bus boycott in the 1950s, the St. Augustine civil rights demonstrations in the 1960s, and the Tampa and Miami race riots of the 1980s clearly indicate the frustrations felt by countless blacks toward the slowness of integration. As we approach a new century, one can only hope that progress will continue to be made in race relations and in the affording of equal opportunity to all.

Chapter 1

American Beach

Amelia Island at the northeastern tip of Florida has had a long and varied history that involved slavery and later an attempt by blacks to establish a beach of their own. Up until the United States acquired Florida from Spain in 1821, the peninsula's many inlets and islands, especially along the east coast, provided smugglers easy access to inland markets. The U.S. outlawed the importation of slaves in 1808, but, because Florida was still under the nominal power of Spain, many smugglers simply moved their operation south and used northern Florida as a means of bringing slaves into the U.S. from Africa. Between 1810 and 1820 smugglers brought in some 60,000 slaves and sold them throughout the South.

Amelia Island's main town of Fernandina prospered from the profits of the slave trade and attracted its share of traders, pirates, and criminals. After the American Civil War and into the middle of the 20th century, segregation throughout the country, but particularly in the South, would not allow blacks to mix with whites in public places, including beaches. Because blacks wanted a beach where they could swim in the ocean and not be subject to the harassment of whites, they settled in **American Beach**, a small community at the southern end of Amelia Island.

American Beach was preceded by another black settlement in the area, an independent community of blacks who had lived at a nearby site, Franklin Town, since 1865. Those early inhabitants had been slaves on a plantation run by Samuel Harrison, a South Carolina planter who had acquired the land during the time when the English controlled Florida (1763-1783).

After the American Civil War ended in 1865, newly freed slaves homesteaded property or bought acreage in the area, earning a livelihood from fishing, farming, and ranching; many of those homesteaders eventually received title to the land during Rutherford B. Hayes's presidency (1877-1881), at a time when Florida land cost as little as 50 cents an acre. The descendants of those early settlers sold the land in 1972 to a development company that later built the luxurious Amelia Island Plantation.

The man behind the establishment of the 200-acre American Beach was A.L. Lewis, the founder and president of the Afro-American Life Insurance Company (see Jacksonville below). In 1901, Lewis and six others had each invested $100 to establish the Afro-American Industrial and Benefit Association, or the Afro as people referred to it, to enable blacks to pay just 10 cents a week for funerals. The company eventually changed its name to the Afro-American Life Insurance Company and did much to provide low-cost health and burial insurance to thousands of blacks, most of whom could not obtain insurance from white companies. The insurance company prospered and by the 1950s became a $5 million corporation.

Besides its own schools, medical staff, and recreation center, the Afro bought the beach on Amelia Island and built several summer cottages for its executives and for those employees who won company sales contests. The company called the beach American to remind everyone, blacks as well as whites, that the people there were just as American as others in this country. American Beach became so popular that up to 10,000 people would gather there on weekends

The seaside resort of American Beach has entertained thousands of black vacationers over the years. Credit: Kevin M. McCarthy

and holidays. In 1935, residents built the first permanent buildings, including houses, hotels, even a candy factory.

The street names in American Beach honored blacks associated with the Afro-American Life Insurance Company that established the resort. Lewis Street, the main street and the only one allowing beach access, was named for A.L. Lewis (1865-1947), one of the founders of the company. Streets that honored his relatives were Julia (for Julia Brown Lewis, his mother), Mary (for Mary F. Lewis, his first wife), and Leonard (for his grandson, J. Leonard Lewis). Other streets named for company officials were Waldron (for Rev. J. Milton Waldron, pastor of Jacksonville's Bethel Baptist Institutional Church from 1892 until 1907 and an organizer of the Afro), Gregg (for Rev. E.J. Gregg, pastor of Mount Zion A.M.E. Church and the first president of the Afro when officials chartered it in 1901), Price (for Rev. Alfred W. Price, president of the Afro after Rev. Gregg), Ervin (for Louis Dargan Ervin, the first full-time agent for the Afro and later its vice president), Lee (for William H. Lee, a vice president and secretary of the Afro), and Stewart (for Ralph Stewart, Sr., a company secretary).

American Beach suffered from major storms over the years, such as Hurricane Dora in 1964, which destroyed some of the town's buildings. Once integration opened up the country's beaches to everyone in the 1960s, the popularity of the black settlement declined. In 1990, officials there dedicated the six-acre **Burney Park Beach Front Park**, the first such park in Nassau County to honor a black. Open to all from 7 a.m. to 7 p.m., the park honors I.H. Burney II, who served as president of the Afro from 1967 to 1975 and was the only president who was not a blood relative or son-in-law of Lewis and his descendants. Today, American Beach finds itself in the midst of very exclusive resorts that cater to the wealthy, some of whom would like to buy large tracts of American Beach. In fact, with more and more whites moving into American Beach, some black residents fear that the town may undergo major changes which may eventually cause people to forget the proud legacy the town has had.

Directions:

American Beach is to the east of AIA on the southern end of Amelia Island in Nassau County.

Further Reading:

Michelle Genz, "Pride and Prejudice," *Tropic*, Sept. 30, 1990.

Pat Keck, "Burney Park Dedication Held at American Beach," *News-Leader* [Fernandina Beach, Florida], Oct. 24, 1990, p. 7A.

Leedell W. Neyland. *Twelve Black Floridians*. Tallahassee: Florida Agricultural and Mechanical University Foundation, 1970, pp. 53-59.

Marsha Dean Phelts, "The Beginnings of an American Beach for African Americans on Amelia Island," *The Florida Star* [Jacksonville], Feb. 5, 1994, p. 14; Feb. 12, 1994, p. 13; Feb. 19, 1994, p. 13; Feb. 26, 1994, pp. 12-13.

Suzie Siegel, "American Beach," *The Tampa Tribune*, February 27, 1993, BayLife, pp. 1, 5.

One other note about Fernandina Beach to the north of American Beach. A black photographer who lived there, Richard Samuel Roberts (1880-1936), operated The Gem Studio and took many photographs of the local community before moving, in 1920, to South Carolina, where he continued taking photographs of blacks. After he died, researchers discovered more than 3,000 of his glass photographic plates, many of which they published to show a good cross-section of Southern blacks.

Further Reading:

Thomas L. Johnson and Phillip C. Dunn, editors. *A True Likeness: The Black South of Richard Samuel Roberts, 1920-1936*. Columbia, S.C.: Bruccoli Clark, 1986.

Chapter 2

Arcadia

Fifty miles southeast of Sarasota is DeSoto County's Arcadia, a small inland town that used to be cowboy country complete with range wars and cattle rustling. It still has an annual rodeo that attracts many participants and was the only Florida town profiled in Norman Crampton's book, *The 100 Best Small Towns in America* (New York: Prentice Hall, 1993). Some have speculated that the name of the town goes back to Arcadia, Greece, and symbolizes peace and serenity, but it actually comes from the first name of the daughter of an early settler.

The town was incorporated in 1887 and became the county seat of DeSoto County. Around 1900 it had its own Chautauqua in a large amphitheater for concerts and lectures, but time and the lack of good jobs have forced many young people to leave town after graduating from high school. Blacks moved to the area in the 19th century to work in turpentining and phosphate and on the building of the Florida East-West Coast Railroad between Arcadia and Bradenton. Racial problems broke out from time to time and lynchings occurred, for example, in 1892, when angry whites lynched a black man for allegedly killing an official of the Arcadia Phosphate Company. Today the population of Arcadia according to the 1990 census is 6,488, of whom 1,958 (30%) are black.

As recently as 1968, writer Richard Nellius could write that the town's 1,800 blacks lived in segregated slums in the southwest part of town called "The Quarters." And while the schools were integrated, the downtown restaurants and lunch counters were not. The bus station cafe tried to justify such segregation with a sign that read:

> This is a privately owned business. It is not based on municipal, county, state or federal property. It is not a public utility, school, church or polling place. We receive no grants or subsidies from any city, county, state or federal funds. We reserve the right to seat our patrons or deny service to anyone.

A series of nationwide race riots in 1967 led to the establishment in Arcadia of an inter-racial group to combat inflammatory rumors, and the sheriff appointed 55 black auxiliary policemen who served without pay to ensure peace in the Quarters. Such steps have helped to secure good relations between the races.

Further Reading:

Canter Brown, Jr. *Florida's Peace River Frontier*. Orlando: University of Central Florida Press, 1991.

George Lane, Jr. *A Pictorial History of Arcadia and DeSoto County*. St. Petersburg: Byron Kennedy, 1984?

Richard Nellius, "Arcadia: Profile of a Small Florida Town," *Floridian* [*St. Petersburg Times*] February 18, 1968: 8-13.

Of significance to blacks is Arcadia's **Hickson Funeral Home**, the town's first black funeral home and possibly the county's oldest continuously operated funeral home, located at 142 S. Orange Avenue three blocks west of U.S. 17 in the downtown area. The funeral home was established in 1924 as the Arcadia Funeral Home and was owned by Mrs. Minnie L. Brown (1884-1975), the step-grandmother of

Eugene Hickson, Sr., the present owner. In 1971, Hickson became the first black elected to the position of City Councilman and later served for four years as vice mayor before becoming mayor of Arcadia in 1979.

Arcadia's black history became front-page news around the country when seven children living at 131 Watson Avenue were poisoned to death in October 1967. Local authorities arrested the children's father, James Richardson, and charged him with the crime, partly because he had taken out a large insurance policy on the children shortly before they died. He was sentenced to die in the electric chair, but had that sentence commuted to 25 years in prison after the U.S. Supreme Court disallowed Florida's death-penalty law.

Washington, D.C., attorney Mark Lane, who wrote *Arcadia* about the killing of the children, was convinced that James Richardson was innocent and wrote in very derogatory terms of Arcadia in the 1960s. In 1989, after spending 21 years in prison, Richardson was freed when an investigator appointed by the governor ruled that the prosecution had obtained his conviction by perjury and the suppression of evidence. From time to time, visitors to the town visit the murdered children's grave site, which is in the very back of **Oak Ridge Cemetery** north of the downtown area and west of U.S. 17.

Directions:

To reach the grave site, enter the main entrance of the cemetery, go .3 miles straight back along the dirt road, and turn right over the little dirt bridge; the graves are on the left at the very back of the rows and near the edge of the cemetery.

Further Reading:

James N. Baker with Howard Manly, "From Tragedy to Travesty," *Newsweek*, April 24, 1989: 68.

Mark Lane. *Arcadia*. New York: Holt, 1970.

"Sheriff Says He's Ready To Act On Murder Charge In Poisonings," *The Arcadian*, November 2, 1967, p. 1+. Plus subsequent editions of this newspaper from Arcadia.

Chapter 3

Avon Park

This pretty little town in Highlands County was created by O.M. Crosby of Danbury, Connecticut, around 1885. As president of the Florida Development Company, he recruited settlers to the area, including several from England's Stratford-on-Avon who gave the town its name. Situated in the geographical center of the state and blessed with many clear lakes, the town has had a history of growing oranges and grapefruits despite some devastating freezes. Crosby began a newspaper, *The Home Seeker*, that successfully lured new residents with such racist advertisements as this one: "Can you imagine a spot where there is no swamp, no malaria, no frost, no mosquitoes, no Negroes, and no liquor sold, and all the people are busy Northerners? Such is Avon Park."

Despite Crosby's intentions to keep them out, blacks began settling in the area in the early part of this century to work in the lumber, turpentine, and railroad businesses, although they were segregated in the southeast part of town called "The Quarters." In 1990, the town had a population of 8,042, of whom 2,431 (30%) were black. One of the most important churches for blacks in the town is **Mt. Olive A.M.E. Church** at 900 S. Delaney Avenue. Church members raised donations to build the structure, whose first pastor

Mt. Olive A.M.E. Church has served the religious needs of this community for over 50 years. Credit: Kevin M. McCarthy

was Rev. A.M. Wardell (or Wadell), and did much of the actual construction themselves. The church is about 10 blocks south of E. Main Street on the corner of E. Green Street and S. Delaney Avenue, which is 1 mile east of U.S. 27 off E. Main Street.

One of its residents that Avon Park honors with a street named after him was Kansas City Royals baseball star Hal McRae (1945-). After attending and playing baseball for Douglas High School in Sebring, he went to Florida A&M University in Tallahassee, where he played baseball for the Rattlers. He then went on to play professional baseball for 19 years, first with Cincinnati (1968, 1970-1972) and then with Kansas City (1973-1987). He played in four World Series and three All-Star Games and also managed the Royals in the 1991 season. He led the American League in doubles (54) in 1977 and runs-batted-in (133) in 1982, all of which helped lead to his induction into the Florida Sports Hall of Fame in 1986.

Further Reading:

Arthur R. Ashe, Jr. *A Hard Road to Glory: A History of the African-American Athlete Since 1946*. New York: Warner Books, Inc., 1988.

Horace J. Fenton. *History of Avon Park, Florida, 1886-1956*. New York: Vantage Press, 1958.

Leoma Bradshaw Maxwell. *The First Hundred Years of Avon Park, Florida*. Avon Park: The Historical Society of The Old Settlers Association, Inc., 1980?

Chapter 4

Bagdad

This small town in Santa Rosa County one mile south of Milton may have been named after the Bagdad of the *Arabian Nights* because both places lie between two rivers on a grassy peninsula. The name may seem strange for a small town in Florida's Panhandle, but, as the famous aviator, Jacqueline Cochran, wrote in her autobiography, *The Stars at Noon*, "Bagdad, Florida, which was my home for about two years, was not like the ancient capital of Persia. But on second thought, maybe it was because I have been to modern Persia and had a look around and for the ordinary folk it leaves almost everything to be desired." (p. 8)

The Florida town, which is between the Escambia and Blackwater rivers, developed from a 19th-century lumber company that relied on slaves to cut trees and work in the mill on Pond Creek. Before the Civil War, those slaves cut and processed the yellow pine lumber and worked in the cotton fields under very difficult circumstances. Insects, diseases like yellow fever, and poor living conditions contributed to the death of many of those workers, but after the Civil War the situation improved somewhat and former slaves were able to own their homesteads and raise their families on their own land.

The plight of the blacks worsened whenever local vigi-

The New Providence Missionary Baptist Church is being restored as a community center and museum. Credit: Kevin M. McCarthy

lante groups took justice into their own hands. Jacqueline Cochran later reported one such tragic incident:

> Once when I was quite a small child I noticed a crowd of men going off into the woods with a Negro prisoner and I tagged along out of curiosity. The Negro was tied to a tree, wood was put all around him and after being sprinkled with kerosene it was set on fire. I was too young then to have any great feeling about the injustice or the loss of life, but I took away from that scene the very bad memory of the odor of burning flesh. (p. 15)

One site of importance to blacks today is the **New Providence Missionary Baptist Church**, one of the oldest churches in Santa Rosa County and the first church built in the county by and for the black community. Emanuel and Delphia Jackson donated the land for a church in 1874, and the sons of pastor Rev. John Kelker, Sr., helped build it. Local residents used the original church structure as a schoolhouse because the area had no public school. The present-day wood-frame building, which was built in 1901, was moved to its present site at 4512 Church Street in the late 1980s, and local authorities have plans to transform the building into a community center and museum about the history of the area. The nearby shotgun-style house is an example of the housing the Bagdad Land and Lumber Company provided for its white workers. The 1990 census showed that Bagdad had a population of 206 blacks (15%) out of a total of 1,416 in the town.

Directions:

Bagdad lies one mile south of Milton and about one mile north of I-10. To reach the church from I-10, take exit 8, drive north 1.8 miles on C.R. 191. Turn left onto Church Street in Bagdad; the church is 1/10 mile on the right, at the corner of Church and Bushnell streets. If you are coming from Milton, drive 1.5 miles south on C.R. 191; turn right on Bushnell Street and go one block to the church.

Further Reading:

Jacqueline Cochran. *The Stars at Noon*. Boston: Little, Brown and Company, 1954.

M. Luther King. *History of Santa Rosa County: A King's Country*. Milton, Fl.: no publ., 1972.

Brian Rucker, "A Bagdad Christmas." Milton, Fl.: Patagonia Press, 1990.

Raymonde Slack-White, "The Grand Old House on School Street," in *When Black Folks Was Colored: A Collection of Memoirs and Poems by Black Americans*. Pensacola: African-American Heritage Society, Inc., 1993, pp. 64-65. It has a description of what Bagdad life was like for blacks in the 1950s, including school, church, and home life.

Chapter 5

Bartow

West-central Florida in the 19th century was very isolated. Because the few white settlers who had begun moving into the area in the early 1830s faced much opposition from the Indians who had been there for decades, the white families clustered near stockades, to which they could retreat if the Indians attacked. In the 1850s, more and more cattle drovers and their families moved into the area, settling down near present-day Fort Meade, while others chose the area around present-day Bartow. Many of those white families brought along their black slaves, forcing them to make the long trip from other southern states on foot with the livestock.

By 1861, enough settlers had moved into the area that officials established Polk County, named after President James K. Polk, who served as the 11th President of the United States from 1845 to 1849. The county seat of Bartow, which was established in the 1860s, honored Confederate General Francis F. Bartow, the first general officer on either side to die in the Civil War. In the Reconstruction period after the Civil War, Polk County became an important citrus and cattle center and later a phosphate mining area. When the South Florida Railroad reached Bartow in 1884 and made the hauling of phosphate easier, many people moved there, and the town prospered.

The Lawrence Brown Home may be the oldest black residence in Bartow. Credit: Kevin M. McCarthy

The railroad, as well as the citrus and phosphate industries, attracted to the town many workers, including blacks, who usually lived in the southeast part of town between Parker and Bay streets and Second and Tenth avenues. Churches, stores, schools, lodges, and a movie theater flourished in that area during the first quarter of this century, but most have long since been demolished. One of the few remaining buildings from that time and possibly the oldest black residence in town is the **Lawrence Brown Home** at 470 Second Avenue. The two-story, wood-frame building, located south of Main Street, west of U.S. 17/98, and north of Stuart Street, has a steeply pitched gable roof, a large veranda porch around the outside, stained-glass transoms, and a porch trim. This architectural style, called Folk Victorian, became popular after the Civil War as magazines featured it and praised its many beauties.

The town's first black school, Union Academy, opened its doors in 1897 under the guidance of principal A.N. Ritchie and four teachers: Miss Emma Bullard, J.P. Hector, Mrs. M.L. Norwood, and Miss Lula Marion Simmons. As the only black high school in southwest Polk County for many years, it served parts of Hardee County and bused in students from Fort Meade, Frostproof, Mulberry, Wauchula, and other small communities. In 1937, James E. Stephens became a teacher at the school and the following year became principal, a position he held for the next 30 years, at which time integration closed down Union Academy. The school sent many athletes to Florida A&M University in Tallahassee in the 1940s and 1950s, but for every athletic scholarship Principal Stephens insisted that the university give one academic scholarship to an "A" student.

One of the black men who came to Bartow in the 1920s was a brick mason, Bradley Mitchell. Like many workers, he realized the importance of education and managed to send through college his three sons and eight daughters, most of whom went on to become teachers. Two other black families, the Hamiltons and the Longworths, joined the Mitchells in producing many of Bartow's excellent black teachers.

Today some 14,700 people live in Bartow, of whom 4,400 (30%) are blacks. One town resident who became a leading civic and education leader was Alice Frederick (see West Palm Beach below). The most famous Bartow black in recent years was Charlie Smith, the oldest man in the United States according to Social Security records. Born in 1842 in Liberia, Africa, he was kidnapped with other blacks in 1854, brought to this country, and sold as a slave. A white Texas rancher, Charles Smith, bought the young man in New Orleans and gave him his own name. Charlie later gained his freedom through President Abraham Lincoln's Emancipation Proclamation in 1863 and traveled throughout the West as a cowboy. He eventually made his way to Florida in the early part of this century, finally settling down in Bartow in 1963. After he died in 1979 at the age of 137, Bartow citizens erected a grave marker at his grave site at the end of a row in the northeast corner of Wildwood Cemetery that gave his

Charlie Smith's gravestone notes his distinction. Credit: Kevin M. McCarthy

name, birth and death dates, and the words "America's Oldest Man."

Directions:

The cemetery, which is open during daylight hours, is at the juncture of Stuart Street and Woodlawn Avenue, about two miles west of U.S. 17-98. To reach the grave site, go in the cemetery entrance nearest to the corner of Vine Street and Woodlawn Avenue; go .1 mile down the main lane, turn right past the fourth rectangular series of graves, and go to the end of the back row of graves. The grave site is the last one at the end of the row and nearest the fence.

Further Reading:

Bartow, Florida. Bartow: The Greater Bartow Chamber of Commerce, 1965.

Canter Brown, Jr. *Florida's Peace River Frontier*. Orlando: University of Central Florida Press, 1991.

Louise Frisbie. *Peace River Pioneers*. Miami: Seemann, 1974.

Joseph G. Mannard, "Black Company Town: A Peculiar Institution in

Pierce, Florida," *Tampa Bay History*, vol. 1, no. 1 (spring/summer 1979), pp. 61-66 [about a town near Bartow].
"New Tombstone a Memorial to America's Oldest Man," *Jet*, August 2, 1982, p. 16 [about Charlie Smith].

Chapter 6

Belle Glade

With a name suggested by a tourist who once remarked that the town looked like the "belle of the 'glades," Belle Glade on the southern shore of Lake Okeechobee has a population that swells from 17,000 to 25,000 during the harvest season. The town also has an extremely high AIDS rate and a history of bad luck that goes back to September 1928, when a monstrous hurricane hit the east coast of Florida near Palm Beach and headed inland to Lake Okeechobee. The eight-foot dike at the southern end of the lake collapsed, and floodwaters, which rose from four to eight feet in one hour, killed or left homeless hundreds of farm workers, many of whom were black. Many of the estimated 2,000 reported dead were transient agricultural workers from the Bahamas who were never reported missing, and so the actual casualty figure will never be known.

Novelist Zora Neale Hurston (1891?-1960) of Eatonville, Florida (see Eatonville and Fort Pierce below) stayed in Belle Glade to write her novel, *Their Eyes Were Watching God*, about the poor blacks who worked in the bean fields. The Belle Glade hotel where she stayed while doing research for her writing is now the **Roof Garden Hotel** at 416 S.W. Dr. Martin Luther King, Jr. Boulevard., formerly Avenue E; the hotel is west of U.S. 441 on one of the major roads in the town. The

Working in the fields all day long is hot and dirty work. Credit: Florida State Archives

hotel, built in 1947 in the black part of town, has served blacks and migrant families for decades. The 8,000 square feet of building is divided into 32 rooms, and plans are underway for converting the hotel into a museum that will collect and preserve information about blacks in the Glades.

A recent book about the exploitation of migrant workers by the large sugar cane companies is Alec Wilkinson's *Big Sugar: Seasons in the Cane Fields of Florida* (New York: Knopf, 1989). During the harvest season in the Belle Glade area black schools used to be shut down so that the children could join their parents in the fields, a practice that reduced the school year for black students from nine to six months. It took much effort by the Palm Beach County Teachers' Association (PBCTA), which was organized in 1941, to halt this practice. The first high school for blacks in the area was Belle Glade's Everglades Vocational High School, the third school in Palm Beach County to go to twelve grades; its principals included Britton G. Sayles and Alton R.F. Williams. Another black school in Belle Glade, Lake Shore, won a state basketball title under coach Arthur King.

CBS television and Edward R. Murrow featured black workers and Belle Glade in a 1960 documentary called "Harvest of Shame." Local officials tried hard to show how the terrible conditions presented in that broadcast were untrue and distorted, but millions of Americans had a very negative view of the town for decades to come because of that broadcast. Local author Lawrence Will wrote a history of the town that showed how many blacks prospered by living and working in that area and how the "Harvest of Shame" documentary was not accurate.

Several black children living in Belle Glade in the 1950s served as the model for Saralee, what is believed to be the first anthropologically correct black doll mass produced. The doll was the idea of Sara Lee Creech, a member of the Belle Glade Inter-Racial Council. Zora Neale Hurston wrote to the originator of the dolls after they came out: "The thing that pleased me most, Miss Creech, was that you, a white girl, should have seen clearly and sought to meet our longing for understanding of us as we really are, and not as some would have us."

Today the official population of Belle Glade is 16,177 people, of whom 9,299 (58%) are black. Many of those blacks have been helped by one of the town's important success stories, the Everglade Progressive Citizens, Inc., one of the largest black-owned businesses in Florida. In 1954, 13 young men each deposited $20 with the founder of the company, W.C. Taylor, and each agreed to deposit $10 a month until they reached a goal of $20,000, at which point they would pay themselves an annual dividend of 5%. When news of the company began to spread, others joined them in investing, soon raised the goal of $20,000, and obtained a charter from the state. Two subsidiaries of the company, the Everglade Progressive Finance Company and the Everglade Mortgage Company, financed many local home-improvement projects. The company's assets of $800,000 included apartment buildings, vacant lots, rolling stock, and second mortgages.

Among local blacks who have had success in the political arena are William A. Grear, who became the first black elected official when voters selected him for the City Council in 1969; two years later he became Vice Mayor and then Mayor in 1975. The second elected black official was attorney Dorothy Walker, whom voters sent to the City Council in 1979. An important appointee was David H. Hill, whom the City Commission appointed to the Civil Service Board in 1966; he later served as chairman of that Board. Also, Oris W. Walker served as an alternate on the Board of Adjustment. Such appointments pointed out the growing influence of blacks in the governance of the city.

An organization founded in 1965 by 13 women under the leadership of Vivian Byrd was the Eldorado Civic Club, which has worked to better the health and general welfare of the community, instill pride in the black heritage, and enhance the social and civic life of the residents; Dorothy Glaze has been one of the club's long-time leaders. Other organizations in the area which have attempted to better conditions are the Elite Community Club, the Women Civic Club, the Friendship Women's Club, Glades Ebonique Ladies Club, Silhouettes Club, the Unity Savings Club, and COBY (Cry of Black Youth).

One modern success story in the town is Harma Miller, a woman who used to pick beans in the muck around the Everglades and lived with her family in a one-room tin house. Against immense odds, she managed to finish school and attend Bethune-Cookman College on a scholarship. She later became a Spanish teacher at the same high school she had graduated from. For 22 years she taught school and somehow found the time to earn a master's degree in linguistics from the University of Pittsburgh. When she looked around her and saw the squalor of so many of her neighbors, she began to register voters, organize protests against segregated housing, and force landlords to clean up their property. In 1985, she was elected city commissioner and four years later became mayor, the second black to be mayor and the first woman to hold the office. She sums up a remarkable life this way: "The folks who knew me when I was a girl see me as an expression of hope. If I can do this—where I came from—then you can do it, too."

Among the important black churches in the area are **Mt. Zion A.M.E. Church of Belle Glade**, which was begun by a midwife, Sister Missouri Vereen, who came to the town from Jacksonville, Georgia, in the early 1900s. When she found that the town had no Methodist church, she obtained a plot of land and organized the church. The Ed Neal and Will Smith families helped establish the **St. John First Baptist Church of Belle Glade** in 1928; one of the later pastors, Reverend J.B. Adams, served the church for over 32 years. The **New Bethel Missionary Baptist Church of Belle Glade**, which had been organized in Chosen, Florida, in 1930, moved to Belle Glade in 1933 and was directed by Reverend Willie Littles. Finally, a nearby church is the **Bible Church of God of Pahokee**, which was established in 1964 under the leadership of Bishop Sylvester Banks.

Further Reading:

Brent Cantrell, "Black Daily Life in Northwestern Palm Beach County: Glimpses from a Half-Century Ago," *South Florida History Magazine*, Spring/Summer 1993, pp. 20-27.

Donald W. Curl. *Palm Beach County: An Illustrated History*. Northridge, Cal.: Windsor Publications, Inc., 1986.

"Harma Miller: From Migrant to Mayor," *Essence*, July 1991, p. 33.

Robert E. Hemenway. *Zora Neale Hurston: A Literary Biography*. Urbana: University of Illinois Press, 1977.

Zora Neale Hurston. *Their Eyes Were Watching God*. Philadelphia: Lippincott, 1937.

Vivian Reissland Rouson-Gossett. *Like a Mighty Banyan: Contributions of Black People County*. Palm Beach County: Palm Beach Junior College, 1982.

Lawrence E. Will. *Swamp to Sugar Bowl: Pioneer Days in Belle Glade*. St. Petersburg: Great Outdoors Publishing, 1968.

Chapter 7

Boca Raton

The name of this town in Palm Beach County means "rat's mouth," referring to a hidden rock in the bay there that could cut ship's cables. In the 1870s, settlers began moving into the area to take advantage of the low prices (about $1.25 an acre) and rich lands to grow citrus and pineapples. More residents moved in after Henry Flagler extended his Florida East Coast Railroad down toward Miami in the mid-1890s. A local newspaper, *The Homeseeker*, meant to attract more settlers and, as quoted in *Pearl City, Florida* (p. 112), mentioned that one of the early settlers was a black man: "C.W. Blaine is a darkey and a good one. He is working on shares. Land and fertilizer are furnished him versus his labor. He has no capital but his own two hands and a little credit. He has shipped over 2 hundred crates of beans selling for 3 dollars and for his six acres of tomatoes he will clear a good thing."

To do the planting and harvesting of the crops, local farmers depended on black laborers, who were sometimes former slaves who had come to Florida after the Civil War in search of jobs and opportunities. In the absence of bulldozers the black men were hired to clear the land with grub hoes, a very backbreaking task. Many of those blacks lived in Deerfield Beach and would walk over to Boca Raton in the morning, work a ten-hour day, and then walk home again in the evening, having earned between 75 cents and a $1 for the day's work. In 1915, George Long surveyed and platted a section of land between Tenth and Twelfth streets on North Dixie Highway that would be used for the blacks moving into the area and working on the growing of pineapples. The 15-acre settlement acquired the name Pearl City either from the name of the first black child born in Boca Raton or from the name of the area's chief street (Pearl Street—now N.E. Eleventh Street) or from a favorite strain of pineapples, Hawaiian Pearls.

Pearl City is located just south of 13th Street (Glades Road) between the Dixie Highway and Federal Highway (U.S. 1). Other nearby black neighborhoods are Dixie Manor, just to the north of Glades Road, and 15th Terrace, to the north of Dixie Manor. Developers concerned about separating the black community from the white community in the 1950s and 1960s built an eight-foot-tall concrete-block wall above 15th Terrace. "The Wall" has tended to keep the black and white communities separated into the 1990s.

Alex Hughes, one of the first blacks in the area and the son of former slaves, arrived in 1914 and two years later built at 1100 North Dixie Highway a house that still stands, although enlarged and changed since then. As more people moved into the area, Hughes began teaching Sunday school in his house, until local residents built a bush arbor of palmettos for religious purposes and began making plans for a church. The engineer for the local developers donated a lot for the church at 128 Northeast Eleventh Street, and the black workers built the **Macedonia African Methodist Episcopal Church** there by 1920. Other residents organized the **Ebenezer Baptist Church** in 1918 and built a church three years later between Tenth and Eleventh streets on what is today Federal Highway. Because the two religious congregations could not have their own minister every Sunday, the two groups alternated having a service, but everyone attended each service. When a 1928 hurricane destroyed the

Baptist church, the congregation built a new structure at 200 Northeast Twelfth Street. After several rebuildings, the new church was finished in 1957.

Alex Hughes also wanted to establish a school in Pearl City, and the Board of Public Instruction told him that they would provide a teacher if he could find eight children for the school. When he found them, the Board sent a teacher, Miss Robinson, and moved a school building to the south side of Eleventh Street off Dixie Highway in 1923. Later the Board built a new school at Dixie Highway and Twelfth Street. A local park honors Alex Hughes, who died in 1977 at the age of 92 after many years of working for the black residents of Pearl City.

Today Boca Raton has approximately 1,734 blacks (3%) out of a total population of 61,491. Around 446 black students (7%) of a total student population of 6,071 attend Florida Atlantic University there. Among winter residents of the city was Arthur Ashe, Jr., (1943-1993), the first black to win the Wimbledon men's tennis championship. Among the modern-day leaders of the city is Wayne D. Barton, a 33-year-old officer with the Boca Raton Police Department and the first black to be named that organization's "Officer of the Year"; he had an after-school program for latch-key children and used his own money to fund trips and prizes for those children who did well in school.

Further Reading:

Jacqueline Ashton. *Boca Raton: From Pioneer Days to the Fabulous Twenties.* Boca Raton: Dedication Press, 1979, esp. pp. 85-93.

Arthur S. Evans, Jr., and David Lee. *Pearl City, Florida: A Black Community Remembers.* Boca Raton: Florida Atlantic University Press, 1990.

H.D. Gates. *Pioneer Days at Boca Raton.* Boca Raton: Gates, 1948?

Chapter 8

Bradenton

The town of Bradenton in Manatee County is near the site where Spanish explorers Ponce de Leon (1521), Panfilo de Narváez (1528), and Hernando de Soto (1539) may have landed to begin exploring Florida. Five hundred years before them, the Timucuan Indians had lived there. White settlers began moving into the area in the middle of the 19th century to take advantage of the closeness to the Gulf of Mexico, the rich soil, and good pasture land. The town of Braidentown, spelled with an *i*, grew up here, honoring in its peculiar spelling the name of a Dr. Joseph Braden, one of the first white settlers and a man who had 95 slaves to work his 1,110-acre plantation. Another slaveholder was Robert Gamble, who had 102 slaves in 1850 to work the labor-intensive sugar cane production he had on his 3,450 acres along the Manatee River in nearby Ellenton. Judah Benjamin, the secretary of state for the Confederacy, used the Gamble Plantation as a hiding place at the end of the Civil War as he fled the United States for England.

Blacks eventually moved into the area as free men after the Civil War, but they often had to be content with menial, back-breaking jobs, for example in the production of sugar cane, feeding sugar cane into the mill to extract the juice from which they would make sugar. Even black youngsters would help out by leading the horses around and around the crude machine that extracted the juice from the cane.

Two retirees from Michigan, Fredi and Ernest Brown, who spent 50 years collecting hundreds of books, magazines, photographs, and recordings about black accomplishments, especially the stories of ordinary citizens, opened in 1990 the **Family Heritage House** resource center behind the Head Start Center at 1707 15th Street E. This house is east of U.S. 301 and north of 26th Avenue E in the Kingston Estates area of town. The center on the East Bradenton property has a comfortable reading room with bookshelves, cabinets, and chairs. Open on Tuesdays, Wednesdays, and Thursdays from 2 p.m. to 7 p.m., the house offers to all a good source of material, including clippings, scrapbooks, and memorabilia by and about blacks.

Today some 43,779 people live in Bradenton, plus many more in the winter season; the official black population is 6,340 (15%). The black baseball players on the roster of the Pittsburgh Pirates, who hold spring training in Bradenton, may well be role models for many of the youth who are seeking a way out of low-income jobs. Another role model is Dr. Jesse L. Burns, who was born and raised in Bradenton and went on to become the 25th president of Jacksonville's Edward Waters College (see below); he received his Bachelor of Science and Master of Business Administration degrees from Stetson University and his Doctor of Business Administration from the University of South Florida and worked as a top resource management and development official with Tropicana Products.

Further Reading:

Arthur C. Schofield. *Yesterday's Bradenton, Including Manatee County*. Miami: Seemann, 1975.

William Zinsser. *Spring Training*. New York: Harper & Row, 1989 [about the Pittsburgh Pirates' 1988 spring-training camp in Bradenton].

Chapter 9

Bushnell

On December 28, 1835, two events occurred that helped start the bloody Second Seminole War (1835-1842). First, Indians killed an Indian agent and a lieutenant outside Fort King near Ocala. Further south and two miles north of present-day Bushnell in Sumter County, Seminole Indians lying in wait ambushed and killed Major Francis Dade and 107 soldiers; from the two companies only three soldiers and one interpreter, a black man, survived. For the next seven years the U.S. Army fought a long, bloody war to remove the Seminoles from Florida.

The black survivor of what became known as the Dade Massacre was Luis Pacheco, who had acted as an interpreter with the Indians for Major Dade. Pacheco (1800-1895) had been born a slave on a plantation south of Jacksonville, but had learned to read and write from the daughter of his master and therefore became more valuable to his masters. Once after visiting his wife, a former slave who had purchased her freedom, he was caught in Tampa and sold to the first of several military commanders. When Major Dade and his soldiers headed out of Tampa to march north, Pacheco went along as an interpreter with the Seminoles, whose language he had learned as a youth.

After the Indians killed Major Dade, they spared Pacheco

The Dade Battlefield was the site of an Indian massacre in 1835. Credit: Kevin M. McCarthy

because of his dark color and took him with them on various missions. Because he joined or was forced to accompany the Indians after the battle, some whites accused him of having aided the Indians in setting their ambush for Major Dade's troops, but no proof exists that Pacheco collaborated with the Indians. However, he did accompany the Indians when they were sent out west to reservations by the federal government. Some 57 years after the Dade Massacre, Pacheco made his way to Jacksonville and located the woman who had taught him to read and write. He took her name, Fatio, and remained with her until he died in 1895.

Battlefield plaques and a museum at the **Dade Battlefield State Historic Site** tell the story of that ambush and the war that followed, the most brutal and expensive American Indian war in our history. The bodies of the slain soldiers were not buried by federal troops until February 20, 1836. In 1842, troops removed the bodies of the fallen warriors and reburied them with honors in St. Augustine, just as the Second Seminole War was ending.

Some people may have thought that Louis Pacheco had collaborated with the Seminoles because blacks had often associated with the Indians and been accepted into their tribes. When runaway slaves from southern plantations reached Florida in the 18th and 19th centuries, they sometimes joined the Seminoles, intermarried with them, and joined them in the fight against those who would send both the slaves to plantations and the Seminoles to western reservations. In the early 1700s some 100,000 Black Seminoles, as they were called, presented a formidable force to the outside world. The Black Seminoles, who had learned English on the plantations, acted as interpreters between the Indians and the whites. When the federal government forced many Seminoles to move to Oklahoma, many Black Seminoles went with them and worked as scouts for the U.S. Army. One of the Florida-born Black Seminoles, Adam Paine, received the Medal of Honor for showing great courage in a battle with the Comanche Indians in Texas in 1874. (For more about the Black Seminoles see Kettle Island below).

Directions:

The site near Bushnell, Florida, about two miles east-south of I-75, is open daily, 8 a.m. until sundown. Phone: (904) 793-4781.

Further Reading:

Mark F. Boyd,"The Seminole War: Its Background and Onset," *Florida Historical Quarterly*, vol. 30 (July 1951): 3-115.

George Klos, "Blacks and Seminoles," *South Florida History Magazine*, Spring 1991, pp. 12-15.

Frank Laumer. *Massacre!* Gainesville: University of Florida Press, 1968.

Daniel F. Littlefield, Jr. *Africans and Seminoles*. Westport, Conn.: Greenwood Press, 1977.

Kenneth W. Porter, "The Early Life of Luis Pacheco Né Fatio," *The Negro History Bulletin*, vol. 7, no. 3 (December 1943), pp. 52+.

Kenneth Wiggins Porter. *The Negro on the American Frontier*. New York: Arno Press and the *New York Times*, 1971, esp. pp. 182-358.

Scott Thybony, "Against All Odds, Black Seminoles Won Their Freedom," *Smithsonian*, August 1991, pp. 90-101.

Chapter 10

Chipley

Washington County, which was established in Florida's Panhandle in 1825 and named after George Washington, has as its county seat the town of Chipley, which began as a railroad camp on the Pensacola and Atlantic line and commemorates in its name a railroad official, Colonel William D. Chipley. The town hosted an Annexation Convention in 1889 to decide whether to try to have Alabama annex the Florida Panhandle, a movement that has surfaced every few years since the early 1800s. Today Chipley, which celebrated its centennial in 1982, has a population of 3,866, of whom 1,014 (26%) are black.

One of the town's schools, **Roulhac Middle School** at 101 North Pecan Street, honors an Orange Hill native, Thomas J. Roulhac, who became supervisor of Washington County's schools for black children in 1913. Having begun his teaching career at the age of 20, he spent the next 49 years in that profession. Each of the ten children of Thomas and Patience Roulhac and many of the 80 Roulhac grandchildren also became educators and education advocates and showed by example how far one can advance through education. Some of those who did not go into the teaching field worked in the fields of medicine, law, business, and religion.

In 1938, Thomas J. Roulhac became principal of Chipley's

first high school for black children, a school that also offered classes for elementary and junior high school students. Up until the mid-1960s Washington County, like many other counties in the United States, maintained two school systems: one for white children and one for black children. The latter schools were often much inferior to the former schools in terms of finances, teacher qualifications, and graduation rates. In 1968-69, the county schools were integrated, and the high school students at Roulhac School were transferred to Chipley High School, the elementary school students went to Kate M. Smith School, and middle school students went to what became known as Roulhac Middle School, a name that honored Chipley's long-time black principal.

Directions:
Roulhac Middle School at 101 North Pecan Street is one block north of U.S. 90 (Jackson Avenue and S.R. 10) across the railroad tracks and Railroad Avenue North at the end of Church Avenue, which runs parallel to U.S. 90. Pecan Street is east of 7th Street and East Boulevard.

Another black, who was known only by his first name, Harry, gave his name to a swampy area near the eastern part of Orange Hill, which is just west of S.R. 273 south of Chipley. Harry's Bay is the name of a wetlands which collected runoff water during the rainy season and slowly released it during dry times. The thick foliage and dense trees made the area a perfect hiding place for Harry, a runaway slave from a nearby plantation. According to local historian E.W. Carswell in *Washington: Florida's Twelfth County* (pp. 35-36), in the mid-1800s Harry became a black Robin Hood, stealing from plantation storehouses and sharing his food with the slaves who could not escape.

Further Reading:

E.W. Carswell. *Tempestuous Triangle: The History of Washington County, Florida.* Chipley: Washington County School Board, 1974.

E.W. Carswell. *Washington: Florida's Twelfth County.* Chipley, Fl.: E.W. Carswell, 1991.

Chapter 11

Clearwater

Spanish explorers like Panfilo de Narváez in 1528 and Hernando de Soto in 1539 may have passed near present-day Clearwater, but they did not remain for long, choosing instead to push north into uncharted areas. After Spain ceded Florida to the United States in 1821 and the Second Seminole War ended in 1842, settlers began moving into the area, attracted by the rich farm lands and the fishing in the Gulf of Mexico. Early residents called the site Clear Water Harbor because of a clear spring that bubbles into the Gulf off the shore. One of the first families to move there was the Stephens (or Stevens) family, but they did not like their land and sold it to John S. Taylor, Sr., for one black slave whom her owners accused of trying to poison the Stephens family. Thus, what is today downtown Clearwater was sold for the price of one unwanted slave.

From a small town in 1900 to a large city and the county seat of Pinellas County today, Clearwater has a population of 98,773, of whom 8,562 (9%) are blacks. Many people have come to this beautiful city to retire but also to live while they commute to work in places throughout the Tampa Bay area. Formerly dependent on retirees and tourists, the city today attracts more and more residents who want to live and work in the area. The Church of Scientology, which owns much of downtown Clearwater, has also attracted many people.

In a 1977 history of the city, Roy Cadwell wrote that "there is no segregation in any part of Clearwater, but there is an economic segregation that makes it difficult, if not impossible, for black persons to live other than in the north Greenwood area." (p. 87) This section of the city is north on Greenwood and west on Palmetto to north Myrtle and east to Betty Lane. The first school for black students was the Pinellas Institute on Palmetto; it later became the Clearwater Comprehensive School and was totally integrated.

Further Reading:

Roy Cadwell. *Clearwater, "A Sparkling City."* Minneapolis, Minn.: T.S. Denison & Company, Inc., 1977.

Hampton Dunn. *Yesterday's Clearwater*. Miami: Seemann, 1973.

Michael Sanders. *Clearwater*. Norfolk, Va.: Donning, 1983.

Diane Tunick, "Clearwater: Still Sparkling," *Florida Trend*, May 1981, pp. 60-67.

June Hurley Young. *Pinellas Peninsula*. St. Petersburg, Fl.: Byron Kennedy & Co., 1984.

The **Dorothy Thompson African American Museum** at 1501 Madison Avenue North houses the private collection of 5,000+ African-American books, 3,000+ records and tapes, 400 cookbooks written by African Americans, and many newspaper articles and artifacts from the first 75 African families who settled in Clearwater. It also features an exhibit about Annie Spyes, a black woman who was born in Clearwater and spent most of her 107 years there. The museum, which opened in 1978, is open by appointment. Phone: 813-447-1037.

Among the other Clearwater sites that should be mentioned here is **Pinellas High School** at 1220 Palmetto Street, which Jazz pianist Ivory "Dwike" Mitchell, Jr., attended. Mitchell, who was born in Dunedin, Florida, on February 14, 1930, attended the Chase Memorial School and played piano at the Shiloh Missionary Baptist Church in Dunedin

Judge Joseph W. Hatchett was Florida's first black supreme court justice. Credit: Florida State Archives

before eventually teaming up with horn player Willie Henry Ruff, Jr., of Sheffield, Alabama, to create a famous and popular jazz duo, as detailed in a profile by William Zinsser. Pinellas High School used to be on the other side of town and was called Pinellas Colored Junior High School, then Pinellas High School, then in 1968 Clearwater Comprehensive Junior High School, and today Clearwater Comprehensive Discovery School.

Further Reading:

William Zinsser. *Willie and Dwike.* New York: Harper & Row, 1984.

Also from Clearwater is Joseph W. Hatchett (1932-), the state's first black supreme court justice. While he was growing up in Clearwater with his three brothers and sisters, his mother worked as a maid and his father worked as a fruit picker. After attending a local school, Joseph went on to Florida A&M University in Tallahassee, spent two years in the U.S. Army, and then went to Howard University Law School in Washington, D.C. After law school, he practiced law in Daytona Beach for seven years, became an Assistant U.S. Attorney in Jacksonville (1966-1971), and then a U.S. magistrate for the Middle District of Florida. When Governor Askew appointed him to the Florida Supreme Court in 1975, Hatchett became the first black to sit on the supreme court in any southern state and later was reelected to the position, becoming the first black since Reconstruction to be elected to a statewide office. He served on that court until 1979, at which time President Jimmy Carter chose him to serve as a federal circuit judge on the Fifth U.S. Circuit Court of Appeals.

Further Reading:

Maxine D. Jones and Kevin M. McCarthy. *African Americans in Florida.* Sarasota: Pineapple Press, 1993: pp. 124-125.

Susan Lykes, "Hatchett Offers 'Real Understanding,'" *Tallahassee Democrat,* October 24, 1975, p. 11.

John Van Gieson, "Hatchett becomes Florida's First Black Justice," *Tallahassee Democrat*, September 2, 1975, p. 1.

Chapter 12

Cleveland

Cleveland, which was named after President Grover Cleveland because he was inaugurated in 1885, the year before this town was named, is a small town in Charlotte County on U.S. 17 along the Peace River and east-northeast of Punta Gorda. Although the 1990 census showed no blacks among the population of 2,922, Cleveland does have two sites of significance to blacks, both places relating to George Brown, a black carpenter who came here in 1890 to work for the DeSoto Phosphate Mining Company at Hull on the Peace River.

The phosphate industry required labor-intensive work by strong men who could stand the long hours in the hot sun. Historian Canter Brown, Jr., wrote that "Like the railroads, phosphate companies turned to black men to perform much of the hardest physical labor connected with the mines. They were paid a dollar a day like all phosphate laborers." (p. 318) Some of the phosphate companies leased black convicts for the difficult work and treated them badly until the Florida legislature finally outlawed the leasing of convicts. In 1897, George Brown bought a small Punta Gorda boat-repair business from another black, Peter W. Miller, and moved it to Cleveland. Around 1916, Brown bought eight more acres to construct the **Cleveland Steam Marine Ways** to build and work on luxury yachts. His crew repaired boats as long as 80 feet and built large pleasure boats, sail or power, for wealthy clients, many of whom wintered in Charlotte Harbor. Today a mobile home park uses the machine shop as a community hall, which visitors can tour.

Directions:
To reach the community hall, turn left on Cleveland Avenue in the middle of the town, then right on Riverside when the avenue dead-ends; the structure is a green building on Georgia Drive in the mobile home park.

After tuberculosis claimed the lives of his first wife and young daughter, Brown married a young woman and built her a large, two-story house on Riverside Drive (Old Highway 17). When he heard that some whites in town were upset that the town's only black man would own the largest home, he sold it to a white family, not wishing to antagonize his neighbors and customers. Brown and his wife, Tommie, moved into a large bungalow at 27430 Cleveland Avenue near the waterfront where they lived for the rest of their lives. The **Brown Home** is now a private residence. Besides an extensive library, Brown also had one of the first automobiles, player pianos, and radios in the area. He and his wife had no children, but they took in several black children who needed homes and also opened up their home to children, both black and white, to see and hear the piano and radio.

Brown was an "equal opportunity employer," hiring whites and blacks and paying equal wages for equal skills. He also bought and sold property throughout the area, especially in the county seat, Punta Gorda; in 1924, he sold prime land in downtown Punta Gorda for the county courthouse. When he finally died in 1951 at age 83, he left behind a legacy of charitable giving and fair treatment of all. He is buried in the **Lt. Carl A. Bailey Memorial Cemetery** in what used to be the black cemetery of Cleveland. The cemetery is named for one of the first black fighter pilots of World War II, a man who survived the war but was later killed in a 1957 automobile accident. The Punta Gorda Colored Investment

The Lt. Carl A. Bailey Memorial Cemetery is where George Brown and his wife are buried. Credit: Kevin M. McCarthy

Company originally platted the cemetery, but the county eventually took it over. (For more about Brown see the Punta Gorda entry below.) When George Brown died and was buried in the Bailey Cemetery, workers put up a double tombstone with his birth and death dates and Tommie's birth date; her death date would be filled in when she died. But when she did die 16 years later, no money remained for the carving of her death date, and so that part is still blank on the marker. The cemetery is off Riverside toward the river to the west of the town; the grave sites are well-marked in the central part of the cemetery.

Further Reading:

Arch Fredric Blakey. *The Florida Phosphate Industry*. Cambridge, Mass.: Wertheim Committee, Harvard University, 1973.

Canter Brown, Jr. *Florida's Peace River Frontier*. Orlando: University of Central Florida Press, 1991.

Vernon Peeples. *Punta Gorda and the Charlotte Harbor Area*. Norfolk, Va.: Donning Company, 1986.

Chapter 13

Cocoa

Brevard County on the eastern coast of Florida was first settled by Indians, like the Ais tribe, and later by the Spanish, pirates, and hardy explorers who pushed down from Georgia and the Carolinas in the 19th century. High temperatures, mosquitoes, hurricanes, and angry Indians did much to discourage permanent settlement, but, as time passed, the pluses of living there attracted more people. Newly freed slaves were some of the first non-Indians to settle in the area. According to historian Glenn Rabac, a group of the freedmen moved to the Cocoa Beach area after the Civil War and claimed all of the land south of the cape between the Atlantic Ocean and the Banana River. An 1885 hurricane flooded out the homesteaders and discouraged others from living near the ocean, but people still headed there by boat and train.

A local black woman may have been responsible for the name of Cocoa. According to Allen Morris's *Florida Place Names* (Coral Gables: University of Miami Press, 1974, p. 37), when some local citizens were trying to decide on a name for the settlement, a black woman saw the label on a box of Baker's Cocoa and suggested that they name the place Cocoa. In any case fishermen founded the town long ago, and officials incorporated it in 1895.

In the 19th and early 20th centuries, blacks came to the

area to work on the railroad, in the orchard fields, and in the homes of wealthy summer residents. By the mid-1920s, blacks made up almost one-third of the town's population, but in those days of segregation they usually lived west of Florida Avenue and south of Willard Street. The focus point was Magnolia Street, which has since been renamed Stone Street to honor Richard E. Stone, a prominent black mortician who did much to improve the area during his long stay there. Blacks had a thriving, self-sufficient community with their own businesses, including grocery stores, a post office, pharmacy, and restaurant. Because the only school open to blacks in the area was an elementary school, those who wanted to attend high school had to move to another city. In the 1930s, officials began busing children to a black high school in Melbourne, something which lasted until desegregation in the 1950s began to give them access to Cocoa schools. Today, Cocoa's population of 17,691 has a black population of 5,079 (29%).

The **Richard E. Stone Historic District** from 121 to 304 Stone Street honors a man who did much to help his fellow blacks of Cocoa. The district, where most of the buildings described here are, is east of U.S. 1, west of Hughlett Avenue, and south of King Street (Route 520). Blacks have lived in this area for most of this century, even when they worked in white areas of the town or at the Florida East Coast Railroad and the East Coast Lumber Company. Cocoa's early black community was settled along the Indian River in the mid-1800s, but gradually moved west to where it is today.

Richard Stone (1902-1985), the son of the owner of Melbourne's first grocery store and stable, established Brevard County's first black funeral home and first black professional baseball team, the Cocoa Black Indians. He also helped establish Cocoa's first civic organization, Liberty League, Inc., which today is known as the Cocoa Rockledge Civic League, and the city's first recreational center. On the national scene, in 1935 he invented and patented a directional signal light for automobiles, and in his professional medical practice patented the trocar, a surgical instrument used in embalming.

Among the important sites in the district are the **Grace Edwards Home** (121 Stone Street) that one of the town's first black families built; the **Greater St. Paul Baptist Church** (213 Stone Street), whose 100-year-old foyer windows came from the original church on that site; the **John Henry Hall Estate** (221 Stone Street), one of the first grocery stores in the area; the **Johnson Home** (225 Stone Street), another early grocery store; the **Dr. B.C. Scurry Home** (231 Stone Street), where Cocoa's first black doctor lived; and the **Brown Home** (241 Stone Street), where the town's first shoe shiner lived. The **Malissa Moore Home,** today a private residence at 215 Stone Street, was home to one of the area's most prominent residents, Malissa Moore. The house, which was first located near the Indian River in 1890, was moved to its present location to become a rooming house and restaurant, for a while the only one in Cocoa and supposedly a favorite eating place for railroad builder Henry Flagler. Having moved to the area in 1884, Malissa Moore decided to build a church similar to the ones she had attended in Atlanta and in her hometown, Monroe, Georgia. Through many Saturday night social gatherings, where she often served her famous fish sandwiches and collected donations of 50 and 75 cents, Mrs. Moore raised enough money in two years to buy land for a church on Florida Avenue and hired a Titusville carpenter to build it. (see next entry)

Mt. Moriah African Methodist Episcopal (A.M.E.) Church at 304 Stone Street (formerly Magnolia Street) has a long history of service to the community. Enough blacks lived in Cocoa by 1886 for Malissa Moore to think about establishing this church. When the original building on Florida Avenue burned down around 1922, Mrs. Moore once again raised money through her well-attended Saturday-night socials to buy land for a new building on Magnolia Street. Workers put up a new building at the present site,

The Mt. Moriah African Methodist Episcopal Church has served a local black congregation for decades. Credit: Kevin M. McCarthy

using bricks for the Gothic structure that were manufactured on the site with sand donated by the generous Richard Stone.

The **Harry T. Moore Center**, a single-story building at 307 Blake Avenue two blocks south of King Street, is today a child-care facility and community center. Cocoa's first black school used to be on this site. The Center honors Harry T. Moore, a civil rights activist who was killed by a bomb in 1951. (See Mims below for more details.)

Further Reading:

Verna G. Langlais, compiler. *Cemetery Census of Brevard County, Florida.* Titusville: no publ., 1984. This booklet lists those buried in the black Cocoa Cemetery at Wilson and Main.

Glenn Rabac. *The City of Cocoa Beach: The First Sixty Years.* Winona, Minn.: Apollo Books, 1986.

Chapter 14

Coconut Grove

*I*n south Miami near the Vizcaya Museum and Gardens is Coconut Grove, one of the oldest settled parts of the area. With a name that recalls a time when the site had coconut palms, Coconut Grove today is the Greenwich Village of Dade County and also the site of the first black community in Miami. The area can trace its history back to the late 1880s, when blacks began arriving from the Bahamas by way of Key West to work as chambermaids, washerwomen, and carpenters at the now-defunct Peacock Inn, the first hotel in the Miami area and originally known as the Bay View House. The first black to arrive, Mariah Brown, lived on the inn property, but, when more and more blacks arrived from the Bahamas, they settled down in a small settlement not far away known as Evangelist Street, later Charles Avenue. The **Mariah Brown House**, which was built in 1890, at 3298 Charles Avenue will be restored to display artifacts from the 19th century and to serve as an educational institution for black history.

Further Reading:

"Mariah Brown House to be restored in Coconut Grove as tribute to Bahamians," *The Miami Times*, May 19, 1994, p. 3A.

Many Bahamian men came to this part of Florida in the 19th century to begin a new life as they developed farms and businesses and later worked on Henry Flagler's railroad, in the fields and hotels, and in the homes of white settlers. Some of the descendants of those Bahamians still live in the beautiful homes those first arrivals built, houses with broad gables and ornate porches running along the front of the houses. The chance to own their own land in a mild climate was also very attractive to northern blacks, especially because they had often experienced racial discrimination in long-established, tradition-bound areas of the North. The newness of the south Florida area held out the opportunity of prosperity based on how hard the people worked.

In the first half of this century, the Grove attracted more and more people of different races, many of them with jobs in Miami and some of them very wealthy. Artists like Augustus St. Gaudens and Maxfield Parrish and writers like Virgil Barker and Hervey Allen moved in and helped make the place an artists' colony with a subsequent rise in land values. However, the section where blacks tended to live deteriorated badly. In the late 1940s, officials discovered that 777 structures in that section housed 3,000 residents, many of them without indoor plumbing; those residents relied on a truck they called the "Honey Wagon," which would collect the excrement each night. Determined to improve the living conditions of those living in the area, many local residents formed the biracial Coconut Grove Committee for Slum Clearance and by 1951 had removed all outdoor privies, connected each residence to water lines, increased police protection in the area, and began a fund for establishing a day nursery.

Further Reading:

Robert Liss, "Coconut Grove: 105-Year Effort to Preserve an Idea," *The Miami Herald*, March 11, 1978, p. 1A+.

Several places are of significance to blacks in the area, many of them near Charles Avenue, which is just below Grand Avenue and off Main Highway. The **Charles Avenue Historic District** is the site of the first black community on the south Florida mainland. A marker at Charles Avenue and Main Highway states the following:

> The first black community on the South Florida mainland began here in the late 1880s when Blacks primarily from the Bahamas came via Key West to work at the Peacock Inn. Their first hand experience with tropical plants and building materials proved invaluable to the development of Coconut Grove. Besides private homes the early buildings included the Odd Fellows Hall, which served as a community center and library, Macedonia Baptist Church, home of the oldest Black congregation in the area, and the A.M.E. Methodist Church, which housed the community's first school. At the western end of Charles Avenue is one of the area's oldest cemeteries.

Blacks in the Grove joined with whites in 1891 to worship in a nondenominational Christian chapel, the Union Chapel, but several years later had their own church: **Macedonia Baptist Church** on Douglas Road, Dade County's first Baptist church for blacks. It began in 1895 when the Rev. Samuel A. Sampson, a black Bahamian, organized the church and called it the Fifty-Six Baptist Church because it had 56 charter members. After meeting at the home of Edith Albury on Williams Avenue, the congregation built the first church building on Charles Avenue in 1903 and changed its name to St. Agnes Missionary Baptist Church. In 1922, they changed the name to Macedonia Baptist Church. Workers completed the present structure on the corner of Douglas Road and Charles Avenue in 1948. In 1993, officials dedicated several historical markers there to commemorate the many contributions that Bahamian and black pioneers made to the area.

Further Reading:

Dorothy Jenkins Fields, "Reflections on Black History: Cocoanut Grove, 1880-1903, A Selected Chronology," *Update* [Historical Association of Southern Florida], December 1975, pp. 3, 12.

Howard Kleinberg, editor. *Miami: The Way We Were.* Tampa: Surfside Publishing, 1989, pp. 54-55: "Black Church in Grove as Early as 1894."

The **Stirrup House** at 3242 Charles Avenue honors Dade County's first black millionaire: Ebenezer W.F. Stirrup, a native of the Bahamas who had come to Key West in 1888 and later moved to Cutler, 14 miles south of the Miami River. He worked in the pineapple fields during the day and then at night cleared the land in the area, sometimes being paid in land instead of cash since money was scarce at that time. After returning to the Bahamas at age 21 to marry Charlotte Jane Sawyer, his childhood sweetheart, he brought her back to Cutler, where they worked in the fields and began building small houses on their property.

At age 25, Stirrup moved his family to Coconut Grove and began slowly buying more and more land until he owned much of what became the downtown. He built over a hundred homes to rent or sell to other Bahamian blacks who came to Coconut Grove around 1900; many of their descendants still live in some of those houses. In 1897, he used tough Florida pine to build his own two-story structure, which still stands today, though now a private residence. Although Mr. Stirrup could barely read and write, he insisted that his children, ten of whom were born in south Florida, acquire as much education as possible. In turn they became productive, influential members of the community. In 1976, the Model City Development Corporation dedicated 26 proposed townhouses in Coconut Grove to Stirrup's memory as a memorial to the many houses he built there; situated off Main Highway at Franklin Avenue and Royal Road, the houses would be called the Stirrup Grove Townhouses.

Although Mr. Stirrup, who worked for some time for Mr.

Charles Deering, the man who bought the town of Cutler and developed it into a beautiful estate, lost much land and money during the Florida real estate bust, he died a very wealthy man in 1957 at the age of 84. In a 1976 interview, three of Stirrup's daughters recalled what it was like growing up in the Grove in the early part of this century. One of them, Mrs. Kate Dean, said that what they liked "in Coconut Grove in those early days of growing up is that everybody seemed to want to take care of everybody else." She continued: "Coconut Grove was and still is one of the few black areas not separated (from the rest of the community) by a railroad track."

Further Reading:

Dorothy Gaiter, "26 Grove Townhouses Dedicated to Builder," *The Miami Herald*, May 1, 1976, p. 2B.

Shelia Payton, "'Everybody Cared in The Grove,'" *The Miami Herald*, May 30, 1976, pp. 1B-2B.

Coconut Grove Cemetery, between Charles Avenue and Franklin Avenue and between Douglas Road and Hibiscus Street, was developed in 1913 by the Coconut Grove Colored Cemetery Association. This cemetery was actually the second one in the black Grove, the first one being further east on Charles Avenue and lasting from 1904 to 1906, at which time city officials shut it down for health reasons. At least 700, maybe as many as 1,200, people lie buried in the Coconut Grove Cemetery, but weather and time have obliterated many of their names. Among those buried there are Willie Bullard, the area's only black casket maker; James Summons, the first black in Coconut Grove to obtain a real estate license; and John E. Sweeting, founder of the early black settlement called Sweetingtown located near what is now South Dixie Highway and Douglas Road.

In order to restore and maintain this important cemetery, members of area churches filed articles of incorporation as the Coconut Grove Cemetery Association in 1989. Under the guidance of local historian Esther Mae Armbrister, this association helped place seven historical markers in Coconut Grove to recognize the contributions of Bahamian and other early black settlers to the area. Two other cemeteries nearby, the **Charlotte Jane Cemetery** and the **Charlotte Jane Annex**, have also been the burial site of many of the black Grove's early residents who were not allowed to be buried with whites.

Further Reading:

Marjorie Valbrun, "Cleanup is just a start for all-black cemetery," *The Miami Herald*, March 15, 1992, p. 2B.

The **Black Heritage Museum** at 3301 Coral Way in the Miracle Center Mall has a permanent collection of tribal artifacts from the west coast of Africa and New Guinea, as well as a large collection of black Americana. Open 11 a.m.-4 p.m. Monday-Friday; 1 pm-4 pm weekends/holidays. Phone: (305) 446-7304 or (305) 252-3535.

Among the other places in Coconut Grove that honor blacks are **George Washington Carver Junior High School**, formerly a senior high; **Scott-Carver Homes Housing Development** named after George Washington Carver (1859-1943), famous for agricultural research at Tuskegee Institute, especially concerning the peanut; **Gibson Senior Plaza** and the **Gibson Building**, named after Father Canon Theodore R. Gibson, who served from 1971 until 1982 as a City of Miami Commissioner and was also a pioneer civil rights leader; and **Frances S. Tucker Elementary School**, which honors Frances S. Tucker, an early elementary school principal at George W. Carver Elementary and the school which bears her name.

Further Reading:

Gene Burnett, "The Peacock Inn Was the Center of Coconut Grove," *Florida Trend*, June 1978, pp. 71-74.

"Coconut Grove Marks Black History," *Florida Heritage*, Summer 1993, p. 6.

From Wilderness to Metropolis: The History and Architecture of Dade County, Florida, 1825-1940. Miami: Metropolitan Dade County, 1982, pp. 7-10.

Arva Moore Parks, "Yesterday," *Coconut Grove U.S.A. Centennial, 1873-1973*. Coconut Grove: no publ., 1974, pp. 6-10.

John Sewell. *Miami Memoirs: A New Pictorial Edition of John Sewell's Own Story* by Arva Moore Parks. Miami: Arva Parks & Co., 1987.

Jean C. Taylor, "South Dade's Black Pioneers," *Update*, June 1976, pp. 10-12.

Jean Taylor. *Villages of South Dade*. St. Petersburg: Byron Kennedy and Company, 1985?

Chapter 15

Coral Gables

George E. Merrick spent much time and money designing Coral Gables, one of the earliest planned cities in the United States, including what became the University of Miami, which opened in 1926. William Jennings Bryan, President Woodrow Wilson's Secretary of State and a three-time Democratic Party nominee for President, would give impassioned speeches around Merrick's fabulous Venetian Pool in the mid-1920s to promote the planned community. The city's blacks, who never numbered very many, today make up only 3% (1,348) of the total population.

A black enclave within Coral Gables is **MacFarlane Homestead Subdivision Historic District**, which is bordered by Oak Avenue, South Dixie Highway (U.S. 1), Brooker Street, and Grand Avenue east, north-east of the University of Miami. The district takes its name from Flora MacFarlane, who homesteaded 160 acres of land here and in Coconut Grove in 1892. Some of the houses in the district predate the expansion of the Gables in 1925 and 1926, while others were built in the 1930s at a time when blacks were not allowed to build in the wealthier parts of the city. One of the early structures, St. Mary's Baptist Church, was built in 1927. Most of the homes in what is called the black Gables are small, single-story homes built from Dade County pine. Many of

Black caddies worked at the Biltmore Golf Course in Coral Gables. Credit: Florida State Archives

the blacks worked in the homes of the wealthy white residents or in the construction of City Hall and the Biltmore Hotel. The area is changing rapidly today, with many architectonically designed homes springing up.

One of the last remaining area schools that were all black before integration is **George Washington Carver Elementary School** at 4901 Lincoln Drive. Built in the 1920s, the school shares a five-acre site with the **George Washington Carver Middle School,** which was built in the 1950s. In 1991, the city's Historic Preservation Board unanimously declared both schools historic. One former student remembered how it was attending the elementary school in the 1930s: "I remember the stone water fountain in the courtyard and how on a cold day the teachers would bring the students out into the sunshine because we had no heat in the building. But we still thought it was the greatest school around."

Further Reading:

Kathryne Ashley. *George E. Merrick and Coral Gables, Florida.* Coral Gables: Crystal Bay Publishers, 1985.

Anthony Faiola, "Black Activists Seek to Preserve School," *The Miami Herald, Neighbors* Magazine, July 28, 1991, p. 2.

From Wilderness to Metropolis: The History and Architecture of Dade County, Florida, 1825-1940. Miami: Metropolitan Dade County, 1982, pp. 93-95.

Chapter 16

Crescent City

Putnam County's Crescent City can trace its history to the mid-18th century, when white settlers began moving in to take advantage of the good soil and access to a lake. The city, which takes its name from the nearby Crescent Lake, so called because of its resemblance to a crescent moon, was incorporated in 1885. Around 1887, black residents began the Village of Whitesville, so called perhaps because of the whitewashed cabins used by the residents near Lake Stella in the southern part of the city. Today Crescent City has a population of 1,859, of whom 688 (37%) are black.

Further Reading:

Susan Clark. *A Historic Tour Guide of Palatka and Putnam County, Florida.* Palatka: Putnam County Historical Society, 1992, pp. 89-95.

A. Philip Randolph (1889-1979), one of the most important civil rights leaders of the 20th century, was born in Crescent City and lived at 1004 S. Reid Avenue in a two-story house that would later burn in 1918. The house that occupies the site now was built and occupied by Richard Holman. Randolph's father, James William Randolph, served as a minister of the African Methodist Episcopal Zion Church in town before the family moved to Jacksonville, where young A. Philip attended school. In 1911, A. Philip settled in New York City and 14 years later organized the all-black International Brotherhood of Sleeping Car Porters, the first important black labor union, and served as the organization's first president. He also organized two large marches on the nation's capital, one in 1941 and the other in 1963, was the first black to serve as International Vice President of the AFL-CIO (1957), and received the Presidential Medal of Freedom from President Lyndon Johnson (1964). Crescent City does not yet have a memorial to A. Philip Randolph, but Jacksonville has the **A. Philip Randolph Northside Skills Center** that teaches students marketable skills.

Further Reading:

Jervis Anderson. *A. Philip Randolph: A Biographical Portrait*. New York: Harcourt Brace Jovanovich, 1973.

Brian E. Michaels. *The River Flows North: A History of Putnam County*. Palatka, Fl.: The Putnam County Archives and History Commission, 1976, pp. 195-207.

Paula F. Pfeffer. *A. Philip Randolph, Pioneer of the Civil Rights Movement*. Baton Rouge: Louisiana State University Press, 1990.

Chapter 17

Crestview

The town of Crestview 40 miles east of Pensacola on U.S. 90 is 223 feet above sea level, the second-highest altitude in Florida and the source of the town's name. In 1916, it became the county seat of the newly established Okaloosa County and later became even more prominent with the establishment of the nearby Eglin Air Force Base in 1944. Today the town has a population of 9,886, of whom 1,930 (20%) are blacks.

The **Carver-Hill Museum** in the 900 block of McClelland Street in the Fairview Park section of Crestview is dedicated to the preservation of black culture, heritage, achievements, and personal contributions of black citizens. Carver-Hill School alumni organized the Carver-Hill Memorial and Historical Society, Inc., in order to preserve the school and various memorabilia at a time when integration was closing black schools. Since its opening in May 1979, the museum has added many reference materials and items of local interest related to the history of the city, county, and nation with a particular emphasis on blacks in the area.

The museum building, which was originally a World War II barracks at Eglin Air Force Base, was constructed in 1942, moved to Carver-Hill School in 1949, and moved to its present site in 1954. This museum to Black Heritage, the only

The Carver-Hill Museum preserves black culture and history of the area. Credit: Kevin M. McCarthy

one of its kind in Okaloosa, Santa Rosa, and Walton counties, began with the efforts of the Okaloosa Negro Civic Club, which acquired property to establish Fairview Park in order to provide wholesome recreational activities; eventually the Club deeded the land to the city for use as a park. Members of the Okaloosa Negro Civic Club used funds from the city to purchase materials, and the men themselves provided their own labor to construct a concrete-block structure which is today used as a recreation center. The Carver-Hill Memorial and Historical Society, which was chartered in 1969 as a non-profit organization, acquired historical documents, photo albums from the different graduating classes, information about Crestview High School after integration, and medals won by local athlete Houston McTear.

Carver-Hill School was closed as part of Okaloosa County's School Integration Plan at the close of the 1968-69 school year. The school, which began around 1915, had been called Rosenwald in honor of Mr. Julius Rosenwald (1862-

1932), a successful American businessman, president of Sears, Roebuck and Company, and philanthropist who used much of his money to establish schools for American blacks. The name of Crestview's school was changed to Carver to honor Dr. George Washington Carver (1864?-1943), famed educator at Tuskegee Institute in Alabama. In 1954, local officials in Crestview added the name Hill to honor Rev. Edward Hill, a man who did much to establish a local school for black children.

Directions:

To reach the museum from I-10, go 1.2 miles north on S.R. 85, turn left on Duggan Avenue and go 6/10 mile, then turn right on McClelland Street and go one block. The museum is on the right across from Hayes Place. The museum's hours are Mon.-Fri., 9-1; Sat. 1-4, and at other times by appointment. Phone: 904-682-3494.

Further Reading:

Edwin R. Embree and Julia Waxman. *Investment in People: The Story of the Julius Rosenwald Fund.* New York: Harper & Brothers Publishers, 1949.

J. Irving E. Scott. *The Education of Black People in Florida.* Philadelphia: Dorrance & Company, 1974, p. 27+—about the Rosenwald Fund.

Chapter 18

Daytona Beach

Daytona Beach is now a part of Volusia County, a section of Florida that used to be in Mosquito County in the days before insect control made life bearable in the state. Wealthy planters like Charles and John Bulow began moving to the area in the early 19th century to take advantage of the cheap land, good soil for producing sugar cane, and accessibility to northern markets by waterways. These planters used many slaves to clear the land, cultivate the crops, and produce sugar, molasses, and rum.

One of the founders of Daytona Beach and the man after whom the city is named, Matthias Day, Jr., of Mansfield, Ohio, came to the area in 1870, determined to operate a saw mill. According to Hebel's racial history of the area, he found a group of freedmen who had gone there after the Civil War. To clear the land and grow crops he employed some of those slaves who had settled north of Port Orange on present-day U.S. 1 in a settlement called Freemanville. Many of their descendants still live in Daytona Beach, a city that has an official population of 61,921, 19,009 (31%) of whom are blacks.

Mary McLeod Bethune stands outside White Hall with some of her students. Credit: Florida State Archives

Further Reading:

Ianthe Bond Hebel. *Daytona Beach, Florida's Racial History*. Daytona Beach: no publ., 1966.

Michael G. Schene. *Hopes, Dreams, and Promises: A History of Volusia County, Florida*. Daytona Beach: News-Journal Corporation, 1976, esp. pp. 37-38 about the working conditions, housing, clothing, and food of the slaves.

Two of the sites of significance to blacks in Daytona Beach relate to Mary McLeod Bethune (1875-1955), one of the great educational leaders of Florida. Born in South Carolina and a student in schools in North Carolina and Illinois, she taught school in Georgia, South Carolina, and Florida before founding in Daytona Beach the Daytona Normal and Industrial Institute for Negro Girls. She also began a hospital for blacks, who could usually not find anywhere else to go for medical treatment. In 1923, she joined her school with Cookman Institute of Jacksonville, Florida, and formed Bethune-Cookman Institute in Daytona Beach. Her school grew to become **Bethune-Cookman College**, at 640 Second Avenue just west of Ridgewood and north of Volusia Avenue, and today has some 120 full-time faculty and 2,230 students.

Further Reading:

Ella Kaiser Carruth. *She Wanted to Read*. New York: Abingdon Press, 1966.

Jesse Walter Dees. *The College Built on Prayer*. Daytona Beach: Bethune-Cookman College, 1953.

J. Irving E. Scott. *The Education of Black People in Florida*. Philadelphia: Dorrance & Company, 1974, p. 55+.

Mrs. Bethune distinguished herself in several fields. In 1924, she was elected president of the National Association of Colored Women, which worked to improve the conditions of black women throughout the United States. She also established the National Council of Negro Women and worked on the Commission on Interracial Cooperation. In 1935, she received the Spingarn Award from the National Association for the Advancement of Colored People (NAACP) for her many accomplishments and was named one of the 50 most influential women in this country. The following year she became the first black woman to head a federal agency when she became director of the National Youth Administration's Division of Negro Affairs.

The **Mary Mcleod Bethune Foundation** at Bethune-Cookman College is the house where this great woman lived and died. The two-story frame house on the campus just north of Second Avenue was built around 1914 and contains citations, plaques, photographs, and artifacts of Mrs. Bethune. With her philosophy of "Not for myself, but for others," she willed her home to the American people. Two years before she died, she had her friend, Eleanor Roosevelt, the widow of President Franklin Roosevelt, dedicate the building as the Mary McLeod Bethune Foundation, near which Mrs. Bethune, who died in 1955 at the age of 79, was buried and which officials named a National Historic Landmark in 1975. (Open Monday-Friday, 9:15 a.m.-12 noon and 1-4:45 p.m. College students lead visitors on a tour of the house.) (For more about Mrs. Bethune see New Smyrna Beach below.)

Further Reading:

Malu Halasa. *Mary McLeod Bethune: Educator*. New York: Chelsea House Publishers, 1989.

Rackham Holt. *Mary McLeod Bethune*. Garden City, N.Y.: Doubleday, 1964.

Patricia C. McKissack. *Mary McLeod Bethune*. Chicago: Children's Press, 1985.

Milton Meltzer. *Mary McLeod Bethune*. New York: Viking Kestrel, 1987.

Another college of significance to blacks was **Volusia County Community College**, one of 12 black junior colleges in Florida (see St. Petersburg below). Established in 1957, the school had as its first president Mr. J. Griffin Greene. The county school board located the junior college in a rented apartment building and had the school take over the running of a very successful vocational program. The courses in cosmetology, electrical appliance repair, masonry, radio and television repair, and tailoring attracted far more students than did the college parallel program, but the school taught marketable skills to many students.

The school eventually merged with Daytona Beach Community College. Ironically, northern visitors who had originally opposed the establishment of a separate black junior college were concerned that the merging of Volusia County Community College with the local white college would force black faculty members at Volusia to lose their jobs. The county school board solved this problem by placing the staff from Volusia in college and public school positions; for example, the president of Volusia became the director of guidance at the white college. The enrollment figures for the community college showed that it served many students in both the college parallel program and the vocational programs:

1958-1959: 141 students
1959-1960: 1,122 students
1960-1961: 2,392 students
1961-1962: 1,802 students
1962-1963: 2,384 students
1963-1964: 5,600 students
1964-1965: 5,245 students

The **Howard Thurman House** at 614 Whitehall Street west of Ridgewood and south of Cedar Street was the birthplace of Dr. Howard Thurman (1900-1981). This two-story, wood-frame vernacular structure, which was built around 1888 and finally recognized as a National Historic Preservation Site in 1990, was in the Waycross community, which was later incorporated as Daytona Beach. Besides the middle-class residential neighborhood of Waycross, blacks could live in Midway (where Mary McLeod Bethune's school was) and Newton (where a public school for black children was located). Blacks worked in the white communities of Daytona and, on the ocean side of the river, Sea Breeze and Daytona Beach, but they were not allowed to live in those areas or even be in them after dark.

Howard Thurman was raised by his illiterate grandmother, a former slave who recognized the importance of education and helped him become the first black in Florida to finish the eighth grade. He then went to Jacksonville's Florida Baptist Academy, Atlanta's Morehouse College (where he majored in economics), and the Colgate-Rochester School of Divinity, before beginning his work as a Baptist minister in 1925. He went on to become an educator, preacher, theologian, and distinguished author of 22 books on race and religion. In 1944, in San Francisco he organized the Church for the Fellowship of All Peoples, one of the first racially integrated churches in this country. At Boston University he served as Dean of Marsh Chapel and became the first black to hold such a position at a predominantly white university in the U.S. In 1953, *Life* magazine named him one of the 12 outstanding preachers of the 20th century.

Further Reading:

"Howard Thurman Home Now National Historic Preservation Site," *The Miami Times*, August 23, 1990, p. 6A.

Lois Kaplan, "Dr. Thurman's Legacy," *Daytona Beach Morning Journal*, July 1, 1985: 1.

Howard Thurman. *With Head and Heart: The Autobiography of Howard Thurman*. New York: Harcourt Brace Jovanovich, 1979.

Elizabeth Yates. *Howard Thurman: Portrait of a Practical Dreamer*. New York: John Day Co., 1964.

Another man who made a contribution to the black history of Daytona Beach was Jackie Robinson (1919-1972), who joined the Brooklyn Dodgers in 1947 and became the first black baseball player in modern times to play on a major league team. He had signed with the Brooklyn Dodgers in the fall of 1945 and was sent to Daytona Beach for spring training with the Montreal Royals, the Dodgers farm team. When he trotted onto the city's Island Ball Park on March 17, 1946, for a spring training game, this future Hall-of-Fame second baseman was making history and breaking organized baseball's color barrier.

In 1988, officials renamed the site on City Island west of Memorial Bridge and east of Ridgewood the **Jackie Robinson Ball Park** and erected a bronze statue outside the park's gates that depicts Robinson standing with two small boys, one black and one white, both of whom represent the future. Montreal sculptor Jules LaSalle, who designed the statue after one at Montreal's Olympic Stadium, modified the Daytona Beach statue to have Robinson wearing a Montreal Royals uniform and with his feet more inward to resemble Robinson's pigeon-toed stance. Behind the statue is a series of curved walls of different lengths and heights that are

The Jackie Robinson statue honors the man who integrated modern major league baseball. Credit: Kevin M. McCarthy

meant to suggest the rippling effect of a pebble dropped into a pond; the result reminds onlookers of the many unforeseen benefits that came from Robinson's integration of modern baseball.

At the 1990 dedication ceremonies of the statue, Bill White of Lakewood, Florida, a former major league ball player and the president of the National League, noted how much Robinson had meant to him: "To me, Jackie represents perseverance. He succeeded despite a lot of obstacles, and I think that's important for any kid to learn. I know I wouldn't be where I'm at now if it hadn't been for Jackie." Robinson had a career batting average of .311, set a fielding record for second basemen, won the league's Most Valuable Player Award in 1949, and was elected to the Baseball Hall of Fame in 1962, his first year of eligibility.

Further Reading:

John Carter, "Rachel Robinson: I Love the Statue," *The News-Journal* [Daytona Beach], September 15, 1990, D1.

Steve Moore, "Robinson: A Hero Honored," *The News-Journal* [Daytona Beach], September 16, 1990, p. C-1+.

Jackie Robinson, "Jackie Robinson's First Spring Training," in *The American Sporting Experience*, ed. Steven A. Riess (West Point, N.Y.: Leisure Press, 1984), pp. 365-370. Excerpts from *Jackie Robinson: My Own Story* by Jackie Robinson and Wendell Smith (New York: Greenberg, 1948).

Jackie Robinson as told to Alfred Duckett. *I Never Had It Made*. New York: Putnam, 1972.

Carl Rowan with Jackie Robinson. *Wait Till Next Year*. New York: Random House, 1960.

Jules Tygiel. *Baseball's Great Experiment: Jackie Robinson and His Legacy*. New York: Oxford University Press, 1983.

Among other sites in the city is **Mount Bethel Baptist Institutional Church** at 700 South Campbell Street. This is the oldest Baptist Church in Daytona Beach, having been organized in 1885 by the late Reverend J.B. Hankerson. At first. the church was in Silver Hill on Fremont Avenue, but a few years later was moved to Church Street (later called Marion Street). Also, the **Museum of Arts and Sciences** at 1040 Museum Boulevard west of Nova Road and south of Volusia Avenue has part of the building devoted to the African cultural history of black Floridians. The collection of African art is one of the best in the Southeast. Open 9 a.m.-4 p.m., Tuesday-Friday; 12 noon-5 p.m., weekends. (904)-255-0285. Finally, black author Zora Neale Hurston (see Eatonville and Fort Pierce below) lived on two houseboats, *Wanago* and *Sun Tan*, in Daytona Beach in the 1940s. She moored them at the Howard Boat Works, 633 Ballough Road, a pleasant place where, she wrote, "All the other boat owners are very nice to me. Not a word about race." Workers recently demolished the boat works after many years of service to the area's boat owners.

Chapter 19

DeLand

In December 1876, industrialist Henry DeLand founded the town in central Florida that bears his last name. Settlers soon began moving in and setting up businesses, including a bank, restaurants, stores, and sawmills. Those settlers suffered a temporary setback when an 1886 fire burned up many wooden stores, but the fire enabled owners to rebuild with sturdier and more attractive brick. The town received a big boost in 1885 when the Florida Baptists established DeLand College, a school which changed its name four years later to the John B. Stetson University to honor one of its donors.

At first, the townspeople relied on citrus products for their livelihood, but the 1894-1895 freezes ruined Henry DeLand, the town, and many other settlements in the state. Determined not to give up, the settlers rebuilt their economy, but diversified into producing naval stores, dairy products, and ferns. Among the black businessmen in town were G.W. Miller, G.D. Taylor, and a Mr. Randall. Today DeLand has a population of 16,491, of whom 3,615 (22%) are blacks.

The prosperity of the town and the influx of northerners necessitated in 1920 the building of a hospital for whites, the Old DeLand Memorial Hospital, and in 1926 one for blacks, the Old DeLand Colored Hospital, both on Stone Street. The name of the Memorial Hospital honored the local soldiers who had died in the service of their country during World War I. Before construction of the **Old Deland Colored Hospital**, blacks had no medical facilities in the town and had to rely on local physicians and on Mrs. Mandy Worthy, a midwife and practical nurse who cared for them in her own home. In 1925, Dr. and Mrs. A.J. Burgess and others began contributing to a fund to build a hospital for blacks near the DeLand Memorial Hospital. The simple, utilitarian, masonry building that local architect Gouveneur Medwin Peek designed for the Old DeLand Colored Hospital contrasted sharply with the two-and-a-half story, Italian Renaissance-style structure for whites.

The smaller size, lack of sophisticated medical equipment, and poorer conditions of the black hospital indicated how the races were kept separate in those days. For example, when doctors needed to perform surgery on a black patient, attendants would wheel the equipment from the white hospital across the parking lot or the doctors would use the basement emergency room of the white hospital or, at night, the main operating room, when hospital officials were away. These practices continued until the mid-1930s, at which time officials began allowing doctors to operate on blacks in the white hospital. Both buildings remained functioning until 1948, when officials transferred the services to the DeLand Naval Air Station. In 1952, a modern hospital, the Fish Memorial Hospital, opened for all the residents of DeLand.

Bradley Hall at 511 S. Clara Avenue north of Euclid Avenue, south of both New York Avenue and Voorhis Avenue and east of 15A, is now a private residence, but at one time the two-story, red-brick house was an orphanage for black children. Built around 1925, this building is one of the very few black orphanages still standing, perhaps the only one. At first called Bradley Hall and then Safe Home Orphanage, the building, which Eva Bradfield ran, was converted to a private residence around 1950.

The **J.W. Wright Building** at 258-264 West Voorhis Avenue

The Wright Building was owned by an important black businessman who did much to improve the lot of other blacks in DeLand. Credit: Kevin M. McCarthy

near S. Clara Avenue was owned by James Washington Wright (1875-1956), who had arrived in DeLand at the age of 15 with $1.50 in his pocket. He worked for 75 cents a day, then $1 a day, until he saved up enough money to begin buying his own land, beginning with his first five acres of citrus after the terrible 1894-1895 freeze. By hard work and many late nights of working his groves by lantern, he saved enough money to buy more land and buildings, one of which is the Wright Building where he and his wife, Ethel, operated a grocery and meat market. He also owned and operated his own shipping business on West Minnesota Avenue, grew crops, and did much to improve the lot of other blacks. Another building of importance to blacks, the **Charles P. Bailey Funeral Home** at 728 Adelle Avenue, was started by Charles P. Bailey of Punta Gorda, who won the Distinguished Flying Cross after flying 133 combat missions over

Europe and shooting down three enemy airplanes as a fighter pilot with the all-black 99th Fighter Squadron.

Further Reading:

Arthur E. Francke, Jr., Alyce Hockaday Gillingham, Maxine Carey Turner. *Volusia: The West Side.* DeLand: West Volusia Historical Society, 1986.

Pleasant D. Gold. *History of Volusia County, Florida.* DeLand: Painter Printing Co., 1927.

Ianthe B. Hebel. *Centennial History of Volusia County, Florida.* Daytona Beach: College Publishing Co., 1955.

Reflections: 100 Years of Progress. DeLand: Bicentennial Commission, 1976, pp. 66-67: "James Washington Wright."

Michael G. Schene. *Hopes, Dreams, and Promises: A History of Volusia County, Florida.* Daytona Beach: News-Journal Corporation, 1976.

Barb Shepherd, "A Landmark of Black Heritage" [about Bradley Hall], *The Orlando Sentinel,* March 15, 1992, p. K-1+.

Chapter 20

Delray Beach

The U.S. government built the Orange Grove House of Refuge in 1876 to give shipwrecked sailors shelter and food in an area that later became Delray Beach. Nineteen years later, seven men from Michigan arrived to settle in the area and established a town called Linton. The name changed to Delray to commemorate the Michigan town of Delray, from which one of the early settlers had come. The new town became part of Palm Beach County, which had been established in 1909. In 1927, the city of Delray on the west side of the intracoastal waterway joined Delray Beach on the ocean side to become Delray Beach. Over the years blacks moved into the area and settled down to a life of hard work in agriculture and business. Today Delray Beach has a population of 47,181, of whom 12,415 (26%) are blacks.

Local officials have placed on the Delray Beach Local Register of Historical Places various sites of importance to blacks in one of the oldest and most permanent parts of the city. When this section, which was incorporated as Linton in 1895 and is bounded on the east by West 1st Avenue, on the west by West 8th Avenue, on the north by Lake Ida Road, and on the south by 4th Street, was part of North Dade County, blacks settled it and established churches, homes, and schools. One early building was **School No. 4, Delray**

Colored on the east side of N.W. 5th Avenue, 100′ south of N.W. 1st Street. In 1894, local blacks petitioned the school superintendent for a school and a teacher, but, because no facilities existed to house the school, it did not open until October 1895. B.F. James, the school's first teacher, opened the four-month school term in a thatched hut on 5th Avenue, now part of the parking lot of Greater Mount Olive Missionary Baptist Church. In 1990, officials dedicated on the original school site a bronze marker with a locator map showing various historic sites. The **B.F. James & Frances J. Bright Mini-park** there honors the first two teachers of the school. The Greater Mount Olive Missionary Baptist Church and its pastor, the Rev. L.C. Johnson, gave the city and the community an easement deed for this mini-park, which became part of the city's Park and Recreation Department by action of the City Commission on February 13, 1990. The inscription on the monument reads as follows:

> Late in the 19th Century, a group of black settlers established a community in this area that became part of the Town of Linton and later the City of Delray Beach. These hardy pioneers established the cultural organization necessary to foster education, fellowship and spiritual needs, despite difficult environmental conditions and isolation.

Greater Mount Olive Missionary Baptist Church at 40 N.W. 4th Avenue was organized in 1896 by a missionary, the Reverend A.B. Williams. Two years later, trustees of the church bought land from the Model Land Company and built what is today the third oldest church in Palm Beach County and the oldest in Delray Beach. Mount Olive built a frame structure on the site and shared it with the African Methodist Church (mentioned next). The original building, constructed in 1898 and able to seat 200 people, was destroyed in the 1928 hurricane that ravaged south Florida, but a year later workers built a new building which doubled the size of the original. In 1959, officials completely remodeled the church and enlarged it to accommodate 1,000 parishioners.

St. Paul African Methodist Episcopal Church at 119 N.W. 5th Avenue was originally organized in 1897 as the African Methodist Episcopal Church in a packing house on the corner of N.W. 3rd Avenue and 2nd Street (now Martin Luther King, Jr. Drive). In 1899, trustees bought a lot from the Model Land Company and shared the building of **Mount Olive Missionary Baptist Church**; their church, originally called Mount Tabor A.M.E. Church, changed its name to St. Paul in 1926. Officials completely remodeled and enlarged it in 1958 and placed in the front yard the large bronze bell, which was part of the original building and was rung by the sexton to announce fires, other public emergencies, and deaths.

Free and Accepted Masons, Lodge 275 at 85 N.W. 5th Avenue houses one of the oldest fraternal organizations in south Florida. These masons, organized in 1899, bought a lot from the African Methodist Episcopal Church in 1904. The original building has been demolished, but the new structure stands on the site of the original. In 1911, the same year that Delray Beach was incorporated, immigrants from the Bahamas who wanted to celebrate the Anglican Episcopal service organized **St. Matthew Episcopal Church** at 404 S.W. 3rd Street. They built the church in 1916 and remodeled it extensively ten years later.

Further Reading:

Vivian Reissland Rouson-Gossett. *Like a Mighty Banyan: Contributions of Black People to the History of Palm Beach County*. Palm Beach County: Palm Beach Junior College, 1982.

Chapter 21

Dunnellon

When Albertus Vogt discovered phosphate in Dunnellon in 1889, hundreds of workers poured into the area hoping to take advantage of the find. Many of those workers were blacks from Georgia and Alabama who had been lured to Dunnellon with the promise of wages and a sharing of the phosphate wealth. At one point, according to Gene Burnett, half the population was black, but "they shared little if any voice in its affairs, even while contributing greatly to its prosperity. They toiled long hours in the mines at subsistent wages—always lower than a white man's—and had to live in the flimsiest of shacks." (p. 114) One black doctor who ministered to the health needs of local blacks was Dr. James F. Sistrunk, who moved to Fort Lauderdale in 1921 to become the only black doctor in the city's black community (see Fort Lauderdale below). Racist whites formed lynching mobs to try to control the blacks, who in turn secretly formed their own Anti-Mob Lynchlaw Society to protect themselves and fight against a particularly racist marshall of the town. The discrimination became so bad that many blacks finally left town and did not return. Today Dunnellon's blacks make up just 12% of the population of 1,624, i.e. 192 people.

The **Second Bethel Baptist Church**, now the Annie W. Johnson Senior Service Center, was originally a school which served the black community. Completed in 1888, it later became Second Bethel Baptist Church. Its first pastor, Rev. Henry Shaw, established the church in an old house, borrowed chairs and boxes for seats, and began ministering to black sawmill and turpentine workers in the area. In time the church moved from the east side to the west side of old U.S. 41; then, when the new U.S. 41 needed room, workers used a mule team to move the church further west to its present location on Test Court.

The church building also served as a school for black children four months a year. Students would kneel on the floor and use the church benches as desks. One of those students was Annie W. Johnson, who later earned degrees from Booker T. Washington High School in Miami, Florida Normal College in St. Augustine, Florida A&M University in Tallahassee, and Columbia University in New York City. She spent 33 years teaching in Dunnellon and Citrus counties, including time at Hernando Elementary School in Citrus County. After her retirement in 1974, she established the Annie Johnson Center that now uses the building of the Second Bethel Baptist Church. With contributions from sources like United Way, the Center provides help to the elderly and others in need. A $20,000 grant in 1987 helped restore the original church building, which serves today as a Human Resource Center for south Dunnellon.

Directions:

Although Dunnellon is part of Marion County, the Second Bethel Baptist Church is actually in Citrus County just below Dunnellon. The turn-off to the original building of the Second Bethel Baptist Church is west of U.S. 41 just south of the Withlacoochee River.

Further Reading:

Arch Fredric Blakey. *The Florida Phosphate Industry*. Cambridge, Mass.: Wertheim Committee, Harvard University, 1973.

Gene Burnett, "Phosphate Lured the Greedy, the Untamed," *Florida Trend*, January 1976, pp. 111-114.

Dunnellon

J. Lester Dinkins. *Dunnellon: Boomtown of the 1890's*. St. Petersburg: Great Outdoors Publishing Company, 1969.
Hampton Dunn. *Back Home: A History of Citrus County, Florida*. Clearwater: Citrus County Bicentennial Steering Committee, 1977?
John Paul Jones, "Dunnellon," *Florida Living*, July 1989, pp. 57-59.
Ken Moritsugu, "A Century's Place of Worship," *St. Petersburg Times. Citrus Times Edition*, February 10, 1992, pp. 1, 7.

Chapter 22

Eatonville

This town in Orange County just off I-4 between Winter Park and Maitland and north of Orlando takes its name from a white man, Captain Joshua (or Josiah) C. Eaton of Maine, a retired Navy paymaster who settled in nearby Maitland after the Civil War and helped a group of blacks buy a 500-acre tract of land west of Maitland. Incorporated in 1888 as a black community, Eatonville attracted many black settlers, including John Hurston, a skilled carpenter, Baptist preacher, one-time mayor of the town, and father of writer Zora Neale Hurston.

Further Reading:

Frank M. Otey. *Eatonville, Florida: A Brief History of One of America's First Freedmen's Towns.* Winter Park: Four-G Publishers, 1989.

Zora Neale Hurston was born in 1901, according to her own testimony, or 1891, according to many scholars, soon after the town was incorporated. She wrote the following in her autobiography, *Dust Tracks on a Road* (1942):

> I was born in a Negro town. I do not mean by that the black back-side of an average town. Eatonville, Florida,

> is, and was at the time of my birth, a pure Negro town — charter, Mayor, council, town marshal and all. It was not the first Negro community in America, but it was the first to be incorporated, the first attempt at organized self-government on the part of the Negroes in America. (p. 3)

She also wrote about the town in novels like *Jonah's Gourd Vine* (1934) and *Their Eyes Were Watching God* (1937), shorter writings like "The Eatonville Anthology" (1926), and short stories like "Sweat" (1926) and "The Gilded Six-Bits" (1933).

Her family's home, long since gone, was in the area bounded today by Lemon, Lime, People, and West streets. Joe Clarke's store, where the young Zora heard many of the stories that later made their way into her writings, is now a grocery story at the northeast corner of Kennedy Boulevard and West Street; Joe Clarke's house was next door to his store. Hurston's father's church, the **Macedonia Missionary Baptist Church**, was then on the south side of Eaton Street between East and West streets; the Macedonia Baptist Church today is in a new building on East Kennedy Boulevard and Calhoun Street. After her mother, Lucy, died and her father remarried, Zora went to Jacksonville to live with a brother while attending school. She later attended Morgan Academy, Howard University in Washington, D.C., and Barnard College in New York City. In the late 1920s, she returned to Eatonville to collect the folklore that would appear in her *Mules and Men* (1935).

The **Zora Neale Hurston Memorial** by the town's fire station is on the former site of a home that belonged to one of Zora's friends that she stayed with on her returns to Eatonville. The Hurston family home was located on what is today a vacant lot across from the fire station. Nearby is the **St. Lawrence African Methodist Episcopal Church**, the first black church in the area and one that dates back to 1882. The **Zora Neale Hurston National Museum of Fine Arts** (phone: 407-647-3307) at 227 East Kennedy Boulevard has

The Zora Neale Hurston Memorial honors a great writer and collector of folklore. Credit: Kevin M. McCarthy

works of black artists in various shows throughout the year, and an annual "ZORA!" festival honors the town's most famous writer. Today Eatonville has a population of 2,192, of whom 2,027 (93%) are blacks.

Further Reading:

Steve Glassman and Kathryn Lee Seidel, editors. *Zora in Florida*. Orlando: University of Central Florida Press, 1991, esp. Anna Lillios, "Excursions into Zora Neale Hurston's Eatonville," pp. 13-27.

Robert E. Hemenway. *Zora Neale Hurston: A Literary Biography*. Urbana: University of Illinois Press, 1977.

Zora Neale Hurston. *Dust Tracks on a Road*. Philadelphia: Lippincott, 1942.

N.Y. Nathiri, editor. *Zora! Zora Neale Hurston: A Woman and Her Community*. Orlando: Sentinel Communications Company, 1991.

Janelle Yates. *Zora Neale Hurston: A Storyteller's Life*. Staten Island: Ward Hill Press, 1991.

The **Robert Hungerford Normal and Industrial School**, now the Wymore Career Educational Center, on Kennedy Boulevard near I-4 used to attract black students from all over Florida, including, possibly, Zora Neale Hurston. Established at the end of the 19th century, it first taught its students academic subjects, as well as industrial trades, agriculture, and the domestic arts. In 1950, the school became part of the Orange County Public School System; in 1967, when desegregation took effect, it became part of the alternative school system that stressed vocational training and careers for those not planning on attending college. Today the Hungerford Elementary School is also on the property.

Further Reading:

J. Irving E. Scott. *The Education of Black People in Florida*. Philadelphia: Dorrance & Company, 1974, p. 44.

Chapter 23

Floral City

*B*efore and after Spanish explorer Hernando de Soto passed through this area in 1539 on his way north, Indian tribes established villages in the vicinity, and in the 19th century white settlers began moving in. Floral City was settled in 1883 and two years later had a population of 300, twice that of Miami in south Florida at the time. The many flowers and crops there gave Floral City and Citrus County (established in 1887) their names. Today Floral City has a population of 2,698, of whom just 28 (1%) are blacks.

Blacks came to Floral City to work in the phosphate mines, sawmills, and turpentine stills and to raise their families. One of the churches they established was the **Pleasant Hill Baptist Church** at 8200 E. Magnolia Street, the oldest religious building of the black community in Floral City and one of three black churches in town, the other two being Mount Carmel Free Methodist Church and Grace Temple Church of the Living God. The wood-frame, folk-styled church was built between 1895 and 1910 and added asbestos siding and modern screen windows about 10 years ago. E. Magnolia Street is west of U.S. 41 below E. Orange and above E. Walnut toward the south end of town.

About one-half mile south of E. Magnolia Street is **Frasier Cemetery** on the southwest corner of E. Tower Trail and S.

Pleasant Hill Baptist Church is the oldest religious structure for blacks in the town. Credit: Kevin M. McCarthy

Great Oak Drive east of U.S. 41; the cemetery took its name from H.C. Frasier, who donated the land in 1908 so that he could bury his son. One grave there was of Arthur Norton, who, when he died in 1986 at age 108, was the oldest-known resident of Citrus County. Like many other blacks, Norton had moved to the area around 1900 to work in the phosphate mines. The Frasier Cemetery graves, which date back to the early 1900s and are scattered over a wide area, have gravestones of family members as well as of former residents, although some markers have no name attached to them.

Further Reading:

Brad Bennett,"Agencies on the trail of African-American history,"*Citrus Chronicle*, August 18, 1991, 1A.

Hampton Dunn. *Back Home: A History of Citrus County, Florida*. Clearwater: Citrus County Bicentennial Steering Committee, 1977?

"Friends, Family Recall Norton's special qualities" [about Arthur Norton], *Citrus Chronicle*, Feb. 12, 1986, p. 1+.

Ken Moritsugu, "Faithful Few Still Come to Worship" [about Pleasant Hill

Baptist Church], *St. Petersburg Times, Citrus Times edition*, February 24, 1992, pp. 1, 3.

Ken Moritsugu, "Silent Reminder of Days Gone By" [about Frasier Cemetery], *St. Petersburg Times, Citrus Times edition*. February 17, 1992, pp. 1, 2.

Norm Swetman, "Arthur Norton Dies; Citrus' Oldest at 109," *Citrus County Chronicle*, February 13, 1986, p. 1+.

Chapter 24

Fort Lauderdale

Among the first settlers to this part of Florida when the Spanish controlled it in the 18th century were slaves escaping from northern plantations. Some of those slaves joined the Seminole Indians who were battling white settlers and bounty hunters looking for escaped slaves, and others went to the Bahamas to escape the harsh conditions of slavery. In the early 19th century, black slaves working for Count Odet Philippe built the first salt-making operation on the area's beaches. In 1839, during the Second Seminole War, a black man by the name of George who was working as an interpreter saved the life of the military commander during a battle with the Indians.

Broward County developed as more and more people moved to south Florida and as Henry Flagler's railroad opened up the area for settlement and cultivation. As Flagler pushed construction of his Florida East Coast Railroad south to Miami and the Florida Keys, he hired many black workers, and, when they finished extending the railroad to Key West, many of them settled down in what became Broward County and became sharecroppers. Even if they did not own their own fields, many owned their own residential lots. Among the blacks who moved here in the late 1880s and early 1890s were the descendants of freed or runaway slaves, immigrants from the Bahamas, and farmers and craftsmen seeking more opportunities. Fort Lauderdale was incorporated in 1911, four years before Broward County split from Dade County.

Further Reading:

Stuart B. McIver. *Fort Lauderdale and Broward County*. Woodland Hills, Cal.: Windsor Publications, Inc., 1983.

Philip J. Weidling and August Burghard. *Checkered Sunshine: The Story of Fort Lauderdale, 1793-1955*. Gainesville: University of Florida Press, 1966.

When blacks moved to Fort Lauderdale, they usually settled in the northwestern section or "colored town" north of Broward Boulevard and west of the railroad tracks. As more and more blacks settled in Broward County, they began demanding schools for their children to prepare them for good jobs and to take them out of poverty. In the Reconstruction period after the American Civil War, politicians had established Black Codes that attempted to keep the former slaves in a new type of bondage. The Codes did not allow blacks to own knives, guns, or other weapons, allowed the police to arrest blacks and sentence them to forced labor, and gave the state the right to execute any black who raped a white woman or who encouraged others to rebellion. The Codes also provided for separate schools for black children. Black men were to pay a dollar tax for the schools, and the children were required to pay tuition, all of which was meant to cost the state nothing. By 1901, when Fort Lauderdale was still part of Dade County, the county had 20 schools for whites but only six schools for blacks.

Further Reading:

Joe M. Richardson. *The Negro in the Reconstruction of Florida, 1865-1877*. Tallahassee: Florida State University, 1965.

Jerrell H. Shofner, "Custom, Law, and History: The Enduring Influence of Florida's 'Black Code,'" *Florida Historical Quarterly*, vol. 55 (January 1977), pp. 277-298.

Jerrell H. Shofner. *Nor Is It Over Yet: Florida During the Era of Reconstruction, 1863-1877*. Gainesville: University of Florida Press, 1974.
Theodore Brantner Wilson. *The Black Codes of the South*. University, Ala.: University of Alabama Press, 1965.

Deerfield Beach above Fort Lauderdale got its first black school in 1903. Four years later, blacks in Fort Lauderdale got their first permanent school when white pioneer Tom M. Bryan donated a one-room, frame building on the west side of N.W. Third Avenue. When workers later tore down the building to build an ice plant, black children who wanted an education had to go to private homes or to the Knights of Pythias Hall at N.W. Fourth Street and Fourth Avenue. Black children were still expected to work in the fields picking crops after school and during the winter harvest, a practice that shortened their school year by one or more months. The first school census of the county showed that in 1915 Fort Lauderdale had 421 white students and 75 black students.

As black parents continued to press for a black school, the Broward County School Board finally agreed in 1923 to open a "colored school" in Tuskegee Park, a black subdivision, on land sold at a modest cost by Frank and Ivy Cromartie Stranahan, two leading white citizens of the city. When the school opened in 1924, Joseph Ely became its first principal and named it to honor James Hardy Dillard, a white man who had done much to foster good relations between the races in the South.

In 1927, the city government helped reinforce segregation by restricting black homes to the northwest quadrant and not allowing blacks to travel to other parts of the city after certain hours. Many blacks worked in tourism, construction, and agriculture, but employers often needed more workers than were readily available. One way that local officials got workers around harvest time in the years of segregation was to arrest blacks on vagrancy charges and "allow" them to pay off the $35 fine by working in the fields.

During the Depression of the 1930s, Lincoln Brown and

J.W. Mickens succeeded Ely as principals of Dillard. Because the school was still not a full high school, students had to leave Broward County and go elsewhere to complete their education, for example black schools in West Palm Beach and Miami. When Clarence C. Walker (1880-1942) became principal of Dillard in 1937, he worked to extend the school's curriculum from eight grades to twelve. The first senior-high school commencement for blacks in Fort Lauderdale took place in 1938, but Walker's efforts to expand the school term for black children to nine months did not have fruition until soon after he died in 1942.

When a new Dillard Elementary School and a new Dillard High School were opened at 2365 N.W. 11th Street just west of the Old Dillard High School between 1952 and 1954, the old 1924 building remained open as an elementary school and was eventually named the Clarence C. Walker Elementary School. In 1974, the old building became an administrative annex for the Division of Instruction. The Broward County Black Historical Society eventually succeeded in restoring the **Old Dillard High School** at 1001 N.W. 4th Street as a black museum and cultural center. Local officials began integrating the schools in 1961 — without incident, and by 1970 were able to integrate all the schools of Broward County, thanks in great part to the efforts of George Allen, the first black to receive a law degree from the University of Florida.

The **Dr. James F. Sistrunk Boulevard Historical Marker** in the 1400 block of N.W. 6th Street honors a man who delivered 5,000+ babies during his many years serving the local black community. Born in Midway, Florida, and educated in Ocala and in Meharry Medical College in Nashville, Tennessee, James F. Sistrunk (1891-1966) came to Fort Lauderdale in 1921 and served as the first black medical doctor in the city and the only one for almost 16 years. When Dr. Von Delaney Mizell, the city's second black physician, came to town in 1938, he and Dr. Sistrunk established Provident Hospital at 1409 N.W. Sixth Street. The city commemorates

Dr. Sistrunk, who served as Chief of Staff of Provident Hospital, in the name of Sistrunk Boulevard and in the name of the bridge over the North Fork of the New River on N.W. 6th Street. The city honors his fellow doctor in the **Von D. Mizell Library**, which serves the community on the same site as the old Provident Hospital.

Further Reading:

Stuart McIver. *Glimpses of South Florida History*. Miami: Florida Flair Books, 1988, p. 131: "'Doc' Sistrunk's 5,000 Babies."

Kitty Oliver, "Early Black Doctors," in *Mostly Sunny Days*, edited by Bob Kearney. Miami: Miami Herald Publishing Company, 1986, pp. 159-161.

In 1927, city officials declared that ocean-front public beaches in the city were off limits to blacks. In searching for another beach, local blacks found the Ocean Mile that developer Arthur Galt of Chicago had bought in 1913. Galt, a Chicago lawyer and the son of the law partner of Hugh Taylor Birch, had tried to sell 8,000 acres of nearby land to a development company, but the Depression and land bust ended that scheme. The blacks used the Ocean Mile, which many called the "black beach" and which they reached by driving across a wooden swing bridge on Oakland Park Boulevard, until Galt eventually sold his land after World War II for $19,000,000, the largest private land transaction up to that time in the history of this country. When builders began constructing a new development, one that would culminate in today's many high-rise condominiums on Ocean Mile worth millions of dollars, the blacks had to move to another beach south of the Port Everglades Inlet.

In 1956, after blacks marched on the county courthouse to demand a beach of their own, the county bought beach-front land where John U. Lloyd State Park is today. Because no road linked the mainland to the beach, blacks had to use a ferry, an inconvenience and expense that angered enough of them to march to the white beaches near Las Olas Boulevard and stage a wade-in on July 4, 1961. Dr. Von D. Mizell later recalled: "I was scared that day. I had to walk through a little corridor there with a human wall on both sides. It was tense, and one little spark could have started a riot. I had to look straight ahead, and I was not at ease at all." The police arrested several black leaders, but the city commission finally agreed to build a road to the black beach.

But local black leaders demanded more; they wanted an end to the segregated beaches. Eula Johnson, a widowed mother of three who had become president of the Broward NAACP in 1958, led seven carloads of young people to the white beaches in late July 1961. The Ku Klux Klan destroyed her car and threatened more violence, and the Fort Lauderdale police tried to convince her to call off wade-ins because her actions would keep away tourists, but she persisted. When officials took Mrs. Johnson to court, a federal judge ruled that blacks had the right to swim at the public beaches.

Integration was finally taking effect. In 1966, a local teacher, Boisy Waters, became the first black elected to a Broward County office, and eight years later Kathleen Wright became the first county-wide black official. The next year Sylvia Poitier became the first black mayor of nearby Deerfield Beach and eventually chairperson of the Broward County Commission. Another local official, Alcee Hastings, became the first black federal judge appointed from south Florida and eventually won a seat in the U.S. Congress.

Further Reading:

Peter Cary, "Fort Lauderdale's Negro Beach," in *Mostly Sunny Days*, edited by Bob Kearney. Miami: Miami Herald Publishing Company, 1986, pp. 162-164.

Stuart McIver. *Glimpses of South Florida History*. Miami: Florida Flair Books, 1988, p. 159: "Galt Had His Mile and Blacks Had a Beach."

Today Fort Lauderdale has a population of 149,377, of whom 41,997 (28%) are blacks. Among other places of importance in this study are the **Carroll Vinnette Repertory**

Company at 503 S.E. 6th Street, which offers black-oriented productions, and the **African American Caribbean Cultural Center** at 1601 S. Andrews Avenue with its permanent exhibits of black art. Finally, the Museum of Art at 1 E. Las Olas Boulevard in downtown Fort Lauderdale has an African Collection worth noting, and the city also has an annual Black Film Festival.

Further Reading:

"Broward County Is Showcasing Its Black Achievers in Extended History Celebration," *The Miami Times*, February 10, 1994, p. 6D.

Chapter 25

Fort Myers

*T*his city on the southwest coast was the site of a 19th-century military outpost, from which military authorities shipped Seminole Indians to western reservations. Right before the Civil War, Major James S. Evans, a surveyor, brought in slaves from his Virginia plantation to cultivate the land, but the war disrupted life in the idyllic site, and it was not until the war ended and the telegraph line reached Fort Myers in 1869 that settlers began arriving in greater numbers. The first free black to settle in the area may have been Nelson Tillis, who arrived in 1867; more than 100 of his descendants still live in Lee County.

Further Reading:

Miller Davis, "Pioneer Club Honors First Black Family in Fort Myers" [about Nelson Tillis], *Fort Myers News-Press*, April 27, 1980, p. 2B. Also see September 16, 1985, p. 1B+.

Fort Myers was incorporated in 1885, and Lee County, named after General Robert E. Lee of the Confederacy, was established in 1887. In 1885, the area had only 500 people, 20 of whom were black, but the coming of the railroad in 1904, connecting Fort Myers with Tampa and the North, attracted more people and increased the prosperity of farmers who could ship their perishable crops to northern markets. The blacks who worked on farms, in hotels, and in the lumber mills prospered until the Depression of the 1930s put many out of work. Fort Myers and the surrounding Lee County have experienced a population explosion this century as more and more people moved south to take advantage of the area's semi-tropical climate. Today Fort Myers has a population of around 45,206, of whom 14,422 (32%) are blacks.

From those early days, black families wanted the best education possible for their children. The minutes of the area's first school board meeting, held in 1887, stated that "the colored people shall be encouraged to organize a school district and receive equal benefits as sub-district No. 3 in New Prospect." According to some records, the school board hired a black teacher, Wesley Roberts, and paid him $20 a month to teach a three-month term in the black district of North Fort Myers near Hancock Creek. The next year, the school board named Prince Robinson as trustee of another black school district in Fort Myers. By 1900, the school-age students in the area were as follows:

	Male	Female	Total
Whites	395	396	791
Blacks	17	15	32
Indians	16	16	32

Eight years later, 70 black students were attending school there. The **Paul Lawrence Dunbar School** at 1857 High Street off Dr. Martin Luther King, Jr., Boulevard (formerly Anderson Avenue) was opened in 1927 and served as the school for the predominantly black Dunbar community. Named for black poet Paul Lawrence (or Laurence) Dunbar (1872-1906) of Ohio and having for its first principal James Robert Dixon, it became so well known for its excellence that children from as far away as Lakeland attended it to com-

The Dunbar School served as a school for the predominantly black Dunbar community since 1927. Credit: Kevin M. McCarthy

plete their high school requirements. In 1963, officials built a new high school one mile away on Edison Avenue and named it Dunbar High School. It remained an all-black high school until 1969, when it became a holding school for the present Riverdale High School and then a middle school for grades 6-8. Today it serves as the Dunbar Community School for adult classes and other community activities.

At the Dunbar School are buildings belonging to the former **Williams Academy**, which opened in 1913 as a black school and later became known as Williams Primary. Its first teachers were K.D. Wilson and Sadda Ford; among its graduates was Edgar Leo Barker, the first graduate to return to Lee County to teach and who later served as principal of Dunbar High School. Located on the northern side of Anderson Avenue at Cranford Avenue, extending back to

Lemon Street, the two-story school with classrooms on both floors and a name which honored J.S. Williams (the Superintendent of the Colored Schools) closed in 1927, when the Dunbar School opened. Its buildings have been altered and moved to the Dunbar School site.

One of the long-time teachers at Dunbar Elementary School was Evelyn Sams, who retired in 1971 after a 47-year career in education. Another Sams, Jessie Bennett Sams, wrote an autobiography, *White Mother* (New York: McGraw-Hill, 1957), about growing up in the black section of Fort Myers. A recent black educator who was appointed to the Florida Board of Regents by Governor Lawton Chiles was Audrea Anderson, a professor of English at Edison Community College.

Further Reading:

Lee Melsek, "ECC Teacher Named Newest Regent" [about Audrea Anderson], *Fort Myers News-Press*, November 10, 1993, p. 1A+.

Donald O. Stone and Beth W. Carter. *The First 100 Years: Lee County Public Schools, 1887-1987*. Fort Myers: School Board of Lee County, 1988.

One section of Fort Myers that attracted many blacks over the years was Harlem Heights, which is southeast of McGregor Boulevard, east of San Carlos Boulevard, and south of Gladiolus Drive. Today the area, which consists of 11 streets and around 700 residents, has a growing number of Hispanics. Dr. Marion Johnson, a black physician who built a settlement for migrant farmworkers in the 1940s, named this site after the country's famous black neighborhood in New York City.

Further Reading:

Mark Stephens, "Harlem Heights," *Fort Myers News-Press*, November 14, 1982, p. 1A, 13A. Other articles on this section are in subsequent issues of the newspaper: November 15, 1982, p. 1A, 9A; November 16, 1982, p. 1A, 9A. Also February 27, 1994, p. 1G+.

McCullum Hall at the N.E. corner of Cranford Avenue and Dr. Martin Luther King, Jr., Boulevard (formerly Anderson Avenue) served for many years as the entertainment center for the black community and hosted such entertainers as Count Basie, Duke Ellington, and Louis Armstrong. During World War II, many black soldiers went to the USO there from nearby Page and Buckingham fields, where they were training for overseas duty. Today one can reach the site, which was built in 1938, by going south on U.S. 41 just over the Caloosahatchee River and turning east on Dr. Martin Luther King, Jr., Boulevard for about 11 blocks.

Further Reading:

"McCullum Hall was full of fun, entertainment," *Fort Myers News-Press*, February 1, 1993, p. 3D.

The **Etta Powell Home** at 2764 Lime Street used to house black major league baseball players who trained at Terry Park but were not allowed to stay at area hotels in the days of segregation. The hospital for blacks, Jones-Walker Hospital on High Street, honored in its name Mrs. Melissa Jones and Candis Walker, who worked hard to raise money for the facility; it operated from the late 1920s until a federal edict closed it in 1965. Finally, the **Dr. Ella Piper Center** at 1771 Evans Avenue honors Ella Mae Piper (1884-1954), who established the first beauty parlor and chiropody (for foot problems) office in Fort Myers.

Further Reading:

Prudy Taylor Board, "Thoroughly Modern Ella" [about Ella Piper], *Fort Myers News-Press*, June 10, 1984, p. 1E+. Also see November 26, 1989, p. 13A.

Prudy Taylor Board and Patricia Pope Bartlett. *Lee County: A Pictorial History*. Norfolk, Va: The Donning Company, 1985.

Prudy Taylor Board and Esther B. Colcord. *Historic Fort Myers*. Virginia Beach, Va: The Donning Company, 1992.

Prudy Taylor Board and Esther B. Colcord. *Pages From the Past: A Pictorial*

Retrospective of Lee County, Florida. Norfolk, Va: The Donning Company, 1990.

Marian Godown & Alberta Rawchuck. *Yesterday's Fort Myers*. Miami: Seemann, 1975.

Karl H. Grismer. *The Story of Fort Myers*. St. Petersburg: St. Petersburg Printing Company, 1949.

Suzanne Jeffries and Lee Melsek, "Far from the Dream," *Fort Myers News-Press*, February 26, 1989, p. 1A+. Also see September 24, 1989, p. 1A+; February 21, 1993, 1F+.

Chapter 26

Fort Pierce

Fort Pierce honors in its name President Franklin Pierce's brother, Lt. Col. Benjamin K. Pierce, who built a fort there on the Indian River in 1838 to fight against the Seminole Indians. In 1843, William Henry Peck arrived with several slaves to help his father settle the land under the Armed Occupation Act of 1842; that Act induced settlers to go to former Indian territory with the promise of 160-acre plots of land. The Pecks lasted only two years, after which the Indians drove them out by murdering some of the settlers. If any of the slaves stayed behind, they probably joined the Seminoles, who took them in and sometimes even made them members of their tribes.

After the Civil War, settlers moved back into the area to cultivate the land and fish the waters offshore. When insecticides began to control the mosquitoes and horseflies, more people moved there, attracted by the warm climate, fertile land, and rich fishing grounds. The railroad that Henry Flagler built along Florida's east coast brought even more people, including many black workers to build the line. The outlets to northern markets that the railroad opened up encouraged many farmers, including blacks, to till the land, especially in the cultivation of pineapple, which required a lot of field labor. The blacks that came to farm the pineapple crops stayed on to become part of the early Fort Pierce settlement. Today Fort Pierce has a population of 36,830, of whom 15,666 (43%) are blacks.

Further Reading:

Walter R. Hellier. *Indian River — Florida's Treasure Coast.* Coconut Grove, Fl.: Hurricane House, 1965.

Walter R. Hellier. *Palmetto Rambler.* New York: Vantage Press, 1973.

Lucille Rights. *A Historical View of Fort Pierce and the Indian River Environmental Community.* Fort Pierce: St. Lucie County Schools, 1979.

Kyle S. Van Landingham. *Pictorial History of Saint Lucie County, 1565-1910.* Fort Pierce: St. Lucie Historical Society, 1976.

Writer Zora Neale Hurston (1891?-1960), who was born in Eatonville, Florida (see above) and went on to become a well-known novelist, folklorist, and anthropologist, lived in Fort Pierce while she worked as a reporter for a weekly black newspaper, C.E. Bolen's *Fort Pierce Chronicle*, and while she wrote her novel, *Herod the Great*. In 1958, she also did substitute teaching at Lincoln Park Academy, the black public school of Fort Pierce.

Further Reading:

Gordon Patterson, "Zora Neale Hurston as English Teacher: A Lost Chapter Found," *The Marjorie Kinnan Rawlings Journal of Florida Literature*, vol. 5 (1993), pp. 51-60.

Dr. C.C. Benton, a successful medical doctor who had sold ten acres of palmetto land to the school board for a new high school for blacks, in 1957 used some of that money to build rental houses on School Court Street, which took its name from the new school one block away. The houses were alternately yellow or green, a color scheme that has not changed over the years, and were an attempt to provide affordable, clean, and safe housing for the poor. The green, one-story, concrete-block **Zora Neale Hurston House** at 1734 School Court Street has two bedrooms, a bathroom, kitchen,

The final resting place of Zora Neale Hurston is peaceful and quiet. Credit: Kevin M. McCarthy

and front room. Hurston was the first tenant to live in the house, now a private residence. School Court Street is off N. 17th St. between Avenue L and Avenue K about three-quarters of a mile west of U.S. 1 and about one mile north of Orange Avenue in the northern part of the city.

Dr. Benton was Hurston's physician, but even he could not prevent the deterioration of her health in 1959. A combination of high blood pressure, obesity, gall bladder attacks, and an ulcer contributed to a stroke she suffered in early 1959. In October, she entered the Saint Lucie County welfare home and, on January 28, 1960, died of hypertensive heart disease. She had once said that "If I happen to die without money somebody will bury me, though I do not wish it to be that way."

Friends raised more than $400 for her burial; even the students for whom she had done substitute teaching raised some money. At the funeral the publisher of the black newspaper she had written for, C.E. Bolen, said that "Zora Neale went about and didn't care too much how she looked.

Or what she said. Maybe people didn't think so much of that. But Zora Neale, every time she went about, had something to offer. She didn't come to you empty. They said she couldn't become a writer recognized by the world. But she did it. The Miami paper said she died poor. But she died rich. She did something."

Her friends buried her in the city's segregated cemetery, the Garden of Heavenly Rest. The grave site was unmarked until, in the summer of 1973, Pulitzer Prize-winning novelist Alice Walker, who wrote *The Color Purple*, came to Fort Pierce "Looking for Zora," as she titled a chapter of *In Search of Our Mothers' Gardens* (San Diego: Harcourt Brace Jovanovich, 1983, pp. 93-116). Walker found the grave site and placed a stone on it which reads:

ZORA NEALE HURSTON
"A GENIUS OF THE SOUTH "
1901 — 1960
NOVELIST, FOLKLORIST
ANTHROPOLOGIST

Today, scholars tend to think that Hurston's birthdate was 1891. The **Zora Neale Hurston Burial Site** is near the street in the Garden of Heavenly Rest Cemetery, which is at the end of N. 17th Street and Avenue S just north of the house mentioned above where she lived.

Further Reading:

Robert E. Hemenway. *Zora Neale Hurston: A Literary Biography*. Urbana: University of Illinois Press, 1977.

James Lyons, "Famous Negro Author Working As Maid Here Just 'To Live a Little,'" *The Miami Herald*, March 27, 1950, p. 1-B.

Lincoln Junior College in Fort Pierce was one of 12 black junior colleges in Florida (see St. Petersburg below). Established in 1958, the school had as its first president Mr. Leroy C. Floyd, Sr. The enrollment figures, which included college parallel courses and vocational courses, for Lincoln Junior College were as follows:

1960-1961: 98 students **1961-1962: 98 students**
1962-1963: 234 students **1963-1964: 386 students**
1964-1965: 667 students

In the mid-1960s, in an attempt to desegregate Indian River Junior College, state officials applied state accreditation standards so rigidly that county officials realized the county would have to spend a great deal of money to improve Lincoln Junior College or lose state accreditation. They chose to integrate the white college and merged Lincoln with Indian River. As with other black colleges throughout the state, the black faculty of Lincoln were not dismissed outright from their jobs, but were placed as well as possible in the integrated college. For example, the president of Lincoln became the administrative dean of Indian River Junior College.

Chapter 27

Gainesville

Soon after the United States acquired Florida from the Spanish in 1821, settlers moved into this area and began farming the land, despite resistance from the Seminoles, who had already been there for decades. In 1824, Alachua County was established as a large area which extended from the Georgia border to Charlotte Harbor in the southwest. The formation of more counties from this large area eventually reduced the county to an inland district with Gainesville as its county seat. The town was named after General Edmund P. Gaines, a commander in the Seminole Indian Wars.

The 1860 census indicated that 46 blacks (21% of the total population) and 223 whites lived in Gainesville. By 1870, the 765 blacks outnumbered the 679 whites in the city limits, partly because many of the black soldiers stationed there during the Civil War, for example the all-black 3rd Regiment, remained after the war, to be joined by newly freed slaves looking for opportunities to make a living. The blacks migrated to two areas in the city: Pleasant Street and Seminary Street. Pleasant Street, the area bordered today by N.W. 1st Street, N.W. 8th Avenue, N.W. 6th Street, and N.W. 1st Avenue, became the religious, educational, and social center of the black community. The **Pleasant Street Historic District** had some 255 historic buildings in this district, including churches, schools, and homes. Skilled blacksmiths, carpenters, tailors, and teamsters found much work in the area and settled down with their families.

With its first building dedicated in 1867, **Mt. Pleasant United Methodist Church** is the oldest black congregation in Gainesville and the religious center for many over the years. Three years after a fire destroyed the building in 1903, the congregation built the present red-brick Romanesque-Revival style building at 620 Northwest 2nd Street. Another important early black church was the **Friendship Baptist Church** at 426 N.W. 2nd Street. In 1888, workers built the first building, which lasted until fire destroyed it in 1911. The congregation then built the present Romanesque Gothic Revival structure with its rusticated concrete block.

One of the most important educational institutions before Santa Fe Community College and the University of Florida and one of the first state-funded grade schools for blacks in the nation was the **Union Academy**, which the Freedmen's Bureau established around 1867 on the southwest corner of N.W. 1st Street and 6th Avenue at 101 N.W. 7th Street. In the early years, the school, which was the city's first public school for blacks and one that offered grades one through ten, had around 17 students, but did not have its first black teachers until the following decade. By 1898, the school had 500 students and was responsible for training many local teachers. Its last principal was A. Quinn Jones, who served from 1921 until it became a recreational center in 1925. When the city eventually razed it because of its rapid deterioration, the students attended Lincoln High School in the 1000 block of N.W. 7th Avenue, where the A. Quinn Jones Center later stood.

Further Reading:

Ben Pickard, editor. *Historic Gainesville: A Tour Guide to the Past*. Gainesville: Historic Gainesville, Inc., 1990.

J. Irving E. Scott. *The Education of Black People in Florida*. Philadelphia: Dorrance & Company, 1974, p. 45.

Cheryl W. Thompson, "Recalling the Days of Union Academy," *The Gainesville Sun*, February 18, 1989, p. 1A+.

Seminary Street (present-day 5th Avenue) was the place where blacks were allowed to buy land and have clubs. Among the stores were Cato's Sundry Store for snacks at 737 N.W. 5th Avenue, Walter's Blue Room for dancing at 912 N.W. 5th Avenue, Plummer's Barber Shop at 743 N.W. 5th Avenue, and the Lyric Theater for movies at 820 N.W. 5th Avenue. Today the **Martin Luther King, Jr., Monument** in the downtown area near city hall honors the many blacks, past, present, and future in the Gainesville area.

The **Josiah Walls Historical Marker** on West University Avenue between N.W. 1st and 2nd streets honors the first black U.S. Congressman from Florida. Josiah Walls (1842-1905) was born in Virginia and later served as a soldier in the Civil War on the Union side. After the war he moved to Jacksonville and Archer, Florida, and worked as a lumberman and teacher. Local voters recognized his skill as a public speaker and elected him to Florida's House of Representatives in 1868 and then the state Senate. In 1870, he was elected to the U.S. Congress, where he served until 1876; for several years he was Florida's only Congressman in the House of Representatives.

In 1873, he bought a newspaper in Gainesville, the *New Era*, which was the first Florida newspaper owned by a black and in which publication he promised that "the wants and interests of the people of color will receive special attention." The paper lasted until the following year, but in the mid-1880s Walls joined Matthew M. Lewey in publishing the *Farmers' Journal*. That same Mr. Lewey established the *Gainesville Sentinel* in 1887 and changed its name to the *Florida Sentinel* when he moved away in 1894 (see Pensacola below). Finally, Josiah Walls served as mayor of Gainesville before eventually returning to farming; he was in charge of the farm at the State College in Tallahassee when he died in 1905. This great man, who was buried in the Negro Cemetery in

Tallahassee, was the last black to represent Florida in the U.S. House of Representatives until the November 1992 election sent Corrine Brown, Alcee Hastings, and Carrie Meek to Washington.

Further Reading:

Maurine Christopher. *Black Americans in Congress.* New York: Thomas Y. Crowell Company, 1976, pp. 78-86: "Josiah T. Walls/Florida."

Peter D. Klingman. *Josiah Walls.* Gainesville: University Presses of Florida, 1976.

World War II brought an influx of black soldiers stationed at Camp Blanding, 25 miles north of Gainesville, and on weekends the soldiers would come into town for a day or two of entertainment. After the war many of those soldiers settled in the area. A school that opened up in east Gainesville right before World War II was **Williams Elementary**, named after Joseph Williams, a civic-minded black who had asked for the school; in its first year it had 150 students and eventually reached 600 students. In 1970, the local schools were integrated with relatively few disturbances, and four years later the city elected a black, Neil Butler, to be mayor; he helped pass an ordinance that prohibited discriminatory practices on the basis of race, religion, creed, sex, marital status, or physical handicap. Today Gainesville has a population of 84,770, of whom 18,211 (22%) are black.

Further Reading:

Derrick Morgan, "African-Americans have rich past in Gainesville," *The Gainesville Sun*, February 27, 1994, p. 1A+.

Finally, the University of Florida, which in the fall of 1991 had 1,549 full-time black students out of a total of 26,670 students or just 6%, named its law school program in which students represent the poor "The Virgil Darnell Hawkins Civil League Clinic" in honor of a man the school had denied admission to in 1949. Hawkins, who was born in Okahumpka, Florida, in 1906, graduated from a Jacksonville high school and attended Lincoln University in Pennsylvania. By selling insurance and teaching school, he saved enough money by the time he was 42 to attend law school, but the University of Florida Law School denied him admission. At that time the law would not allow black and white students to attend school together.

The Board of Control, which ran the universities, decided to open a new law school at Florida Agricultural and Mechanical College for Negroes (later Florida A&M University) in Tallahassee in order not to have the races mix at the white law schools, but Hawkins asked the Florida Supreme Court for permission to attend the University of Florida Law School. When the Florida Supreme Court denied his request, he took his case to the U.S. Supreme Court, which in 1956 ordered the University of Florida Law School to admit him. The University still refused, arguing that violence would result if he were admitted to the school.

In 1958, a federal district court judge ordered the University to admit qualified blacks to its graduate schools, but this time the University would not admit Hawkins on the basis, according to the school, that he did not meet their admission standards. Other blacks were able to enter the University's graduate programs, but not Hawkins, the man who had begun the litigation process in the first place. He then entered the New England School of Law in Boston, Massachusetts, and graduated in 1964, but Florida officials would not permit him to take the Florida Bar Exam, which all lawyers had to pass to be able to practice law in Florida, because he had not attended an accredited law school. In 1976, the Florida Supreme Court allowed him to become a lawyer without taking the bar exam. At age 70, Hawkins finally became a lawyer and opened his office in Leesburg. He died in 1988 after spending a lifetime fighting the racial practices of the state's educational system. Today, the Florida university system has a Virgil D. Hawkins Scholarship for minority students in law school.

Further Reading:

Algia R. Cooper, "Brown V. Board of Education and Virgil Darnell Hawkins," *The Journal of Negro History*, 64 (Winter 1979), pp. 1+.

Maxine D. Jones and Kevin M. McCarthy. *African Americans in Florida.* Sarasota: Pineapple Press, 1993, pp. 103-105: "Virgil D. Hawkins, 1906-1988."

Gilbert L. Porter and Leedell W. Neyland. *The History of the Florida State Teachers Association.* Washington, D.C.: National Education Association, 1977, p. 101+.

Chapter 28

Haines City

*I*n the 1870s and 1880s, settlers who had gone to a place in central Florida they called Clay Cut on the South Florida Railroad could not convince railroad officials to put a station there until they renamed the town Haines City to honor a railroad official. Located in northeast Polk County in the center of peninsula Florida, the city, which calls itself "The Gateway to the Scenic Highlands," is near highways U.S. 27, 17-92, and I-4. That prime location helps in the shipping of the city's primary product, citrus. The city had 4,000 people by 1940, 5,000 by 1950, 9,000 by 1970, and 11,683 by 1990, of whom 4,641 (40%) are black.

The first blacks settled there in 1902, when the Malloy-Miller turpentine company relocated from Huston, Florida. Two years after the first black school opened in 1915 in St. Marks Church on 7th and Church Street, workers built a wooden school building near the site of what much later became Oakland High School. In 1928, Oakland School opened with the first eight grades, but students who wanted to go to high school had to travel to Bartow or Lakeland. In 1930, the school was accredited as a senior high school, at which time students came from Loughman, Davenport, Dundee, and Lake Hamilton. The first graduating class in 1930 had four students; the second in 1931 had three. Over the years and before integration merged schools, the graduates of Oakland High School distinguished themselves as doctors, lawyers, educators, and business people. The school, which is on 8th Street near Avenue D and E near lakes Tracy and Boomerang and west of 17th Street, is now called **Bethune Neighborhood Center** and provides the community with recreation programs, child day-care, reading and writing programs, and other activities.

Further Reading:

Bernice More Barber. *From Beginnings to Boom.* Haines City: Barber, 1975, pp. 187-190: "Haines City's Black Community (1907-1926)."

Chapter 29

Inverness

Inverness, the county seat of Citrus County, was named by a Scotch settler after the Scottish city of Inverness because of the similarities of topography, namely lakes and the highlands nearby. Voters approved the transfer of the county seat of Citrus County, which was established in 1887 with some 400,000 acres, from Mannsfield to Inverness in 1891, but not without much fistfighting and many arguments. The county did well in the citrus boom before the 1894-1895 freeze, but suffered much damage in that freeze and others. The 1990 population of the Florida town was 5,797, of whom just 389 (7%) were black, but the town has an important place related to the black history of the area:the northeast section of **Oak Ridge Cemetery**, where blacks used to bury their dead.

Unofficially called Pine Ridge Cemetery, the site is at the south edge of Oak Ridge Cemetery, which is several blocks due south of Citrus Memorial Hospital; to reach Pine Ridge, turn left at the end of S. Line Avenue and proceed to the top of the small hill, where you can see dozens of small, white columns marking the sites where black families in the area buried their dead for over 50 years. In 1988, when the county learned that it owned the 1.8 acre black cemetery, workers cleaned up the neglected site and used ground-penetrating radar to locate unmarked graves. The workers placed column markers on those sites and cleaned the metal markers that showed the name of the deceased, as well as the name of the funeral home that arranged for the burial. The East Dampier Street Funeral Home, owned and managed by Mr. Eli White, arranged many of the burials and carefully maintained the black cemetery until he was no longer able to. One can still read the headstones or markers of over 100 of those buried there, at least 23 of whom were U.S. servicemen.

Further Reading:

Karen Dukess, "County to Restore Neglected Cemetery," *St. Petersburg Times*, Citrus Times edition, June 2, 1988, p. 1.
"Inverness," *North Florida Living*, June 1986, pp. 6-12.
Jim Twitty, "Cemetery Forgotten by County," *The Tampa Tribune*, Citrus/Sumter edition, May 14, 1988, p. 1.

Chapter 30

Jacksonville

When the Timucuan Indians lived in this area on the St. Johns River, they called the site "wacca pilatka," which meant "place where cows cross." After the United States gained control of Florida in 1821, the name of the town, which had been Cow Ford under the British, became Jacksonville to honor Andrew Jackson, the governor of the territories of East and West Florida and later the seventh president of the United States.

The 1860 census showed that 908 of the city's 2,118 inhabitants were slaves and only 87 were free blacks. Slave labor did much to build the city's hotels, railroad, and port facilities. During the Reconstruction period after the Civil War, blacks had to contend with Black Codes and other forms of discrimination, but by the end of the 19th century blacks were operating small businesses and owned property, although most worked as laborers, barbers, laundresses, or servants; in 1894, 62% of the city's black workers were unskilled laborers. A poll tax and a confusing ballot system meant to confuse illiterates had virtually disenfranchised them. Many blacks saw education as a way to good jobs and stressed this to their children to such an extent that by 1900 73% of the city's blacks were literate. Today the county seat of Duval County has a population of 635,230, of whom 160,421 (25%) are black.

Further Reading:

Barbara Ann Richardson. *A History of Blacks in Jacksonville, Florida, 1860-1895: A Socio-Economic and Political Study.* Dissertation. Carnegie-Mellon University, 1975.

Among the institutions of importance to blacks in Jacksonville is **Edward Waters College** at 1715 Kings Road. This four-year, liberal arts college associated with the African Methodist Episcopal Church is the oldest independent institution of higher education for blacks in Florida. It began in 1883 as the East Florida Conference High School, changed in 1885 to the Florida Normal and Divinity School, and expanded in 1891 to become a college named after Reverend Edward Waters, the third bishop of the African Methodist Episcopal Church. The 1901 Jacksonville fire burned down the school building on East Beaver Street, but officials rebuilt it several years later on the present Kings Road property. Among its many distinguished graduates was A. Philip Randolph, founder of the Brotherhood of Sleeping Car Porters and an important figure in the Civil Rights movement. Today some 670 students attend the college.

The oldest building on the 20-acre campus is Centennial Hall, which dates back to 1916, is on the National Register, and commemorates in its name the 100th anniversary of the A.M.E. Church. The contractor for this building, which became the college library in 1979, was Richard Lewis Brown (1854-1948), the city's first-known black architect. Born into poverty in South Carolina before the Civil War, he later moved with his family to Florida, where he worked as a farmer, carpenter, and minister. He bought several acres of land in east Jacksonville, including the site of the **Richard L. Brown Elementary School** at 1535 Milnor Street, served two terms (1881-1884) in the Florida House of Representatives, and worked for the Duval County School Board in the construction and repair of schools. Dr. Jesse L. Burns of Bradenton (see above) became the 25th president of EWC in 1994 at a time when the school was undergoing several new construction and renovation projects, for example a new dormitory, a state-of-the-art science laboratory, and a new student assessment center.

Further Reading:

"EWC Inaugurates New 25th President," *The Florida Star* [Jacksonville], April 2, 1994, p. 6.

Rev. Charles Sumner Long. *History of the A.M.E. Church in Florida.* Philadelphia: A.M.E. Book Concern, 1939, p. 87+.

J. Irving E. Scott. *The Education of Black People in Florida.* Philadelphia: Dorrance & Company, 1974, p. 49+.

Samuel J. Tucker. *Phoenix From the Ashes: EWC's Past, Present, and Future.* Jacksonville: Convention Press, 1976.

Wayne W. Wood. *Jacksonville's Architectural Heritage.* Jacksonville: University of North Florida Press, 1989. This book is very useful for the other city sites mentioned here.

The **Bethel Baptist Institutional Church** at 1058 Hogan Street dates back to 1904, from which time this Neo-classical Revival-style building has served the community well. The congregation was first organized in 1838 and included two slaves belonging to the Rev. J. Jaudan. Within two years, the congregation built Jacksonville's first church building on the northeast corner of Duval and Newnan streets and called it Bethel Baptist Church. The congregation later sold the property to the Presbyterians and constructed a new building in West LaVilla. During the Civil War, the church was used as a hospital. In 1868, the black members of the church received $400 for their interest in the church property and left to build a new church with the Bethel Baptist name. After the 1901 fire destroyed that building, members of the congregation built an impressive structure that still dominates the local scene. Today the church's main bell tower and its two small towers anchor the rectangular building, which is now on the National Register of Historic Sites. The pastor of the church from 1892 until 1907 was Rev. J. Milton Waldron, who also helped organize the very important Afro-American Life Insurance Company in 1901 (see below) and is honored today by Waldron Street in American Beach (see above).

The **Catherine Street Fire Station #3** at 12 Catherine Street replaced the nearby Fire Station #3, which the devastating 1901 fire had destroyed. Opened in 1902, the new station with its large, arched door that was large enough for horse-drawn fire wagons was manned by black firemen until 1905, when an all-white crew took over. Officials decommissioned the unit in 1933 and began using the building as a storage facility for the Fire Department. Workers were to tear down the building in 1972 to make room for a new police administration building, but historians pointed out the significance of the site and convinced authorities to build the new building around the old one. It then became a museum for the city's firefighting history.

The **Masonic Temple Building** at 410 Broad Street is also on the National Register of Historic Sites. The Most Worshipful Union Grand Lodge of the Most Ancient and Honorable Fraternity of Free and Accepted Masons of Florida and Jurisdiction, Inc., founded in 1870, has been the Masonic organization for blacks in this state. The group decided to construct this building in the early part of this century as a meeting place for blacks and as a site for offices and stores. After ten years of fund-raising, they built this tall, red-brick structure in 1912 at the northwest corner of Broad and Duval streets; the 1926 *Negro Blue Book* called it "one of the finest buildings owned by Negroes in the world." It has served as the headquarters of the Masons of the State of Florida Grand East, and the first black bank in Jacksonville, the Anderson Bank, also occupied one level. Over the years many black businessmen used this building, including dentists, physicians, and insurance agents.

Mount Olive A.M.E. Church at 841 Franklin Street dates back to 1887, when workers built the first wooden sanctuary of the church on this site. Builder Richard L. Brown, the city's first black architect (see above for Centennial Hall), drew up plans for a new building in the early 1920s and workers finished the present structure in 1922. The brown mortar used throughout the structure, as well as a large portico at the entrance, and the three huge columns at the front all add a distinctive style to this building.

Mount Zion A.M.E. Church at 201 East Beaver Street traces its history back to 1866, when a group of freed slaves, who had organized themselves into the Society for Religious Worship, formed the church. They built a small structure there for worship services, replaced it in 1870 with a large wooden building, and replaced that one 20 years later with a larger brick structure that could seat 1,500. The 1901 fire destroyed the building, but the congregation soon built the present Romanesque Revival-style building with its large bell tower.

Old Brewster Hospital at 915 West Monroe Street was originally the home of Hans Christian Peters, a meat dealer. His family sold the house in 1901 to the Women's Home Missionary Society of the Methodist Church, which used a $1,500 gift from Mrs. George A. Brewster to establish the Brewster Hospital and Nurse Training School there, the first hospital for blacks in the city. The hospital moved to larger facilities until it finally closed in 1966, two years after the 1964 Civil Rights Act, which opened the city's other hospitals to blacks. Today it serves as a private residence.

Further Reading:

Jacksonville Looks at Its Negro Community. Jacksonville: Council of Social Agencies, 1946, pp. 5-6.

Several black cemeteries in Jacksonville should be mentioned here: **Memorial Cemetery, Sunset Memorial Cemetery,** and **Pinehurst Cemetery** on the Northside. These cemeteries, which are near Moncrief Road around Edgewood Avenue West and Avenue B, were developed between 1909 and 1928 and were owned by Memorial Cemetery

Association, which A.L. Lewis formed to provide plots for blacks who were excluded by segregation from being buried in white cemeteries. James "Charley Edd" Craddock, the owner of the famous Two Spot nightclub on Moncrief Road and 45th Street, developed **Mount Olive Cemetery** south of the other three cemeteries in 1946; his own mausoleum is in Sunset Memorial Cemetery. These four cemeteries declined with neglect and with the opening of formerly all-white cemeteries in the 1960s.

Further Reading:

"Restoration of 4 Historic Black Cemeteries Underway in City," *The Florida Star* [Jacksonville], May 14, 1994, p. 1.

Tonyaa Weathersbee, "Saving a Heritage: City to help Clean Black Cemeteries," *The Florida Times-Union* [Jacksonville], June 20, 1993, p. A-1+.

The **A.L. Lewis Mausoleum** in Memorial Cemetery on Moncrief Road near Edgewood Avenue was for the family of A.L. Lewis (1865-1947), one of the founders of the Afro-American Industrial and Benefit Association, which later became the Afro-American Life Insurance Company, one of the largest black-owned businesses in Florida. Born into poverty in Madison, Florida, at the end of the Civil War, he moved with his family to Jacksonville, where he worked in a lumber mill for over 20 years and eventually saved enough money to buy part of a shoe store. In 1901, he and six other blacks contributed $100 each to establish an insurance company to provide low-cost health and burial insurance to poor blacks in the city. Lewis also helped found the Negro Business League and the Negro Insurance Association and established recreational facilities at American Beach on Amelia Island (see above), as well as contributing generously to many funds, including scholarships for black students.

Further Reading:

Leedell W. Neyland. *Twelve Black Floridians*. Tallahassee: Florida Agricultural and Mechanical University Foundation, 1970, pp. 53-59.

The **Afro-American Life Insurance Company** at 101 East Union Street is the building that houses the offices that A.L. Lewis helped found. As the oldest life insurance company in Florida and one of the most successful black businesses in the state, it has done much to help thousands of blacks over the years. Other locations of the company have included 722 Main Street and 105 East Union Street.

The **James Weldon Johnson Birthplace** at 1307 Lee Street is where one of Florida's most distinguished blacks was born. James Weldon Johnson (1871-1938) learned the value of education from his parents and attended Stanton Grade School and Atlanta University before returning to Jacksonville to become principal of Stanton High School. He also became a lawyer, writer, newspaper man who started in Jacksonville *The Daily American* (the nation's first daily newspaper for blacks), U.S. consul to Venezuela and Nicaragua, co-writer with his brother of a song entitled "Lift Ev'ry Voice and Sing" (which became the Negro National Anthem), and an official of the National Association for the Advancement of Colored People (NAACP). A plaque at Third and Lee streets notes the birthplace of Johnson.

Further Reading:

James Weldon Johnson. *Along This Way: The Autobiography of James Weldon Johnson*. New York: Viking Press, 1968.

Jerrell H. Shofner, "Florida," in *The Black Press in the South, 1865-1979*, edited by Henry Lewis Suggs. Westport, Conn.: Greenwood Press, 1983, pp. 91-118.

Ellen Tarry. *Young Jim: The Early Years of James Weldon Johnson*. New York: Dodd, Mead, 1967.

Stanton High School at 521 W. Ashley Street is where James Weldon Johnson attended school and where he served as principal from 1894 to 1902. Established as the first public school for black children in Jacksonville and named for Edwin M. Stanton, an abolitionist and President Lincoln's Secretary of War, the school can trace its history back to 1868, when Jacksonville blacks bought the land from Ossian B. Hart, the son of Jacksonville's founder and the tenth governor of Florida. In 1869, financing from the Freedmen's Bureau built a school there. Fires destroyed that structure, first in 1882 and then in 1901, but insurance money was enough to rebuild it each time, although at a lower level than before. When trustees of the school realized the school was no longer adequate for its students, they sued the Board of Public Instruction in 1915, at which time the Board agreed to build a new, three-story school, which was finally finished in 1917 and which served as the place where many Duval County blacks received their education. A 1965 court ruling ended segregated schools in the county, and the building was closed down in 1971. Local officials made plans to turn the structure into a multi-use community building.

Further Reading:

J. Irving E. Scott. *The Education of Black People in Florida*. Philadelphia: Dorrance & Company, 1974, p. 45+.

Another important institution in the city was the **Boylan-Haven School**, which the Missionary Society of the Methodist Episcopal Church founded around 1885 as Boylan Home to provide students educational and cultural opportunities and foster Christian character. Miss Harriet Emerson, a white missionary from New Hampshire, organized the school and became its first director. At first the school taught practical homemaking skills like cooking and sewing to a small group of girls, and then later added elementary and high school classes. Miss Artell Beaver from Montana became the second director. The school moved in 1910 to a block bounded by Odessa, Bridier, Franklin, and Jessie streets in East Jacksonville. In 1932, the school merged with Haven Home of Savannah, Georgia, to become Boylan-Haven School and continued to attract black girls until it closed in 1959 and moved to Camden, South Carolina, where it merged with Mather Academy, a co-educational preparatory school.

The **Ritz Theatre** at 825 Davis Street between State and Union streets northwest of downtown Jacksonville had an Art Deco style and neon lights which may have been among the earliest such fixtures in the city. Opened in 1929, at the time of the Depression, the theater contained spaces for shops and offices. The 600-seat theater in the LaVilla neighborhood became the center for the arts, entertainment, and shopping activities of the black community. Besides showing films for a black audience, the theater also attracted over a period of three decades such stars as Louis Armstrong, Cab Calloway, Ray Charles, Duke Ellington, Ella Fitzgerald, Earl Hines, The Ink Spots, and the Mills Brothers. The theater, which closed in 1972 and stood vacant for many years, may undergo much-needed restoration which will do much to revitalize the area.

The **Clara White Mission** at 611-13 West Ashley Street honors Clara English White (1845-1920) and her daughter, Eartha Mary Magdalene White (1876-1974), whom many called an "angel of mercy" for her unselfish efforts to make life better for Jacksonville's blacks. Eartha nursed soldiers during the Spanish-American War in 1898, taught school in a poor country school in Duval County, and worked for the city's Afro-American Life Insurance Company. After the terrible 1901 fire, which destroyed much of the city, Ms. White became a social worker in the black community and started the Union Benevolent Association to help those in need. In 1922, she honored her mother by opening the Clara White Mission, which helped many during the Great Depression. In 1936, she helped secure a tuberculosis rest home for blacks and also helped obtain better prison facilities for inmates. The three-story framed building on West Ashley Street is a living memorial to two great women.

One other site associated with Eartha M. White is the large

structure attached to a feed-store building at 7420 Roscoe Avenue. It used to be **Bayard Schoolhouse**, where Eartha White taught school for several years, beginning in 1899. Arriving in Bayard, she convinced Bartolo Genovar to donate land, organized black volunteers into building a schoolhouse, and had others contribute building materials. That one-room wooden schoolhouse, the oldest public school building in Duval County, served many black students for several decades before it became a church and, in 1985, part of the feed-store building several blocks from its original site.

Further Reading:

Charles E. Bennett. *Twelve on the River St. Johns.* Jacksonville: University of North Florida Press, 1980, pp. 137-148.

Leedell W. Neyland. *Twelve Black Floridians.* Tallahassee: Florida Agricultural and Mechanical University Foundation, 1970, pp. 33-41.

Just north of Jacksonville at the northern end of Fort George Island off Highway A1A is the **Kingsley Plantation State Historic Site**. As one of the few remaining examples of the plantation system of Territorial Florida, the plantation has a large house where Zephaniah Kingsley (1765-1843) directed a group of slaves in growing sea island cotton, sweet potatoes, sugar cane, and citrus from 1813 until 1839. Kingsley was married to an African princess, but he was also involved in the African slave trade and believed that slavery was the best means to grow agricultural crops in the South. After the United States took over Florida in 1821, Kingsley stopped smuggling slaves into Georgia and began arguing that people should treat slaves better. Toward the end of his life he established a colony in Haiti where former slaves would be free and where he sent some of his own former slaves. At the site above Jacksonville one can take a guided tour of the main house and see the slave cabins. The grounds are open daily 9 a.m. to 5 p.m.; free admission. Phone: (904) 251-3537.

The Kingsley Plantation is a good example of the wealthy homes built by slave traders. Credit: Kevin M. McCarthy

Further Reading:

Charles E. Bennett. *Twelve on the River St. Johns*. Jacksonville: University of North Florida Press, 1980, pp. 89-113.

Carita Doggett Corse. *The Key to the Golden Islands*. Chapel Hill, N.C.: University of North Carolina Press, 1931.

Zephaniah Kingsley. *A Treatise on the Patriarchal, or Co-operative, System of Society As it Exists in Some Governments, and Colonies in America, and in the United States, Under the Name of Slavery, With its Necessity and Advantages*. 1828. Reprinted Freeport, N.Y.: Books for Libraries Press, 1970. This pamphlet contains Kingsley's ideas about slavery.

Philip S. May, "Zephaniah Kingsley, Nonconformist (1765-1843)," *Florida Historical Quarterly*, 23 (January 1945), pp. 145-159.

Edith Pope. *Colcorton*. New York: Scribner, 1944; reprinted New York: Plume, 1990. This is a novel about Kingsley.

Chapter 31

Kettle Island

On a small island on the Sumter County side of the Withlacoochee River, archaeologists have unearthed remains probably related to a former settlement of Black Seminoles. There on Boggy Island (present-day Kettle Island) between 1813 and 1823, blacks associated with Sitarkey's band of Seminoles retreated into isolated areas to escape slave raiding and American incursions and to settle down with their families. Having worked on coastal plantations in the Carolinas and Georgia and having learned some technology from their American and European owners, the ex-slaves were able to join forces with the Seminoles for their mutual survival. Although the relationship between the blacks and Seminoles is not entirely clear, it does appear from existing documents that the Seminoles considered the blacks to be their legal property, despite the blacks' living in a state of virtual independence.

Some of the blacks settled 12 miles south of Okahumpka in the town of Pilaklikaha, which was between the present-day towns of Bevilles Corner and Center Hill just east of Bushnell, near where Dade's Battle took place (see Bushnell above). The blacks living in this area were probably involved in that battle. Other blacks settled in the remoteness of the Withlacoochee Cove on Boggy Island. Having learned the languages of the whites and the Seminoles, the blacks were able to act as interpreters between the two groups. Federal forces finally drove the Indians and blacks from the area during the Second Seminole War in the move to make the area more open for white settlers.

Directions:

Kettle Island is not accessible by car. The island is located on the Sumter County side of the Withlacoochee River about four miles west of the southern part of Lake Panasoffkee and about eight miles northwest of Bushnell.

Further Reading:

Piers Anthony. *Tatham Mound*. New York: Morrow, 1991. This is a novel about an Indian mound near the Withlacoochee River.

Daniel F. Littlefield, Jr. *Africans and Seminoles*. Westport, Conn.: Greenwood Press, 1977.

Kenneth Wiggins Porter. *The Negro on the American Frontier*. New York: Arno Press and the *New York Times*, 1971, esp. pp. 182-358.

Scott Thybony, "Against All Odds, Black Seminoles Won Their Freedom," *Smithsonian*, August 1991, pp. 90-101.

Brent Richards Weisman. *Like Beads on a String: A Culture History of the Seminole Indians in Northern Peninsular Florida*. Tuscaloosa, Ala: University of Alabama Press, 1989.

Chapter 32

Key Biscayne

In 1497, long after the Vizcaynos Indians had lived there, explorer John Cabot sailed to the land that became Key Biscayne and returned again in 1498, 15 years before Spanish explorer Juan Ponce de Leon visited the area. In the 16th century, Spanish treasure fleets sailed north in the Gulf Stream and sometimes wrecked on the offshore reef near what Spanish cartographers called "Cabo Florida" (Cape Florida). Pirates also frequented the area, including Black Caesar (see Key Largo below).

In the early 19th century, escaped slaves and black Seminole Indians came to Cape Florida, especially after the United States took control of Florida from Spain in 1821, to try to escape by boat to the Bahamas. During the Civil War, blockade runners used Biscayne Bay to bring in supplies for the Confederacy, and in the 20th century, rumrunners brought in illegal liquor from the Bahamas. Many wealthy people, including former President Richard Nixon, have built homes on the bay and transformed the site into a popular beach. Another much-frequented beach on Key Biscayne is Crandon Park, which opened in the late 1940s. Today Key Biscayne has a population of 8,854, of whom 26 (less than 1%) are black.

The lighthouse at the tip of Key Biscayne was the place where a brave black man died. Credit: Florida State Archives

Further Reading:

Jim Woodman. *The Book of Key Biscayne*. Miami: Miami Post, 1961.

At the southeastern tip of Key Biscayne in the Bill Baggs Cape Florida State Recreation Area stands the only lighthouse in Dade County and one that saw an act of great bravery by a black man in 1836. Workers built **Cape Florida Lighthouse** in 1825, just four years after the United States gained control of Florida from Spain. Soon after the Second Seminole War started in the mid-1830s, Indians attacked the two men stationed at the lighthouse, intent on driving out them and other whites in the area. The lighthouse keeper and his assistant, a black man named Henry, rushed into the lighthouse, bolted the door, and fired on the Indians from the window of the tower. When the Indians set fire to the door and then burst through, the two men inside quickly climbed up the ladder, cutting it out from beneath them to prevent the Indians from pursuing them. The Indians aimed their muskets up at the fleeing men, killing the brave Henry and wounding the keeper. U.S. troops eventually rescued the keeper from the top of the tower and probably buried Henry in the area, but records of this are hard to find.

Further Reading:

Kevin M. McCarthy. *Florida Lighthouses.* Gainesville: University of Florida Press, 1990, pp. 41-44.

Off the northern edge of Key Biscayne is **Virginia Key**, which played an important part in the history of blacks in the 1950s. At that time blacks were not allowed to enter Miami Beach or Palm Beach unless they had identification cards that indicated they were employees who worked there. Those black workers could work at the beaches but were not allowed to swim there. In the 1920s, blacks had been allowed to swim at Fisher Island because Mr. D.A. Dorsey, Miami's first black millionaire, had bought the whole island in order to provide blacks with a place to swim; that was fine until he had to sell the island in the mid-1920s because of rising property values and taxes.

In the following decades, blacks were continually denied access to public beaches, but they finally became so angry over that discrimination that they planned protests and peaceful demonstrations. Many white people, when they learned that blacks could not go to any public beach, also pressured officials to solve the problem. L.E. Thomas, a lawyer who later became a municipal judge, tried in 1944 to be arrested at Baker's Haulover Beach in North Dade in order to make a test case out of it, but the police refused to arrest him, instead handing the problem over to the Dade County commissioners, who in 1945 finally designated part of Virginia Key as a black beach. Until a causeway to Virginia Key and Key Biscayne was completed in 1947, the Dade

County commissioners arranged for a ferry to take the blacks to and from Virginia Key.

FURTHER READING:

Peter Cary, "Fort Lauderdale's Negro Beach," in *Mostly Sunny Days*, edited by Bob Kearney. Miami: Miami Herald Publishing Company, 1986, pp. 162-164.

Dr. S.H. Johnson as told to Dorothy Jenkins Fields, "Reflections on Black History: Fun and Games Overtown" [about Virginia Key Beach], *Update*, August 1977, p. 8+.

Chapter 33

Key Largo

Two sites near Key Largo in the Florida Keys are of interest here: Caesar's Creek and Caesar's Rock, named in honor of the infamous pirate Black Caesar. According to legend, in the early slave-trading days in the Caribbean, slave traders captured a huge African chief and transported him and other slaves across the Atlantic. When the slave ship approached Florida, a storm sank the ship, drowning many of the crew and most of the slaves shackled down below. By some means Black Caesar and a mate that had befriended him escaped from the ship and made it to land, where they began preying on ships passing off the Florida Reef. The two pirates were very successful in their attacks and accumulated many goods and jewels on their island.

When the two men eventually had an argument, Black Caesar killed his friend and continued carrying on his piracy as a one-man band. He soon enlisted more pirates and used larger boats to attack the passing ships. When his crew had to hide from danger, they would escape into Caesar's Creek (near Elliott Key) and other inlets between Old Rhodes Key and Elliott Key. There they would use a metal ring embedded in a rock (today called Caesar's Rock), run a strong rope through the ring, heel the boat over, and hide it in the water until the patrol boat went away. Or they would lower the mast and sink the ship in shallow water, hidden from prying eyes; later they would cut the rope or pump out the water, raise the boat, and continue with their raids.

Although piracy was wrong and hurt many people, it offered escaped slaves like Caesar a liberty they could not have obtained at that time. In the early 1700s, Black Caesar left Biscayne Bay to join the more infamous Blackbeard, Captain Edward Teach, to prey on shipping up and down America's east coast, especially around North Carolina. In 1718, government forces finally defeated and killed Blackbeard near Ocracoke Island off the tip of Cape Hatteras. The British took Black Caesar to Virginia for trial and hanged him in Williamsburg.

Further Reading:

Love Dean, "Pirates and Legends," *Florida Keys Magazine*, 1st quarter, 1981, pp. 10-14.

Howard Kleinberg, editor. *Miami: The Way We Were*. Tampa: Surfside Publishing, 1989, pp. 12-13: "Black Caesar."

Albert Payson Terhune. *Black Caesar's Clan*. New York: George H. Doran Company, 1922.

David O. True, "Pirates and Treasure Trove of South Florida," *Tequesta: The Journal of the Historical Association of Southern Florida*, 1947, pp. 3-13.

Chapter 34

Key West

The town of Key West, at the southern end of U.S. 1, has a long history unlike that of any other American place. Isolated for most of its existence from the mainland, it finally became accessible from land when Henry Flagler extended his Florida East Coast Railroad to the town in 1912. Before that time, this small outpost, which is only one mile long and four miles wide, attracted many hardy souls who were willing to endure the hardships of isolation, hurricanes, and attacks from pirates and Indians to earn a living from the sea. That living might consist of fishing, salvaging wrecked ships along the Keys, or guiding ships among the dangerous reefs.

Key West and the other islands along the Florida Reef became the destination of many slaves brought over from Africa in the 18th and 19th centuries. Before the United States ended the slave trade around 1807, slave traders brought over millions of Africans to work on plantations in Brazil, Jamaica, and the southern United States. Whenever U.S. patrol boats would capture a slave ship near the Florida Keys, they would take the slaves into Key West, where doctors would treat them and try to help them recover from the long trip across the Atlantic Ocean from Africa.

Sometimes those slave ships wrecked on the reef off the

U.S. patrol boats brought slaves into Key West in 1860 after rescuing them from slave traders. Credit: Florida State Archives

Keys. For example, the *Henrietta Marie,* a ship that could transport as many as 400 slaves to America, sank on **New Ground Reef** near Key West in 1701. The many sets of iron leg shackles and wrist shackles that divers found on the remains of the ship indicate that the slave traders kept the slaves imprisoned under the decks during the passage. In 1993, the National Association of Black Scuba Divers placed a memorial near the site of the shipwreck in memory of all those slaves who had died on ships like the *Henrietta Marie*.

Further Reading:

Herbert S. Klein. *The Middle Passage: Comparative Studies in the Atlantic Slave Trade*. Princeton: Princeton University Press, 1978.

"Knight Foundation donates $75,000 to exhibition involving Henrietta Marie," *The Miami Times*, June 16, 1994, p. 6A.

Daniel P. Mannix. *Black Cargoes: A History of the Atlantic Slave Trade, 1518-1865*. New York: Viking, 1962.

Kevin M. McCarthy. *Thirty Florida Shipwrecks*. Sarasota: Pineapple Press, 1992, pp. 29-31.

Dinizulu Gene Tinnie, "Divers Honor Ancestors at Site of Wreck of Slave Ship," *The Miami Times*, May 20, 1993, p. 9A.

The **Bahama Village**, a 12-block area in Key West, surrounded by Whitehead, Louisa, Fort, and Angela streets, is the chief black residential area of the town. Persons of African descent who had arrived from the U.S. mainland, the Bahamas, and the Caribbean began settling here in the mid-1800s. Some of them came looking for freedom; others came looking for work in the sponge and turtle industries. Among the important blacks who had homes in the area were Robert Gabriel (Monroe County's representative in the state legislature in 1879) and Mildred Shaver (principal of the Frederick Douglass School in the early 20th century). The Douglass School was organized in 1870, just five years after the end of the American Civil War, to educate black children in Key West.

The **Cornish Memorial A.M.E. Zion Church** at 702 Whitehead Street, which was built in 1903, honors Sandy Cornish, an early immigrant from the Bahamas who founded the congregation in 1865. Because no ordained black minister lived in Key West at the time, Cornish and another black man, Cataline Simmons, conducted the services. Simmons later went on to Jacksonville to be in charge of a church there.

The tall, stately Cornish Memorial A.M.E. Zion Church remains today a strong force in the lives of Key West's blacks, who number some 2,584, 10% of the total population of 24,832. Fires and hurricanes have destroyed the building several times, but members of the congregation have rebuilt it each time.

Cornish, who was known as the strongest man and the best farmer on Key West, was born in Maryland in the 1790s. After buying his freedom for $3,200, he moved with his wife to Florida to work on the railroad. When his house burned down and he lost the papers proving he was free, a mob attacked him with the intention of selling him as a slave in New Orleans. Cornish beat them off with his great physical strength, but, when he learned that a bigger mob was planning on sending him off into slavery, he mutilated himself so badly (cutting off one of his fingers and cutting the muscles in his leg) that the mob left him alone. Everyone had to be impressed with how much he hated slavery and how far he was willing to go to remain free.

In the Bahama Village on the corner of Thomas and Amelia streets is **Nelson English Park**, a recreation area named for the black civic leader who served as the postmaster in Key West from 1882 to 1886. Running such a post office in the 19th century was difficult because the island was not yet connected to the mainland by road and therefore depended on boats arriving with mail and newspapers. The first postal service to Key West began in 1829, when sloops from Charleston, South Carolina, made regular calls; later, mail ships came from St. Marks, a small town in the Florida Panhandle that was closer to the Keys than was South Carolina. When Nelson English served as postmaster in the 1880s, mail came regularly by ship, but not as regularly as when the railroad would link Key West to the mainland beginning in 1912. Mr. English also worked in the customs house at a time when Key West had the ninth largest port in the U.S., and he was the leader of the Key West Cornet Band, a group of musicians that became famous for accompanying funeral processions from the black churches to the cemetery.

Another public official working in the town's customs house was John Willis Menard, called by historian Jerrell Shofner "the most influential black editor speaking for and to blacks in the 1880s...." (p. 93) Menard began publishing the Key West *News* in 1882, renaming the newspaper the following year to the *Florida News* to give it a wider tone and coverage. He took the newspaper to Jacksonville in 1885 and continued using his editorial powers to help the educational, political, and economic aims of blacks.

Further Reading

Christopher Cox. *A Key West Companion*. New York: St. Martin's Press, 1983, especially pp. 73-78: "Whitelaw Reid Visits Sandy Cornish" and "Cornish Memorial AME ZION Church."

George Hall. *Key West*. London: Osprey, 1991.

Maxine D. Jones and Kevin M. McCarthy. *African Americans in Florida*. Sarasota: Pineapple Press, 1993, pp. 25-26.

Joan & Wright Langley. *Key West: Images of the Past*. Key West: C.C. Belland & E.O. Swift, 1982.

Jerrell H. Shofner, "Florida," in *The Black Press in the South, 1865-1979*, edited by Henry Lewis Suggs. Westport, Conn.: Greenwood Press, 1983, pp. 91-118.

Sharon Wells. *Forgotten Legacy: Blacks in Nineteenth Century Key West*. Key West: Historic Key West Preservation Board, 1982.

The waters off Key West played a part in one of the most unusual trials in the state's history. In the 1840s, Abolitionists, who were determined to end slavery in the South, came to Florida to try to free as many slaves as possible. One of them was Jonathan Walker, a man from Massachusetts who came to Florida in the 1800s to help the slaves. He took a group of them in his boat from Pensacola to try to make it to freedom in Nassau, but was captured near Key West in July 1844. Officials took him back to Pensacola, where the letters "SS" for slave stealer were burned into his right hand. The New England poet, John Greenleaf Whittier, wrote a poem entitled "The Branded Hand" about that incident.

Further Reading:

Jonathan Walker. *Trial and Imprisonment of Jonathan Walker, at Pensacola, Florida, for Aiding Slaves to Escape from Bondage.* 1845. Reprinted Gainesville: University Presses of Florida, 1974.

About 70 miles west of Key West in the Gulf of Mexico on the 16-acre Garden Key lies one of the most remarkable structures in the state and one that slave labor did much to build: **Fort Jefferson**. Spanish explorer Ponce De Leon had named the islands the Dry Tortugas in the 16th century because they had no fresh water and were full of Loggerhead turtles ("tortugas" in Spanish). The seven small coral keys that make up the Dry Tortugas were isolated, barren, and mosquito-infested for centuries until the U.S. government decided in 1846 to build a huge stone fort, the "Gibraltar of the Gulf," to prevent British and Spanish forays into the Gulf and to protect American shipping in the area.

Hundreds of workers, including many slaves, toiled for almost 30 years to build the six-sided fort; it rose 60 feet from its coral bedrock, and each side was 450 feet long and five feet thick at the top. They painstakingly placed 243 monstrous cannon on the fort to guard the outside sea lanes. Inside the fort, the workers built officers' quarters, barracks to house some 800 men, and a large parade ground. Around the fort they dug a 70-foot-wide, 10-foot-deep moat (complete with sharks and barracudas) to dissuade the prisoners from escaping. Although its guns never fired a shot against the enemy, the structure did serve as a federal prison during the Civil War for many prisoners, including Dr. Samuel Mudd, the Maryland doctor who unwittingly set the broken leg of John Wilkes Booth, the assassin of President Abraham Lincoln.

Building the fort was very hard work. The workers had to endure the blazing sun, hordes of mosquitoes, hurricanes, dysentery, scurvy, and typhoid to build what turned out to be one of the most massive fortresses ever constructed in the western hemisphere, a structure which contained 40,000,000

Fort Jefferson was a massive stone structure that slaves helped build. Credit: Florida State Archives

bricks. While most of the skilled workers were Yankees from the North and most of the slaves did the hard, manual labor, a few well-trained slaves were able to work as masons and carpenters. When the ordinary workday was over, the 30-35 slaves on the job sometimes continued working or did some fishing in order to gain a few cents to buy some extra food. At one point in 1847, seven blacks escaped by boat into the Gulf, but very few of the others were successful in their attempts to flee.

The men worked ten hours a day, six days a week, but the harsh conditions made one officer comment that in better conditions one man could do the work of two men at Fort Jefferson. The slaves came from Key West slave owners, some of whom bought more slaves to work at the fort. The slave owners were happy to rent out their slaves to the government and also wanted their slaves isolated at the fort and away from Key West, where they would be away from northern visitors who might encourage the slaves to rebel. Also the slave owners discouraged any education among the slaves, even simple reading and writing, on the grounds that ignorant slaves would be less susceptible to abolitionist ideas. The fort, which ended its usefulness as a prison in the 1870s and was virtually abandoned for decades, is now a national monument and a reminder how harsh a life slave-workers had in the 19th century.

Further Reading:

Rodman Bethel. *A Slumbering Giant of the Past: Fort Jefferson, U.S.A. in the Dry Tortugas.* No place: R. Bethel, 1979.

Gene Burnett, "The 'Gibraltar' Gripped by an Ancient Curse," *Florida Trend,* vol. 17 (February 1975), pp. 54-55.

Writers' Program. *History of the Fort Jefferson National Monument.* No place or date.

Chapter 35

Kissimmee

The name of this town, with the accent on the second syllable, may come from an Indian name that means "mulberries yonder." The town was incorporated in 1883 and four years later became the seat of government for Osceola County. When financier Hamilton Disston bought 4,000,000 acres of central Florida land at 25 cents an acre in 1881 and began draining and developing the land, coupled with the coming of the South Florida Railroad, many people moved to the area. The population of Kissimmee reached 1,086 by 1890 and 2,200 by 1915, despite devastating freezes that hurt the local citrus industry. The arrival of Disney World in the 1960s brought more settlers and visitors to the area. Today the town has a population of 30,050, of whom 2,827 (9%) are black.

Among the blacks who have made many contributions to the history of the town are two in particular: Lawrence Silas, a wealthy black cattle rancher who built up a large herd of cattle, and Scipio Lesesne, a farmer. In an article entitled "Lawrence of the River," Zora Neale Hurston (see above at Eatonville and Fort Pierce) wrote the following about the first man: "Lawrence Silas is in, and of, the cow lands. He is important because his story is a sign and a symbol of the strength of the nation. Lawrence Silas represents the men

Bethel A.M.E. Church is associated with Lawrence Silas, a local rancher. Credit: Kevin M. McCarthy

who could plan and do, the generations who were willing to undertake the hard job, to accept the challenge of the frontiers. And remember, he had one more frontier to conquer than the majority of men in America." Silas also helped establish Bethune-Volusia Beach below Daytona Beach (see New Smyrna Beach below).

One can see the name of Lawrence Silas in the cornerstone of the **Bethel A.M.E. Church** at 1702 North Brack Street, on the northeast corner of Brack Street, two streets east of Main Street (U.S. 17-92, 441), and East Walnut Street, which is two blocks north of Vine Street (the main east-west street in town). This one-story masonry church building was constructed in 1916 by a congregation that had been founded in 1888 to serve the black community. Two other black churches in town are **St. Luke's Missionary Baptist Church** on Columbia Street and **St. James African Methodist Episcopal Zion Church** on Bermuda Avenue.

Scipio Lesesne, who was born in Barbados and came to Kissimmee in 1883 from South Carolina to work on a sugar plantation, eventually cultivated a 100-acre potato farm near the present airport. He also had a farm at the northwest corner of Main Street and Vine Street; he and his family lived upstairs in a two-story building there, on the first floor of which was a movie theater. While working in the Gilbert Knox Hotel across from the railroad depot, Scipio's youngest son, William Buster Lesesne, started Buster's Cabs in 1941, the same year his father died. Buster later worked as deputy hotel commissioner under Governor Collins and in various positions under governors Askew and Graham, often bridging the gap between the white and black communities.

Black students of Kissimmee were able to attend a local school up until the eighth grade, after which they had to go elsewhere for further schooling. The Federal Emergency Relief Administration took down the old school in the northeast section of town and rebuilt it where Central Avenue Elementary is located today: 1502 N. Central Avenue. Little by little officials added grades until the school became Kissimmee High School, which had its first graduating class in 1945. Its principals were Lamar Forte, S.T.E. Pinckney, and W.E. Patterson, who served from 1946 until the integration of schools in 1968. One of its teachers was Mrs. Theresa Helms, who may have been Osceola County's first native black to graduate from college; after beginning her teaching career in 1937 at Kissimmee High School and St. Cloud Middle School, she retired after 35 consecutive years of teaching in county schools.

Further Reading:

Al and Bob Cody, "The Past Hundred Years...Contributions of the Black Community." Kissimmee: First Florida Bank, 1987.

Zora Neale Hurston, "Lawrence of the River," *Saturday Evening Post*, September 5, 1942, pp. 18, 55-57. The same article was condensed in *Negro Digest*, 1 (March 1943), pp. 47-49.

Betty Metzger, editor. *The History of Kissimmee*. St. Petersburg: Byron Kennedy & Company, 1983?

Minnie Moore Willson. *History of Osceola County*. Orlando: Inland Press, 1935.

Chapter 36

Lake City

This picturesque town, which has a population of 9,927, of whom 3,824 (39%) are black, has three places of importance to blacks: two in the town and one in nearby Olustee. The first one in the city is the **Florida Sports Hall of Fame**, which members of the Florida Sports Writers Association (FSWA) founded in 1958. Later the Florida Sportscasters Association (FSA) joined in, and each year members of both organizations elect a new class of inductees, each of whom must be a native of Florida or established/prolonged a reputation of excellence in sports while living in the state. Until 1975, the Hall of Fame did not have a permanent location; in that year it moved to Cypress Gardens near Winter Haven, where it remained until 1985. It then stayed in a temporary location in Orlando until it moved to its present 9,000-square-foot facility in Lake City in 1990. Special exhibits, video displays, and a 45-seat theater make up this impressive facility on a seven-acre complex near the intersection of U.S. 90 and I-75.

Among the 130+ inductees in the Hall of Fame are many blacks, including athletes from baseball (Andre Dawson, Hal McRae [see Avon Park above], and Tim Raines), basketball (Artis Gilmore), football (Ottis Anderson, Wes Chandler, Alonzo S. "Jake" Gaither, Willie Galimore [see St. Augustine below], Bob Hayes, Deacon Jones, Larry Little, Jack "Cy"

The Hall of Fame honors many black athletes from the state.
Credit: Kevin M. McCarthy

McClairen, Nat Moore, Ken Riley, Lee Roy Selmon, and Paul Warfield), golf (Charlie Owens), and tennis (Althea Gibson). The museum is open daily 8 a.m.-6 p.m. Phone: (904) 758-1311.

The other place in Lake City, **Richardson High School**, formerly a school for blacks before integration and now the site of Richardson Community Center at 221 North Street, was the school that Alfonso (Al) Lofton graduated from before becoming Florida's first black state trooper. Lofton (1945-1984) graduated from Richardson in 1963 and then joined the U.S. Marines and served in the Vietnam War. In 1968, after an honorable discharge from the Marines, he was hired by the Department of Corrections before joining the Florida Highway Patrol in 1970 and becoming the state's first black state trooper. Two years after his retirement in 1982, after a distinguished career in which he won many commendations, he died of multiple sclerosis. In 1988, officials dedicated the Florida Highway Patrol station at 1011 N.W. 11th Avenue in Miami in his honor.

Further Reading:

"Florida's first Black State Trooper Was Good Role Model," *The Miami Times*, February 24, 1994, p. 3D.

For more about an important Civil War battleground to the east of Lake City, see Olustee below.

Chapter 37

Leesburg

*T*his town in Lake County was named by Calvin Lee, an early resident who named it after himself. The Lee family came from Alabama in the 1840s to take advantage of the rich lands and the lakes. Black families also moved there and began raising their families. In the 1949-1966 period, local blacks, like many throughout Florida, wanted an institution of higher learning below the senior-college level to provide a post-secondary education. The 12 black junior colleges established in Florida allowed those Floridians who were not able financially to attend Florida A&M University in Tallahassee or out-of-state colleges to live at home and obtain the first two years of college at minimal cost.

Leesburg's **Johnson Junior College** was one of those 12 black junior colleges in Florida (see St. Petersburg below). Established by legislative act in 1961 to serve black students in Lake and Sumter counties and offering classes for the first time in the fall of 1962, the school had as its first president Mr. Perman E. Williams. Like the other 11 black junior colleges and white junior colleges, Johnson was to have courses both for those who wanted to transfer to a four-year university and for those who wanted to learn a technical trade. The college began meeting in two portable classrooms on the campus of Leesburg Negro High School and shared the facilities of the high school. The enrollment figures for Johnson Junior College showed that it served a good number of students:

1962-1963: 250 students **1963-1964: 318 students**
1964-1965: 397 students

In 1965, when the college merged with Lake-Sumter Junior College, local officials did their best to employ the black faculty from Johnson in the integrated college or in high schools. As was often the case in Florida, administrators at the black school had to settle for reduced responsibilities in the integrated college; the president of Johnson Junior College, for example, became the dean at Lake-Sumter Junior College.

Chapter 38

Live Oak

In the 1850s, settlers arriving in the Suwannee County area began petitioning the Florida Legislature to establish a new county, something which finally happened in 1858. One of the first legal documents entered into the records of the new county was the transfer of title to a male slave; the slave's owners, Margaret and John Demere, sold Adam for $1200. The county's first census of 1860 listed 1,467 whites, 835 slaves, and only one free black. By the end of the Civil War in 1865 all of the blacks were freed, and many of them stayed in the area because the Suwannee Valley region had rich soil to grow tobacco and cotton. By 1893, the town also had a black, Thomas Harris, as postmaster. Today Live Oak, the county seat of Suwannee County, has a population of 6,332, of whom 2,490 (39%) are black.

Further Reading:

"Focus on Live Oak Centennial, 1878-1978." Live Oak: Suwannee Democrat, 1978.

John Paul Jones, "Suwannee County — Florida's New Frontier," *Guide to North Florida Living*, May-June, 1982, pp. 25-33.

"Live Oak: 'Belle' of the Suwannee," *Florida Living*, November 1989, p. 10+.

A typical black home in Live Oak in the 1930s was simple but adequate. Credit: Florida State Archives

One might-have-been for the town was the plan to establish Brown Theological Institute there after the Civil War. In 1870, the African Methodist Episcopal Church of Florida planned to build the school in Live Oak for the newly freed slaves on 640 acres of land donated by friends of the Church. When a school official absconded with the money, authorities had to wait another decade and then built the school, which became Edward Waters College (see above), in Jacksonville.

The **African Missionary Baptist Church** at 509 Walker Avenue S.W., two blocks south of U.S. 90, traces its history to the First African Baptist Church, the oldest church for blacks, which was organized in January 1868, three years after President Abraham Lincoln's Emancipation Proclamation went into effect. The first church building was located on the corner of Parshley Street and Houston Avenue on land donated by Mrs. Nancy Parshley, a wealthy white woman. Workers later moved the building to its present site on Walker Avenue. One of its most important pastors was Dr.

George P. McKinney, Sr., who began his 26-year tenure as pastor there in 1890. He also served as editor of such denominational newspapers as *The Florida Baptist, The Florida Baptist Herald,* and *The Florida Baptist Watchman.*

Mrs. Parshley also gave land for another black church, the **Ebenezer African Methodist Episcopal Church**, also on the corner of Parshley Street and Houston Avenue. This church also began in 1868, five years before congregation members built the first building. Rev. Frank Sylbel and a small band of members held their first services in a small, frame house at the site of the present church. In 1892, the congregation built a brick structure on land they purchased. In 1973, Rev. T.E. Shehee and congregation members built the present structure.

Douglass High School, which was renamed the **Douglass Center**, on Douglass Street in Live Oak has served as an educational center since 1868. The high school was originally located on Houston Avenue; later the New Douglass High School was built on 10th Street, which was renamed Douglass Street. The original building, which had just one door and was built in 1868, operated for only four months a year: June, July, August, and September. In 1949, a new school was built to house grades 1 to 12 and had 680 students. The enrollment jumped to 889 after the consolidation of rural schools. The school was renamed Suwannee Middle School in 1969. In 1990, a new middle school was built, and the school was renamed Douglass Center. (For more about a local educator see Punta Gorda below for information about Benjamin Joshua Baker of Live Oak. For more about a legislator from Live Oak who represented Miami in the Florida Legislature for 14 terms see Joe Lang Kershaw in Miami below.)

Chapter 39

Madison

The county (established in 1827) and town (established in 1838) honor in their names James Madison, the fourth president of the United States. In the first half of the 19th century, the county had many slaves (2,688 out of a total population of 5,490 in 1850, for example), but whites and blacks worshiped together even in the days of segregation; of the 46 members of the Hickstown/Madison Baptist Church in 1851, for example, 38 were white and 8 were black, probably slaves. After the Civil War, the two races often worshiped in different churches. Today the town has 1,194 blacks (36%) out of a total population of 3,360.

Further Reading:

Elizabeth H. Sims. *A History of Madison County, Florida.* Madison: Madison County Historical Society, 1986.

An early Spanish explorer in the area was Panfilo de Narváez, a man who led a group of some 400 men through Florida in 1528. One of the men in that group and one of only four who survived Indian attacks, shipwreck, and an eight-year journey to Mexico was a slave, Estevanico the Black, who originally came from Morocco in Africa. He was the first black man to travel through Florida and much of the southwestern part of the present-day United States.

Further Reading:

Maxine D. Jones and Kevin M. McCarthy. *African Americans in Florida.* Sarasota: Pineapple Press, 1993, pp. 9-10.

John Upton Terrell. *Estevanico the Black.* Los Angeles: Westernlore Press, 1968.

One black from Madison who went on to become well-known was Abrams Lincoln Lewis (1865-1947), a founder of the Afro-American Industrial and Benefit Association, which later became the Afro-American Life Insurance Company, one of the largest black-owned businesses in Florida (see Jacksonville above).

Suwannee River Junior College, which was established in 1958, was one of 12 black junior colleges in Florida (see St. Petersburg below). Mrs. Jenyethel Merritt and Mr. James Gardener served as presidents of the school, which enrolled the most students, 402, in the 1964-65 school year. In 1966, the school, which had several buildings near the Madison County Training School, merged with North Florida Junior College, at which time Mrs. Merritt became vice-president of the integrated junior college and the director of the Learning Resources Center, which honors her in its name. The enrollment figures for Suwannee River Junior College were as follows:

1959-1960: 90 students
1960-1961: 170 students
1961-1962: 234 students
1962-1963: 202 students
1963-1964: 261 students
1964-1965: 402 students
1965-1966: 250 students

Chapter 40

Marathon

About midway between Key Largo and Key West in the Florida Keys on Key Vaca is the small town of Marathon, which received its name from the workers who used it to refer to the endurance contest or difficulties the workers overcame in building Henry Flagler's Florida East Coast Railroad to Key West. Apparently, one of the engineers in charge of the railroad urged his workers to "make a marathon effort to complete the line" before Flagler died, which is exactly what they did, a year ahead of schedule. The Indians who inhabited the Keys for decades before the first Europeans arrived in the 16th century did not take kindly to the invaders and killed many of them, including shipwrecked sailors. As federal forces pushed the Indians off the Keys, settlers moved in, including pirates and wreckers who used the inlets and islands in the vicinity. Around 1818, local fishermen established a small village in what became Key Vaca. Henry Flagler began extending his railroad down the Keys in 1905 in a job he called the toughest he ever undertook. By the time the 156-mile Overseas Railroad reached Key West in 1912, 20,000 men had worked on it and it cost $50 million, which would be more than half a billion in today's dollars.

Some 800 of Flagler's construction workers were blacks

from Florida and the Bahamas attracted to the Keys by the work. Flagler's workers had a base camp at Key Vaca that they abandoned when they finished building the Seven-Mile Bridge just southwest of Marathon, and the population slowly diminished until it reached just 17 by 1926. Little by little the town of Marathon developed between the railroad line, where U.S. 1 runs today, and the bay. In the 1950s, the town began to develop rapidly, acquiring its first dial-system telephones, the Florida Highway Patrol station, a volunteer fire department, and the first full-time doctor.

In the middle of Marathon is the Crane Point Historic and Archaeological District, which contained the black pioneer settlements of Adderley (or Adderly) Town, which developed between 1903 and 1912. The town had six people in 1910, all members of the Adderley and Curry families. Among those blacks was George Adderley (or Adderly) (1870-1958), a black Bahamian who came to Florida in 1890. In 1903, he bought 32 acres of land from Annie Crain for $100 and moved to Key Vaca, where he built his house and where he worked in sponging and charcoal making. The town also had a small wooden church where George Adderley, an Anglican lay preacher, preached.

The **Adderley** (or **Adderly**) **House** at 5550 Overseas Highway behind the Museum of Natural History of the Florida Keys is a small, white, one-story building in the Bahamian architecture style that George Adderley and his wife, Olivia, built sometime after they bought the property in 1903 on part of the 32 acres they owned. The house was built of tabby, a building material consisting of lime, shells, gravel or stones, and water. When this concrete-like material dried in the sun, it became hard enough to withstand the hurricanes that buffeted the area over the years. The house withstood the terrible 1935 hurricane, which destroyed much of Flagler's railroad track in the Keys and made the area less accessible until the U.S. government finished the Overseas Highway in 1938. Adderley sold his property in 1950 to Mary and Frances Crane, who built a new winter house on

The Adderley House in Marathon was home to a black Bahamian immigrant who worked in the area in the early 1900s. Credit: Kevin M. McCarthy

Rachel Key and connected the small island to the mainland. By then all of the blacks had left the property. George's wife died that year, and George died eight years later; they are buried in unmarked graves in the Key West cemetery.

Today Marathon has a population of 8,857, of whom 586 (7%) are black. For many years the town's blacks lived in what is known today as **Marathon Beach Subdivision**, a name that dates back to the 1920s, when William A. Parrish bought up land between 35th and 43rd streets on the gulf side of the highway. Many of the early settlers who bought land there were blacks, who settled down and renamed the place "The Rock." The segregated school for black children later became the Grace Jones Community Center, honoring in its name the town's first black teacher.

At the southwestern edge of Marathon is Knights Key, where the famous Seven Mile Bridge begins. The bridge, completed in 1911, withstood the hurricanes that hit the

Keys, including the 1935 one that destroyed Flagler's railroad. Workers then constructed the Overseas Highway using Flagler's railroad line. The bridge led to Pigeon Key, where railroad workers and their families lived; later the University of Miami used the island for marine research. Workers built a new bridge in 1982 and cut off Pigeon Key from the main highway.

The **Pigeon Key Historic District** at mile marker 45 off U.S. 1 has seven frame buildings which workers used while building the Overseas Railroad. One of the buildings is a 1912 "Negro Workers' Cottage" where black workers were housed. Officials have plans to make the area into a recreational facility with displays about the building of the railroad. The site is not accessible from the new bridge, but must be reached by way of the old trestle.

Further Reading:

Rodman Bethel. *Flagler's Folly: The Railroad That Went to Sea and Was Blown Away*. Key West: Bethel, 1987?

Stuart McIver. *Glimpses of South Florida History*. Miami: Florida Flair Books, 1988, p. 49: "Working on the Overseas Railroad."

Pat Parks. *The Railroad That Died At Sea*. Brattleboro, Vermont: Stephen Greene Press, 1968.

Jerry and June Powell. *Marathon: Heart of the Florida Keys*. Marathon: Seagrape Publications, 1980.

Mike Smith, "Waxing and Waning with the Times, Pigeon Key Remains a Keys Constant," *Florida Keys Magazine*, June 1994, pp. 14-15.

Larry Thompson, "'The Rock': Marathon's historic black area changes," *The Key West Citizen*, September 27, 1993: p. 5A.

Joy Williams. *The Florida Keys: A History & Guide*. New York: Random House, 1987.

Chapter 41

Marianna

*M*arianna, the county seat of Jackson County, was established in 1823 and named by the original site owners for their two daughters, Mary and Anna, or for the wife, Anna Marie, of the town's founder. A Scottish immigrant laid out the town of Marianna in 1827, and little by little businesses and families moved to the town. A Civil War skirmish, called the "Battle of Marianna," took place near the town, with the result that Union troops seized 600 slaves from the area. Throughout the 19th and into the 20th century, farmers have grown peanuts and cotton, crops that demand hard work, much of it performed by black workers. Today the town, which lies near U.S. 90 and I-10 in the state's Panhandle, has a population of 6,292, of whom 2,422 (39%) are black. (For more about one of the town's blacks, see St. Augustine below: the Cary A. White Complex.)

Further Reading:

Rita Dickens. *Marse Ned: The Story of an Old Southern Family*. New York: Exposition Press, 1959. This is the story of a slave plantation near Marianna in the 19th century.

John Paul Jones, "Florida's Cavern City," *Florida Living*, July 1986, pp. 6-13.

Steve Liner, editor. *A Brief History of Marianna*. Marianna: City of Marianna, 1979.

Jerrell H. Shofner. *Jackson County, Florida: A History*. Marianna: Jackson County Heritage Association, 1985.

Julia Floyd Smith. *Slavery and Plantation Growth in Antebellum Florida, 1821-1860*. Gainesville: University of Florida Press, 1973.

J. Randall Stanley. *History of Jackson County*. Marianna: Jackson County Historical Society, 1950.

The **Joseph W. Russ, Jr. House** at 4318 (formerly 310) W. Lafayette Street is now a private residence, but it used to be the main plantation house near where a famous black journalist was born a slave: Timothy Thomas Fortune (1856-1928). When the Civil War ended, Fortune joined adults and other children of Marianna in a small church, where two Union soldiers taught them how to read and write. Later he began working at a local newspaper, *The Marianna Courier*, and learned skills he would keep with him the rest of his life. When his father was elected to the Florida legislature, the local Ku Klux Klan threatened the whole family, and so they had to move to Jacksonville. There young Timothy worked on another newspaper, *The Daily Union*, and learned more about the power of journalism.

He later went on to Howard University and to New York City, where he worked on several important black newspapers: *The New York Globe*, *The Freeman*, *The New York Age*, and *The Negro World*. By the time he died in 1928, he was known as the dean of black journalism and had established the National Afro-American League to fight for the rights of blacks in this country. His published books include *Black and White; Land, Labor, and Politics in the South* (1884), *The Negro in Politics* (1885), and *Dreams of Life* (1905).

Directions:

The large, wooden Russ House is on the north side of West Lafayette Street just west of Russ Street and between Russ and Daniels streets.

Further Reading:

Gene Burnett, "T.T. Fortune: Florida's Black Militant," in *Florida's Past:*

T. Thomas Fortune became a famous journalist who championed the rights of blacks throughout America. Credit: Florida State Archives

People and Events that Shaped the State. Sarasota: Pineapple Press, 1986, vol. I, pp. 50-53.

Emma Lou Thornbrough. *T. Thomas Fortune, Militant Journalist*. Chicago: University of Chicago Press, 1972.

Fortune would have been pleased with an educational institution established in Marianna in 1961 near the Jackson County Training School for blacks, **Jackson Junior College**, one of 12 black junior colleges in Florida (see St. Petersburg below). Its first president was Mr. William H. Harley, Sr., the principal of the black high school there. In the mid-1960s it merged with Chipola Junior College, which was founded in 1947 as the state's third junior college. The enrollment figures for Jackson Junior College were as follows:

1961-1962: 47 students **1962-1963: 83 students**
1963-1964: 97 students **1964-1965: 333 students**
1965-1966: 443 students

Two tragic events associated with the **Courthouse** in the

middle of Marianna show how difficult the plight of the black has been even in recent times. The first event was the 1934 lynching of a black man, Claude Neal, who was accused of raping and murdering a white woman, the daughter of one of his employers. After authorities arrested Neal and took him to a jail in Alabama for his protection, a mob of angry whites found out where he was, kidnapped him, returned him to the scene of the murder, tortured him, and then lynched him. They then hung his corpse from a tree near the Marianna courthouse. The horror of that torture and execution so incensed much of the country that lynching began to decline in popularity in this country. Lynching had become a means by which white racists, who lynched almost 3,000 blacks since the 1880s, were able to control the blacks after the Civil War.

Further Reading:

Jacquelyn Dowd Hall. *Revolt Against Chivalry: Jessie Daniel Ames and the Woman's Campaign Against Lynching*. New York: Columbia University Press, 1979.

James R. McGovern. *Anatomy of a Lynching*. Baton Rouge: Louisiana State University Press, 1982 [about the Claude Neal execution].

Arthur F. Raper. *The Tragedy of Lynching*. Chapel Hill: University of North Carolina Press, 1933.

Walter White. *Rope and Faggot: A Biography of Judge Lynch*. New York: Knopf, 1929.

The other tragic event associated with the courthouse was the second trial of two black men, Freddie Pitts and Wilbert Lee, who were falsely accused of killing two men in Port St. Joe in 1963. The first trial of the two innocent men that year sentenced the men to death, but the Florida Supreme Court ordered a new trial in 1971 because the state had suppressed evidence and excluded black jurors in the trial. The Marianna courthouse was the scene of the second trial, 74 miles north of Port St. Joe, but another all-white jury convicted the two black men even though another man had already confessed to the crime. Pitts and Lee spent nine years on death row, but Governor Reuben Askew and three other Cabinet members believed the men were innocent and pardoned them in 1975.

Further Reading:

Kevin Metz, "Looking for Justice," *The Tampa Tribune*, February 20, 1994, pp. 1, 18.

Chapter 42

Melbourne

By the time the railroad arrived in 1893, this Brevard County town on the Indian River, which was named after Melbourne, Australia, was already developed because of steamboat accessibility. Three of the first non-Indians to arrive before then were blacks: Balaam Allen, Wright Brothers, and Peter Wright. According to *The Melbourne Bicentennial Book* (p. 39), they were freedmen "who after the Civil War had been reluctant to leave their former owner. But, their master, unable to support them, sailed with them beyond the last southern outpost and staked out for each of them what he considered was about 160 acres for a homestead. There he left them to shift for themselves." Weona Cleveland in her *Crossroad Towns Remembered* (p. 96) doubts this story because each of the three black men had been born in different states.

One of those men, Peter Wright, was the largest landholder in the area as well as a trader and boatman and also the first postal carrier in the area, bringing the mail twice a week from Titusville on his sailboat. Another of those first three black men to arrive here was Wright Brothers; his one-story **Wright Brothers House** at 2310 1/2 Lipscomb Street, which is a private residence, one block north of Brothers Avenue and one block west of U.S. 1, was built around 1892. Today the **Brothers Park** in south Melbourne honors him.

Further Reading:

Weona Cleveland. *Crossroad Towns Remembered: A Look Back at Brevard & Indian River Communities*. Melbourne: Florida Today, 1994. See esp. pp. 95-98: "A Remembrance of Melbourne's Forgotten Pioneers"; pp. 101-102: "Still going strong after 75 years" [about teacher and activist Flossie Bryant]; pp. 112-113: "Historic Past Shapes Present" [about Leola Price Harper]; and pp. 122-123: "First Black Officer Got City Badge but No Gun or Car" [about patrolman James R. Ryoland].

Jackie Reid, "Brothers Park Ills Recounted," *The Times* [Melbourne], August 11, 1971.

Mary Silas Brothers, who helped her husband, Wright, grow citrus on the 7.5 acres of land they lived on near Crane Creek, gave birth in 1882 to William Rufus Brothers, the first black child born in Melbourne. William attended school at the little red schoolhouse, the first school in Melbourne, in Tarheel on what is now South Riverview Drive. Then in 1909 workers built a one-room school for blacks on the corner of Line and Lipscomb streets, where the Church of God in Christ now stands. The school had two rows of seats with two students sitting in a seat. About 16 students attended school there.

When that school became too small, workers built the Melbourne Vocational School in the area where Brothers Park is located today. Black students attended that school until it burned in 1953, at which point they attended school at the old Naval Base at Melbourne Airport, until the present Stone School was built in 1958. Officials considered calling the new school Hopkins since the area had been called Hopkins when the Union Cypress Sawmill was there, but decided in favor of Stone because Mr. Stone had been such an important educational leader in Melbourne. The first graduating class from Stone School took place in 1955. Today **Stone Junior High School** is at 1101 E. University Boulevard.

Further Reading:

Weona Cleveland, "Stone School history aired," *The Times* [Melbourne], February 18, 1976, p. 8A.

William Rufus Brothers, the first black child born in Melbourne, later married Estelle Stone, and they had three children, including John Brothers (1907-1981). William's mother, Mary Brothers, was one of several black women, including Lydia Duncan, Anneda Harris, and Estella Jackson, who became midwives at a time when the area had few doctors. Other blacks opened up successful businesses, for example Stone Funeral Home and Tucker Plumbing.

Further Reading:

Bart Bachman, "John Brothers is a proud man with a rich past," *The Times* [Melbourne], June 11, 1980.

Elaine Murray Stone. *Brevard County*. Northridge, Cal.: Windsor Publications, 1988.

"Pioneer Brothers dies," *The Times*, November 25, 1981, p. 9A.

Julie Williams, "Brothers' Roots Deep in Melbourne," *Florida Today* [Melbourne], July, 1979.

In the home of Wright and Mary Brothers, local residents like Carrie and Robert Lipscomb and Balaam Allen and his wife established the **Allen Chapel A.M.E. Church** in the late 19th century and built the first structure on the northern end of Lipscomb Street in 1885. In 1964, they built a new church at 2416 S. Lipscomb Street. The church bell, which members acquired in 1928 and which is in the new building, is made of solid brass and weighs about 1,000 pounds.

Carver Junior College, which was established in 1959, was one of 12 black junior colleges in Florida (see St. Petersburg below). Its first president was Mr. James R. Greene. The school, which was about 10 miles from Cape Canaveral, 15 miles from the Kennedy Space Center, and 12 miles from Patrick Air Force Base, merged with Brevard Junior College in 1963 after an NAACP official complained to the U.S. Commission on Civil Rights that the school had cost the taxpayers $100,000 a year for three years, had been using high school teachers and facilities, and had graduated poorly educated black students. The enrollment figures, which included college parallel courses and vocational courses, for Carver Junior College were as follows:

1960-1961: 168 students **1961-1962: 263 students**
1962-1963: 143 students

Early black settlers of the Brothers, Ford, and Stone families established a **cemetery on Line Street** in south Melbourne that over a period of 80 years after its establishment became forgotten and overrun with weeds, trees, and garbage, until it was recently restored. In 1980, Boy Scout Troop 730 cleaned up the cemetery and the five tombstones found there, including those of Alice Chambers, Franklin Johnson, Carrie E. Lipscomb, John H. Whitfield, and the cryptic Wm. W.W. (probably referring to Wm. W. Whitfield).

Directions to Cemetery:
Turn west off U.S. 1 onto Line Street and go beyond Lipscomb Street; the cemetery is on the north side of Line Street south of Brothers Street.

Further Reading:

Weona Cleveland, "Graveyard Revitalized," *The Times* [Melbourne] November 26, 1980. Also articles by the same author in the same newspaper, September 10, 1980 and June 18, 1980.

Verna G. Langlais, compiler. *Cemetery Census of Brevard County, Florida.* Titusville: no publ., 1984. This booklet lists those buried in the Line Street cemetery as well as in the black Stone Cemetery behind Brothers Park, the Bull Creek Cemetery near Deer Park, and the Eau Gallie Cemetery; the latter two cemeteries are not black cemeteries.

An early black church of the community was **Macedonia Baptist Church**. Because the Florida East Coast Railroad had not reached Melbourne by 1891, the church's pastor, Rev. Parson Miller, had to transport the lumber for the first sanctuary by boat from Titusville. Twelve members of the congregation, including J.E. Austell, built the first church building on East Brothers Avenue. Between 1970 and 1975 the congregation built a new sanctuary on Lipscomb Street. Among the distinguished pastors of the church was Rev. James Massey, who served a term of 20 years.

Further Reading:

Weona Cleveland, "Church Was Built on Faith," *The Times* [Melbourne], October 10, 1979, p. 2B.

Georgiana Greene Kjerulff. *Tales of Old Brevard*. Melbourne: The Kellersberger Fund of The South Brevard Historical Society, Inc., 1972, esp. pp. 103-104: "The Black Community."

By 1900, only about 200 people lived in Melbourne, but the land boom of the 1920s brought many new settlers to the area, and the development of the National Aeronautics and Space Administration (NASA) facility at Cape Canaveral (later Cape Kennedy) brought in thousands more. Among those who worked hard to desegregate the schools in the area in the 1950s and 1960s was Harry Lawrence, the one-time president of the South Brevard Civic League; the **Harry Lawrence Park** at the juncture of New Haven and Strawbridge avenues in Melbourne honors him.

Further Reading:

Weona Cleveland. *Crossroad Towns Remembered: A Look Back at Brevard & Indian River Communities*. Melbourne: Florida Today, 1994, pp. 128-129: "Long-time Melbourne Resident Gets a Park Named after Him."

Brevard County had many demonstrations in the 1960s as local blacks sought an end to segregation. Interracial advisory committees met to make the move to integration as painless as possible, despite the efforts by the Ku Klux Klan to harass the blacks. Black leaders in Melbourne included John Brothers, descendant of one of the first settlers there; U.F. Gibbs, the principal of the all-black Stone High School; and Henry Jackson, the president of the local NAACP. As a result of many discussions, one-fourth of local restaurant owners agreed to integrate their facilities, and the Melbourne Country Club was desegregated.

The integration of Brevard schools took place in 1964. Soon after that, Ted Nichols, a Stone High School teacher, won a two-year term on the Melbourne City Commission, the first black elected to public office in the county. The 1980s saw further progress. For example, local Melbourne officials made a decision in the 1980s to change the name of Lynching Tree Drive to Legendary Lane; according to local legend, a black man who had been involved in trying to free a cow tangled in a rope in 1926 was accused of accosting several children playing nearby. He was arrested and taken to an oak tree where he was hanged. The name of Lynching Tree Drive had perpetuated a sad chapter in the city's history and had offended enough people to have it changed. Today Melbourne has a population of 59,646, of whom 5,624 (9%) are black.

Further Reading:

Noreda B. McKemy and Elaine Murray Stone, editors. *The Melbourne Bicentennial Book*. Melbourne: The Melbourne Bicentennial Committee, 1976.

Melbourne: A Century of Memories. Melbourne: The Melbourne Area Chamber of Commerce Centennial Committee, 1980. See esp. pp. 21, 24, 27-28, & 105.

Stephen Olausen. *Historic Buildings of Melbourne*. Melbourne: S. Olausen?, 1991.

Chapter 43

Miami

This city of 358,548, of whom 97,822 (27%) are black, developed in the last 100 years after having an earlier army outpost on the Miami River, Fort Dallas. When Henry Flagler brought his railroad to the area in 1896, Miami's first land boom began. Among the blacks who played a significant role in the city's early history were Rev. A.W. Brown, who threw the first shovel of dirt in the building of Flagler's Royal Palm Hotel in what is now the Dupont Plaza area; W.H. Artson, the first person to sign the original city charter on July 28, 1896; and the 162 black voters out of a total of 368 pioneers who voted to create the city of Miami. Many of those black pioneers are buried in the **City of Miami Cemetery** at 1800 N.E. 2nd Avenue, including Father Theodore Gibson, who served as a Miami City Commissioner and local president of the NAACP; A.C. Lightburn, who helped establish the Bethel A.M.E. Church; and Judge Lawson E. Thomas, Miami's first black judge.

Further Reading:

Alma J. Crawford, "Old-style Procession Marks Tribute to Miami Pioneers," *The Miami Times*, April 14, 1994, p. 1A.

Derek T. Davis, "Theodore Gibson Carried on Civil Rights Battle in Miami," *The Miami Times*, January 13, 1994, p. 4B.

Dorothy Jenkins Fields, "Reflections on Black History: Miami's Incorporation," *Update* [Historical Association of Southern Florida], August 1976, p. 10. This article lists all the blacks who were present at the incorporation of Miami.

Howard Kleinberg, editor. *Miami: The Way We Were*. Tampa: Surfside Publishing, 1989, pp. 46-47: "Early Black Workers Played Big Role."

Miami grew rapidly in this century, especially after World War II, when so many of its sons and daughters returned to live after serving in the Armed Forces, and many of the soldiers who had trained in the area decided to live there also. The population of the area nearly doubled between 1940 and 1950 and then nearly doubled again the following decade. Many returning soldiers used the G.I. Bill of Rights to attend the fledgling University of Miami, transforming it into a major educational institution. Black veterans moved to segregated subdivisions like Bunche Park in North Dade and Richmond Heights in South Dade. In time, blacks entered the Miami work force as policemen, mail carriers, and attorneys, slowly making gains as integration provided more opportunities.

That history has been clouded in recent years by racial riots and unrest. In 1980, after insurance executive Arthur McDuffie was allegedly killed by police and an all-white jury acquitted white Dade County police officers of his death, black residents of the city rose up in disgust and rioted, with the result that 15 more people died and more than $100 million in physical damage scarred the city.

Further Reading:

The Negro Almanac: A Reference Work on the African American, compiled and edited by Harry A. Ploski and James Williams. Detroit: Gale Research Inc., 1989, p. 250.

When South African leader Nelson Mandela visited the city in June 1990 to address a labor union convention, no local official publicly welcomed him. That led to a tourism boycott by black attorneys that spread to much of the black community and, after lasting 1,030 days, eventually resulted in gains by blacks in the community. In 1992, voters chose Alcee Hastings and Carrie Meek, along with Corrine Brown, as the first blacks elected to Congress from the state since Reconstruction.

Among the sites of importance to blacks is the **Vanguard** in the Historical Museum of Southern Florida, 111 Flagler Street. The Urban League of Greater Miami commissioned a mural entitled "The Vanguard—Black Miami's Mural of Purpose" to commemorate the 25th anniversary of the passage of the 1965 Civil Rights Bill. Miami artist Carl Latimore created the mural with photographs of the city's black personages, past and present, all of whom made important contributions to the city's black progress in the past 25 years. To prepare the mural, the artist conducted oral history interviews, did research in the archives, and used high technology to create a unique collage of photographs and images.

When Henry Flagler was building his railroad down to Miami in the 1890s and eventually to Key West, he needed a place for his workers to live. At that time, because blacks were not allowed to live within the white community, the land west of the railroad tracks within the city limits of Miami between today's N.W. Sixth and Twelfth streets was called "Colored Town" and became the basis of what later would become **Overtown**. By 1915, the area had most of the city's 5,000 blacks, although some lived in other so-called "colored districts" on what is now S.W. Eighth Street, in Coconut Grove (see above), and near Lemon City. It did not take long before many churches and businesses flourished in Overtown, but the poor living conditions often led to poverty, disease, and crime. And hate groups like the Ku Klux Klan remained active throughout Florida.

Avenue G (now N.W. Second Avenue) was the main street of Colored Town, which had more than 100 black-owned businesses and a Colored Board of Trade which encouraged blacks to own their own stores. Six doctors, several pharma-

The Ku Klux Klan marched in Miami in 1925. Credit: Florida State Archives

cists, an attorney, nine ministers, and many grocers, tailors, dress-makers, repairmen, even two undertakers provided services for the black community. As World War I erupted, many black Miamians enlisted in the Armed Forces; residents would often hold a parade down Avenue G before sending off a group of its young men to begin their training at Tuskegee Institute in Alabama. Several decades later, in 1935, St. Francis Xavier Catholic School opened as south Florida's first private school for blacks.

Further Reading:

Dorothy J. Fields, "Reflections on Black History: Stevedores," *Update,* June 1975, p. 9.

Dorothy Jenkins Fields, "Reflections on Black History," *Update,* October 1975, p. 8.

Paul S. George, "Colored Town: Miami's Black Community, 1896-1930," *Florida Historical Quarterly,* vol. 56 (April 1978), pp. 432-447.

Paul S. George, editor. *A Guide to the History of Florida.* New York: Greenwood Press, 1989. This is an excellent bibliographical reference, e.g. Chapter 12: "Black Floridians" by Joe M. Richardson and Maxine D. Jones.

In the 1930s, another Miami suburb developed for blacks northwest of Overtown. **Liberty City** took the overflow from Overtown and developed the first public housing in Florida, the Liberty Square Housing Project between N.W. 12th and 15th Avenues. Among the places in Liberty City that honor blacks is **Lillie C. Evans Elementary School**, named after a long-time teacher and principal of the Washington Graded School; and the **Alonzo Kelly Park**, named after one of black Miami's first real estate developers. One of the places that visiting black entertainers stayed at was the **Georgette Tea Room** at 2550 N.W. 51st Street, once a meeting place/guest house for black celebrities and entertainers and today a private residence on Dade County's list of historic places.

Further Reading:

Derek T. Davis, "Georgette Tea Room Is Example of Black Identity in Miami," *The Miami Times*, April 8, 1993, Lifestyle, p. 1.

One particularly successful black businessman was Dana Albert Dorsey (1872-1940), who came to Miami in the late 1890s to farm. He slowly began to buy property in the area, and his real estate holdings eventually included an island, which later became Fisher Island, that he developed as a black bathing beach until selling it in the 1920s. He also opened the first black hotel and gave land for a black high school, Dorsey High, at N.W. 71st Street and 17th Avenue. Before he died in 1940, he had become the area's first black millionaire. Named in his honor are Dorsey High School, which is now the **Dorsey Skills Center** in Liberty City, **Dorsey Park**, and **Dorsey Avenue** (also N.W. 3rd Avenue), both in Overtown. Miami's Heritage Conservation Board has had erected at the site of his house at 250 N.W. Ninth Street a replica of the house, which had been destroyed.

Further Reading:

Shelia Payton, "Looking Back at Being Black," *The Miami Herald,* February 1, 1976, p. 1G+.

Another successful businessman was Henry Ethelbert Sigismund Reeves, who came to Miami from the Bahamas in 1919. As a former printer for the *Nassau City Press,* he wanted to stay in the newspaper business, and so he joined with Rev. Samuel Sampson, Dr. Alonzo P. Kelly, and M.J. Bodie to form a printing company and publish a newspaper, the *Miami Sun,* for the black community. After publishing the newspaper for eight months, they had to suspend operations because of the lack of newsprint caused by World War I. In 1923, Reeves began another black weekly newspaper, *The Miami Times,* which is today the South's largest black weekly in circulation. **Reeves Park** in Overtown honors him to this day. His son, Garth C. Reeves, Sr., and grandson, Garth C. Reeves, Jr., have continued the newspaper over the years. Today, Rachel J. Reeves is publisher and chairman of the newspaper. Another business that Henry Reeves began, the Magic City Printery, did well enough to tide the newspaper over during the difficult times of the Depression. Other black newspapers in Overtown in the early days were *The Industrial Reporter, The Miami Journal, The Biscayne Messenger, The Tropical Dispatch,* and the Florida edition of the *Pittsburgh Courier*. The **Garth C. Reeves, Sr. Hall** at Miami-Dade Community College honors the man who served as chairman of the Board of Trustees of the college.

More recent black newspapers include the *Coptic Times* published by the Ethiopian Zion Coptic Church in Miami Beach (1978?-1980); *Liberty News* (1961?-), which claimed to be "Miami's largest circulated Afro-American Daily"; *Newsletter of African American Activist* (1980-1980?) about the Miami riots; *The Orthodox Messenger — The Voice of Washington Heights* (1941?- ?), "A Negro Catholic Monthly" and the "Official Organ of the Southern Jurisdiction of the African Orthodox Church"; *Yahweh* (1987- ?), published by Yahweh

Ben Yahweh Temple of Love Publishers; and *Haiti en Marche* (1987?-).

Further Reading:

Dorothy Jenkins Fields, "Reflections on Black History: Miami's First Newspaper" [about *The Industrial Reporter*], *Update*, February 1976, p. 10.

Thomas F. Fleischmann, "Black Miamians in *The Miami Metropolis*, 1896-1900," *Tequesta*, vol. 52 (1992), pp. 21-38.

"The Industrial Reporter," *Update*, August 1976, p. 4.

Well-known black entertainers like Count Basie, Cab Calloway, Nat King Cole, Ella Fitzgerald, Aretha Franklin, and Billie Holiday had to stay in Overtown when they performed in white nightclubs on Miami Beach or in Miami, but they also performed in Overtown places like Sir John Hotel (formerly at Sixth Street and Third Avenue), the Mary Elizabeth Hotel (N.W. 2nd Avenue and 7th Street), and other nightclubs. Vacationers in Overtown included distinguished Americans like author W.E.B. DuBois, folklorist Zora Neale Hurston, boxer Joe Louis, and baseball players Roy Campanella and Jackie Robinson.

A center of entertainment which opened in 1919 at N.W. 2nd Avenue and 8th Street was the **Lyric Theater**, a building whose theater, movies, and meeting space were frequented by many people. Advertisements for the theater, which Gedar Walker owned, called it the "most beautiful and costly playhouse owned by colored people in all the Southland." Today this masonry building is all that survives of what was known as "Little Broadway" that prospered in the 1930s and 1940s. When desegregation and the construction of an expressway through the district led to the moving out of many black families, the area deteriorated, but officials have plans to revive the district. The Black Archives bought the Lyric Theater in 1988 and has progressed greatly in its restoration work on it.

Further Reading:

Dorothy Fields, "Black Entertainment, 1908-1919," *Update*, December 1974, p. 11.

Bea Hines, "Overtown: Good Times, Bad Times," *Mostly Sunny Days: A Miami Herald Salute to South Florida's Heritage*, edited by Bob Kearney. Miami: Miami Herald Publishing Company, 1986, pp. 96-98.

Dr. S.H. Johnson as told to Dorothy Jenkins Fields, "Reflections on Black History: Fun and Games Overtown," *Update*, August 1977, p. 8.

Eve Reed, "Funky Nights in Overtown," *South Florida History Magazine*, Spring/Summer 1993, pp. 8-14. This article includes a list of performers who appeared in Overtown in the 1940s, 1950s, and 1960s.

John Sewell. *Miami Memoirs: A New Pictorial Edition of John Sewell's Own Story* by Arva Moore Parks. Miami: Arva Parks & Co., 1987.

Booker T. Washington High School at 1200 N.W. 6th Avenue was the first school in south Florida that allowed black students to complete the 12th grade. It opened in early 1927 for 1,340 students and had its first graduation for six students the following year. The first school for black children in Miami's Colored Town was a wooden building that stood on N.W. 8th Street between 2nd and 3rd avenues where the Berrien Hotel later stood. Started around 1896, "Old Washington," as it was called, had only grades one through six. Later the Fort Dallas Land Company gave the land on 12th Street for a new school building where Douglass Elementary School now stands.

In 1924, high school classes were moved to Dunbar School on 20th Street. When the school board acquired land on N.W. 6th Avenue several years later for Booker T. Washington High School, some white residents in the area protested; concerned blacks then took turns guarding the site at night. Over the years the school expanded its facilities and activities like playing its first football game (1928), becoming A-rated (1934), organizing its first band (1941), and establishing its first School Supply Store (1947). The last senior class was in 1967, just before integration took place. In 1970, the school had only the 9th grade and was paired with Ada Merritt Junior High School for the 7th grade and Citrus Grove Junior High School for the 8th. Among the many

Booker T. Washington High School provided educational opportunities to thousands of black students from 1927 on. Credit: Florida State Archives

graduates of Booker T. Washington who went on to success was John D. Johnson, who became a judge in Miami. Also, Joe Lang Kershaw, who graduated from Booker T. and coached track there; he later served 14 terms (1968-1982) as a representative from Miami in the Florida Legislature.

Further Reading:

Lisa Jacques, "Joe Lang Kershaw: Teacher, Family Man, Political Pioneer," *The Miami Times*, September 30, 1993, p. 6A.

Lisa Jacques, "John Johnson Rose From Humble Origins to Become Pioneering Judge," *The Miami Times*, February 18, 1993, p. 3D.

Schools For the Miami Area. Tallahassee: State Department of Education, 1940.

Booker T. Washington School might have been expected to share facilities with a black junior college that might be established in the area. Throughout Florida, officials had established 12 black junior colleges, despite the fact that the

1954 Supreme Court had outlawed segregated schools. (See St. Petersburg below.) When the Dade County School Board began attempts to establish a black junior college, the local NAACP chapter objected, arguing that establishing such a junior college would be a continuation of segregation. Although enough liberal, forward-thinking citizens lived in Dade County to support an integrated junior college, the local school board feared that a segregationist legislature in Tallahassee would punish the local school system for establishing an integrated junior college. The school board also worried that the lack of good preparation among black students at the segregated high schools would not prepare them for college work.

The school board decided to open a separate branch of Dade County Junior College (Northwestern Center) rather than establish a separate black junior college. The faculty at the center would be black, but would share the advisory committee and administration of the main campus (Central Center). This may have been the first time in the nation that such an arrangement was attempted. When several black students requested admission to the all-white Central Campus of the junior college, the school board allowed seven of them to register in the fall of 1960, thus establishing one of the first desegregated public schools in Florida and the whole Southeast.

By the early 1960s, officials closed down the black center and transferred its black students and 11 black teachers to the main center. That November, the Greater Miami Urban League gave the college, Miami-Dade Junior College, an award for totally integrating itself in just two years. Little by little black students became more and more involved in activities on the central campus, including the student newspaper, and all extracurricular activities became integrated. The 1966 election of a black to be student body president indicated that the integration of students was succeeding.

Further Reading:

Arthur M. Cohen, "The Process of Desegregation: A Case Study," *The Journal of Negro Education*, vol. 35 (fall 1966), pp. 445-451.

Arthur M. Cohen, "Racial Integration in a Southern Junior College," *Junior College Journal*, vol. 35 (March 1965), pp. 8-11.

Arthur O. White, "The Desegregation of Florida's Public Junior Colleges, 1954-1977," *Integrated Education*, vol. 16, no. 3 (May-June 1978), pp. 31-36.

The **Greater Bethel A.M.E. Church** at 245 N.W. 8th Street is a Mediterranean Revival-style church in Overtown that was built during the difficult times of Florida's Real Estate Bust and subsequent Depression (1927-1942). Miami's oldest congregation, the Greater Bethel A.M.E. Church was organized in 1896, even before the city was incorporated. The first building, called "Little Bethel," was a simple frame structure with a dirt floor; built before 1899, it was moved to N.W. 8th Street that year. Congregation members began the present structure in 1927 with a building fund of $7,000. Adopting a "pay-as-you-go" policy, members did not finish the structure until 1942, at a total cost of $150,000. Engineers designed the building well so that the thick walls, small windows, and high ceilings keep the inside of the church cool without the use of air conditioning.

Further Reading:

Howard Kleinberg, editor. *Miami: The Way We Were*. Tampa: Surfside Publishing, 1989, pp. 54-55: "Black Church in Grove as Early as 1894."

One of the active members of the Greater Bethel A.M.E. Church was Dr. William A. Chapman, Sr., the first black appointed to the Florida Department of Health and possibly the first black doctor to travel through Florida with an education program about communicable diseases; from Tallahassee to Key West he met with groups in churches, schools, and homes to explain about health issues. His Overtown home at 526 N.W. 13th Street, out of which he practiced medicine for a while and which the city declared a historic site in 1983, is of special significance to the history of blacks in Florida and therefore became the site of the Chapman House Ethnic Heritage Children's Folklife Educational Center; this center will emphasize the city's diverse cultural influences. The School Board took over the property in 1984 as part of a new campus for the rebuilt Booker T. Washington Middle School. On the grounds where the **Chapman House** stands is the new Black Archives, History and Research Foundation of South Florida, an organization that Dorothy Fields helped establish and direct.

Further Reading:

Charisse L. Grant, "Restoring Pioneer Home Skyrockets to $800,000," *The Miami Herald*, September 12, 1991, p. 1B+.
Erick Johnson, "Kids Get Preview of Restored Chapman House for Opening," *The Miami Times*, April 15, 1993, p. 4C.

Other early black medical doctors to practice in Miami included a Dr. Rivers, who practiced medicine in the city in 1896 before moving to Tampa; Dr. J.A. Butler, who also owned The Magic City Drug Store on the corner of Avenue G and Fifth Street; Dr. Solomon Frazier, who arrived in 1904 and began a practice that lasted for over 60 years in the city; and Dr. William B. Sawyer, who joined others in 1918 to start the Christian Hospital—complete with twelve bedrooms in a wooden structure—to care for blacks after other hospitals refused to do so.

Overtown was renamed Culmer-Overtown in 1967 to honor Father John Edwin Culmer (1891-1963), an early civil rights leader from the Bahamas; beginning in 1929, he served as pastor of Overtown's **St. Agnes Episcopal Church**, Miami's oldest black episcopal church, having been established in 1898. **Culmer Library** and **Culmer Community Center** also honor him. Another important civil rights champion this century was Lawson E. Thomas, the first judge that the city commission appointed to serve on what was then the

Negro Municipal Court; he meted out black-on-black justice in the 1950s in the segregated court, but earned the respect of many for his tough fairmindedness.

Further Reading:

Derek T. Davis, "Lawson E. Thomas Was Pioneering Judge Who Was Tough but Fair," *The Miami Times*, July 22, 1993, p. 11A.

Eugene C. Thomas, "EpiscopaL Church Was Born of Struggle for Dignity of Blacks," *The Miami Times*, February 10, 1994, p. 4D.

Other places in Overtown that honor blacks are **Douglas Elementary School** named after Frederick Douglas (1817-1895), a leading spokesman for blacks in the 1800s; **Dunbar Elementary School** named after Paul Lawrence Dunbar (1872-1906), a famous black poet and novelist; **Athalie Range Park**, named after the first black and the second woman elected to the Miami City Commission, and the first black secretary of Community Affairs in a Florida Cabinet; **Phyllis Wheatley Elementary School**, named after the first famous black woman poet in America (1753-1784); and the **Williams Park and Pool**, named after Charles Leofric Williams, a well-liked principal of Booker T. Washington school.

Among many places in Miami named after blacks are the following: the **Belafonte Tacolcy Center**, a youth activity center in Liberty City, which honors singer and actor Harry Belafonte; the **Joseph Caleb Community Center** at 5400 N.W. 22 Avenue; the **Annie M. Coleman Gardens** at 2610 N.W. 48th Street, a housing complex which honors a woman who did much to establish a local library and have the police department hire black officers; **Charles Hadley Elementary School** at 8400 N.W. 7th Street; and **Kelsey L. Pharr Elementary School** at 2000 N.W. 46 Street, which honors a man who came to Miami in 1914 and later established a funeral parlor for area blacks, as well as the Lincoln Memorial Park for the burial of blacks.

Further Reading:

Derek T. Davis, "Annie M. Coleman Led Way for Library, Hiring of Black Officers," *The Miami Times*, February 18, 1993, p. 4D.

From Wilderness to Metropolis: The History and Architecture of Dade County, Florida, 1825-1940. Miami: Metropolitan Dade County, 1982.

Chapter 44

Milton

This town on U.S. 90, 20 miles east of Pensacola, was named after Governor Milton of Florida or a local pioneer or was a contraction of Milltown; in any case, the name is definitely more refined than its former names: Scratch Ankle and Hard Scrabble. The town had a good location since it was on the Blackwater River, at the terminus of an old Indian and trading trail, and in the center of a forested area of long-leaf yellow pine, all of which made it a good trading and shipbuilding site. Its county, Santa Rosa, was established in 1842, one year before Milton became the county seat and three years before Florida entered the United States as a slave state (1845). Today Milton has a population of 7,216, of whom 1,056 (15%) are black.

Mount Pilgrim African Baptist Church on the northwest corner of the intersection of Clara and Alice streets one block west of Canal Street and one block south of U.S. 90 is Florida's only identified work of Wallace A. Rayfield, one of the most important black architects in the South in the early 20th century. The church is also an excellent local example of Late Gothic Revival architecture.

The church property includes the entire block bounded by Alice, Ann, Mary, and Clara streets. The history of the church begins in 1845, when the First Baptist Church of Milton was

Mount Pilgrim African Baptist Church was designed by one of the most important black architects in the South. Credit: Kevin M. McCarthy

established; four years later the church had a membership of 83 whites and 33 blacks. Some of those black members may have been slaves on a nearby plantation owned by Jackson Morton, who owned 118 slaves in 1830 and by 1860 was among the 100 largest slave-holders in Florida. In 1866, black members of First Baptist Church established Mount Pilgrim Baptist Church. In 1880, church members bought property on Canal Street and built a frame church. When membership continued to increase, the church trustees bought more land on Clara Street in 1911. When their 1880 church building burned down in 1916, the congregation built another church on Clara Street under the leadership of the Rev. King David Britt. At that time the building was the only brick church in Santa Rosa County.

Wallace A. Rayfield, an important black architect in the South in the early 20th century, designed the present church. Rayfield was born in Georgia, educated at Howard University in Washington, D.C., and at Pratt Institute in Brooklyn, N.Y., trained in architecture at Tuskegee Institute in Alabama, and worked in Birmingham, Alabama, specializing in designing churches, especially Baptist and African Methodist Episcopal Zion ones. Mount Pilgrim African Baptist Church in Milton was the first of his works outside of Birmingham to be listed in the National Register.

Directions:

To reach the church from I-10, take exit 8 and drive north 3.3 miles through Bagdad (see above) on C.R. 191. Turn left at Alice Street and go one block to Clara Street. The church is on the northwest corner of the intersection.

Further Reading:

M. Luther King. *History of Santa Rosa County*. Milton: no publ., 1972.

Brian Rucker. *Blackwater and Yellow Pine: The Development of Santa Rosa County*. Tallahassee: Florida State University, 1990.

Chapter 45

Mims

This small town, which today has a population of 9,412, of whom 1,194 (13%) are black, was the scene of a double murder in 1951 that has still not been solved. On Christmas night of that year, Harry and Harriette Moore retired for the night after spending the holiday with relatives in this quiet Brevard County town. They had spent a pleasant evening celebrating their 25th wedding anniversary with their 24-year-old daughter and Harry's mother. Soon after Harry and Harriette got ready for bed at around 10:15 that fateful night, a huge explosion ripped open the house, destroying the bedroom and killing one of this state's most effective civil rights activists. His wife would die nine days later from injuries suffered in that blast. To this day, investigators have never been able to solve that crime, the nation's first assassination of a civil rights leader, although FBI agents suspected it was the work of the Orange County Ku Klux Klan. Harry Moore's assassination would be the first of several that would later include Medgar Evers in Mississippi and Martin Luther King, Jr., in Tennessee.

The 46-year-old Moore had spent his adult life fighting for civil rights. In 1941, he became president of the Florida National Association for the Advancement of Colored People (NAACP). In 1947, after 20 years working in the Brevard

County school system, he lost his job as a junior high school principal because of his civil rights activism, but continued organizing blacks around the state, concentrating on three areas: trying to have a new trial for two blacks sentenced to death for raping a white woman in Lake County, obtaining equal pay for the state's black public school teachers, and registering black voters. He was succeeding in all three areas and was therefore considered a threat by the segregationists of the state.

At the time of their death the Moores were visiting relatives in Mims from their home in Riviera Beach, Florida, where Harriette Moore was working as a teacher. The house where the explosion took place was in an isolated orange grove about one mile south of Mims set back about 100 yards from the Dixie Highway in an orange grove. Harry and Harriette were buried from **St. James Missionary Baptist Church**, which is at 2396 Harry T. Moore Avenue (formerly Palmetto Avenue); this avenue is behind the water tower, which says, "Welcome to Mims, The Friendly Town," and about 1/4 mile east of U.S. 1 across the railroad tracks.

The grave site of the Moores is in **Lagrange Cemetery** on Old Dixie Highway south of Mims. To reach the cemetery, go 4/10 mile south of S.R. 40 in Mims, take a right at West Parker Street, then an immediate left onto Old Dixie Highway; go 1.4 miles to the first gate of Lagrange Cemetery on the east side opposite Diamond Road. The grave site is about 75 feet northeast from that gate. Harry T. Moore is also commemorated by a small bust outside the **Harry T. Moore Social Service Center** at 725 DeLeon Street in Titusville.

Further Reading:

James C. Clark, "Death Found Suspects Before Justice Could," *The Orlando Sentinel*, October 11, 1991, p. A-1+.

"Harriet [sic] Moore Buried," *Orlando Morning Sentinel*, January 9, 1952, p. 13.

Verna G. Langlais, compiler. *Cemetery Census of Brevard County, Florida.* Titusville: no publ., 1984. This booklet lists those buried in the La-Grange Cemetery, including the Moores.

The gravestone of the Moores in the cemetery near where they were killed. Credit: Kevin M. McCarthy

"Moore's Funeral Held Without Trouble," *Orlando Morning Sentinel,* January 2, 1952, p. 11.

Leedell W. Neyland. *Twelve Black Floridians.* Tallahassee: Florida Agricultural and Mechanical University Foundation, 1970, pp. 85-91.

Don Rider, "FBI Joins In Hunt For Killers," *Orlando Morning Sentinel,* Dec. 27, 1951, p. 1+. Also p. 13: "Mother Of Slain Negro Tells of Fatal Explosion."

Chapter 46

New Smyrna Beach

This town in Volusia County on the ocean was first developed by British entrepreneur Dr. Andrew Turnbull (1720-1792), who named the Florida settlement after his Greek wife's former home of Smyrna in Asia Minor. He wanted to use indentured servants from the Mediterranean, especially the island of Minorca, to grow indigo for the making of dye, and also bought a number of black slaves to do the more onerous tasks, but the ship carrying the slaves sank in the Florida Keys — with the loss of the slaves. In 1777, the Minorcans at New Smyrna Beach rebelled against Turnbull and fled to the safety of St. Augustine, where their descendants live today.

Further Reading:

Patricia C. Griffin. *Mullet on the Beach: The Minorcans of Florida, 1768-1788.* Jacksonville: University of North Florida Press, 1991.

E.P. Panagopoulos. *New Smyrna: An Eighteenth Century Greek Odyssey.* Gainesville: University of Florida Press, 1966.

Jane Quinn. *Minorcans in Florida: Their History and Heritage.* St. Augustine: Mission Press, 1975.

Philip D. Rasico. *The Minorcans of Florida: Their History, Language, and Culture.* New Smyrna Beach: Luthers, 1990.

The New Smyrna area did not become settled by whites until the federal government was able to control the Indians in the 1850s. During the Civil War, blockade runners used the area to bring in supplies for the Confederacy from the Bahamas. After the Civil War, among the settlers who came by steamer up the St. Johns River were blacks, who settled west of U.S. 1. in what became known as the Westside. Many of them had farms and gardens and caught fish and crabs in the river. When a second railroad connection arrived in New Smyrna Beach in 1891 and the Florida East Coast Railroad built a locomotive repair shop and roundhouse in 1926, many blacks found work on the railroad, but a 1963 strike for higher wages put many of those men out of work and forced many black families to leave the area in search of good jobs. Today only 1,335 (8%) of the city's population of 16,548 are black.

Further Reading:

Zelia Wilson Sweett, "New Smyrna Beach and Neighboring Communities," in *Centennial History of Volusia County, Florida, 1854-1954*, edited by Ianthe Bond Hebel. Daytona Beach: College Publishing Company, 1955, p. 83+.

Zelia Wilson Sweett and J.C. Marsden. *New Smyrna, Florida: Its History and Antiquities*. DeLand: Painter, 1925.

Old Sacred Heart/St. Rita Mission Church at the northwest corner of North Duss and Jefferson streets is a small wooden structure with a seating capacity of 80 people and a boxed steeple with the original bell. In 1899, workers built the church, called at that time Sacred Heart, on Faulkner Street near the downtown as a mission outpost from Saint Peter parish in DeLand to serve a small group of white Roman Catholics. When the congregation built a new parish church in 1956 on another site, they had this frame structure moved to its present location in the heart of the city's black section.

Old Sacred Heart/St. Rita Mission Church served the needs of Roman Catholics in New Smyrna Beach. Credit: Kevin M. McCarthy

Members renamed it Saint Rita Mission and used it to replace a chapel of the same name in an old boarding house that had served the needs of black Catholics. The church was near the Madonna House, a two-story building where the Sisters of the Christian Doctrine lived; the nuns ran a daycare center and kindergarten. When integration took effect in the 1960s, church officials merged Saint Rita Mission with the new Sacred Heart Parish, and the Duss Street building was used as annex space for a child-care project. The church, which has not been used much in the past few years, is just west of U.S. 1 and north of Washington Street.

The **Chisholm Academy** is a one-story wood frame building located in the subdivision of the Sams Estate. The Chisholm School, which was the first school for black children in southeast Volusia County, began when one of the two houses where classes were being held burned; the owner of the houses, Leroy Chisholm, built and donated a two-story frame building in the 500-block of Washington Street to house the black students. The new elementary school, built in 1910 with funds raised by Chisholm and other concerned citizens, had grades one through six. Later, Mrs. Clara Wallace raised funds to add grades seven and eight, with a ninth grade to be added later. The school was officially called "Chisholm Academy," and Chisholm became the supervisor. In 1916, the white children attending Mary Avenue Elementary were transferred to the new Faulkner Street Elementary School, and black elementary school students in grades one through four were transferred to the Mary Avenue school, which was named Kimball Elementary after its first principal. The next principal, Fannie Walden, remained in that position until integration took place.

S.F. Harris served as principal of Chisholm from 1930 until 1935, during which time grades 10, 11, and 12 were added. During the 1935-1942 administration of J.B. Jones, the school's name was changed to Chisholm High School, and the school year was increased from eight to nine months. C.W. Harris, who became principal in 1942, saw more changes, including the addition of music to the curriculum and the construction of an annex to house the home economics department; he was principal when the students moved to the new Chisholm High School site on Ronnoke Lane in 1954. W.O. Berry, who became principal in 1957, saw the building of a gymnasium, a bandroom, and an industrial arts complex and the addition to the curriculum of agriculture and drivers education. L.W. Kennedy became principal in 1962 and had the school fully accredited by the Southern

Association of Colleges and Schools. When New Smyrna Beach Senior High opened in 1969, the students from Chisholm High School were transferred there, and the elementary school students went to Faulkner and Read-Pattillo schools. Today Chisholm School at 588 Washington Street is called the **Alonzo "Babe" James Youth Center**.

Further Reading:

A Pictorial History of New Smyrna's Westside. New Smyrna Beach: Senior Ushers, 1991.

A grave site in the town is also worth mentioning. Douglas Dummett, a white orange grower who developed Indian River citrus, had a black son, Charles Dummett (1844-1860), who killed himself or was accidentally killed while hunting at the age of 16. Author John McPhee wrote that "his death was called an accident, but some people on Merritt Island thought he had done it because of the shame he was made to feel for having Negro blood" (p. 95). His family buried him in part of the vast acreage they owned then, but in time the city grew, more roads were built, and soon the grave site stood in the middle of a street. Road builders have respected his final resting place and have built Canova Drive around the site; Canova Drive was named for entertainer Judy Canova's brother, who owned property there. The slab at the grave site reads: "Sacred to the Memory of Charles Dummett, Born August 18, 1844—Died April 23, 1860." The young man's father, Douglas, became sick in 1872 and traveled to Merritt Island to seek treatment; he died there and is buried in an unmarked grave. Charles's grave site is in the middle of Canova Drive, which is south of Riverview Hotel. To reach Canova Drive, go east across Indian River North Causeway, then onto Columbus Avenue and immediately onto Canova Drive, which is near the river.

Further Reading:

History of New Smyrna. New Smyrna Beach: G. Luther, 1987, p. 15: "Mt. Pleasant and a Grave in the Street."
John McPhee. *Oranges*. New York: Farrar, Straus and Giroux, 1967.

Six miles south of New Smyrna Beach in Volusia County over on A1A was **Bethune-Volusia Beach**, a 2.5-mile-long beach established for blacks in the 1940s by prominent Florida blacks, including educator Mary McLeod Bethune, insurance executive G. Rogers of Tampa, rancher Lawrence Silas of Kissimmee, and other black investors who wanted to develop a black residential resort community and recreation area. For a while, that beach was apparently the only year-round one in the state where blacks could own property. Amenities eventually included a bath house, picnic facilities, and a snack bar. Today one can see signs indicating Bethune Beach and Bethune Park, but the area is completely integrated.

Further Reading:

"Florida's First Negro Resort," *Ebony*, vol. 3, no. 4 (February 1948), pp. 24-26.

Chapter 47

Ocala

The name of this town, the county seat of Marion County, is of Indian origin, but the meaning is unknown. After the Indians left the area, white settlers moved in and began to farm the land. Some of those settlers had slaves. In fact, the 1860 census indicated that 62% of the 8,609 residents of Marion County were slaves, a fact that worried those whites who thought that Union sympathizers might incite the blacks to attack their owners, especially because so many white men were away at war. To raise money in 1863, local officials put a value on the slaves to raise taxes; they valued slaves according to age, although skilled mechanics, no matter what their age, were assessed at $2,500 each. Black children eight years of age and younger were valued at $800 each; workers between 16 and 25 were valued at $1,200 each, those between 35 and 50 at $900, and those over 50 at $300 each.

When the Civil War ended in 1865, more and more people moved to Florida to take advantage of the opportunities for making a living and raising families. In the Reconstruction period after the war, officials organized a company of black soldiers to enforce the rulings of the local administrators and placed ex-slaves in county offices. Ex-slaves like Singleton Coleman, Scipio Jasper, and Samuel Small represented

Black businessmen in Ocala in the early 1900s helped establish the Metropolitan Bank. Credit: Florida State Archives

Marion County in the Florida Legislature for several years, and H.E. Chandler, a black educator from the North, represented the county in the Florida Senate. Samuel Small also served as chairman of the Board of County Commissioners. Marion County has grown rapidly in the last 100 years as more and more people moved in to take advantage of the rich farmland, good horse-grazing facilities, and natural beauty. Today Ocala has a population of around 42,045, of whom 10,060 (24%) are black. For an account of growing up black in the area see the book by Idella Parker noted below.

Further Reading:

Barbara E. Janowitz. *Historic Marion County.* Ocala: Marion County Historical Society, 1990.

Eloise Robinson Ott and Louis Hickman Chazal. *Ocala Country: Kingdom*

of the Sun, A History of Marion County, Florida. Oklawaha, Fl.: Marion Publishers, 1966.
Idella Parker. *Idella: Marjorie Rawlings' "Perfect Maid."* Gainesville: University Press of Florida, 1992.

Mount Zion A.M.E. Church at 623 South Magnolia Avenue (the northeast corner of S.E. 7th Street and South Magnolia Avenue) is on one of the major north-south thoroughfares of Ocala. Reverend Thomas W. Long, a circuit rider who traveled by horseback throughout Florida for the African Methodist Episcopal Church, helped establish the church in 1866, as did Reverend S. Morgan two years later. In 1891, the congregation decided they wanted a new brick building so that it would be more secure from fires such as one that destroyed much of Ocala in 1883. Rev. J.W. Dukes and then Rev. John H. Dickerson formulated the plans for the construction, the men of the congregation donated their time, and the women raised money by giving dinners and holding bazaars. Levi Alexander, Sr., was the architect of the building, the first brick church owned by black people in Ocala. Other groups have held many functions there, for example Howard Academy and Howard High School commencements, concerts, and other activities of the black community. The fine acoustics and large seating capacity (up to 600 persons) of the building have made it an ideal location to hold such functions. The church is now on the National Register of Historic Places.

Further Reading:

Mount Zion African Methodist Episcopal Church. 1984.

Another early church was **Mount Moriah Baptist Church,** founded in 1866 under the leadership of Samuel Small. Before the Civil War, blacks had attended services of white congregations, usually sitting in galleries reserved for blacks. After the war they established their own churches.

The Freedmen's Bureau with financing from northern

benefactors organized **Howard Academy** as a school for black students in 1867. It honored in its name either James H. Howard, a former slave-owner who donated the land for the school in the block bounded by Osceola, Orange, Sixth, and Seventh streets, or Gen. Otis Howard, the ex-Federal officer who was in charge of the Freedmen's Bureau and was interested in the education of blacks. By 1880, a group of black teachers replaced the white teachers of the school. After fire destroyed the original building on Orange Avenue, workers built a new one at Academy and Adams streets.

Further Reading:

J. Irving E. Scott. *The Education of Black People in Florida*. Philadelphia: Dorrance & Company, 1974, p. 47.

Hampton Junior College, which opened in 1958 at 1014 N. 24th Street, was one of 12 black junior colleges in Florida (see St. Petersburg below). Its first and only president during its eight years of operation was William H. Jackson, principal of **Howard Senior High School** in northwest Ocala which shared its facilities with the new junior college; the high school honored in its name a white person who had donated land on which the black high school had been built. Originally called Howard Junior College, the school changed its name to Hampton to honor a local black dentist, the late L.R. Hampton, Sr., who had done much to encourage educational opportunities for black youth. As was true elsewhere in the state, the black junior college shared the facilities of the local black high school in order for the facilities of the college to revert back to the high school at the time of the merger/integration of the black and white colleges. President Jackson continued serving as supervising principal of Howard High School for three years after becoming president of Hampton Junior College.

Unlike other black junior colleges that relied on hiring the faculty of local black high schools — a practice that led some local activists to criticize the junior colleges — Hampton

Junior College hired faculty from other colleges, especially from outside the state. When it merged with the predominantly white Central Florida Junior College (CFCC) in 1966, half the faculty of the black college transferred to CFCC and the other half transferred to Marion County public schools. President Jackson became Associate Dean of Academic Affairs, eventually retiring in 1985 as Director, Institutional and Sponsored Research. The enrollment figures, which included college parallel courses and vocational courses, for Hampton Junior College were as follows:

1958-1959: 146 students	**1959-1960: 193 students**
1960-1961: 366 students	**1961-1962: 407 students**
1962-1963: 426 students	**1963-1964: 699 students**
1964-1965: 890 students	**1965-1966: 778 students**

The number of graduates during these years (1958-1966) was 317 (8%) out of a total of 3,905 students who attended the school.

Further Reading:

Portia L. Taylor. *Community College Education for Black Students, A Case Study*. Dissertation. Gainesville: University of Florida, 1986, esp. pp. 78-109: "A History of Hampton Junior College, 1958-1966."

A school to the northwest of Ocala and south of Reddick, Lowell, and Martin is **Fessenden Academy** at 4200 N.W. 90th Street, now being used as an integrated elementary school, but for 123 years an important institution for the county's black students. When a number of black families settled in the suburb of Martin, they asked the county school board for a school for their children. The school board granted their request and hired a northerner, Emma Hodd, to be the teacher of what was called the Union School. The students attended class in a small log cabin, beginning in 1868, and had white instructors until 1877. As more and more students wanted to attend the school, a larger building was built. During the winter of 1889, Ferdinand Stone Fessenden of Boston, a sickly man who had traveled to Florida to try to

The Fessenden Elementary School provided educational opportunities for countless black youth over the years. Credit: Kevin M. McCarthy

regain his failing health, was staying in Martin on the advice of his doctor. When he visited the Union School one day, he noticed how poor the facilities were for the 250 black students and resolved to do something about it.

Mr. Gilbert Maynor donated two acres of land a mile south of Martin for a new school, and by 1890 workers had completed the building. On the recommendation of Mr. Fessenden, the American Missionary Association in New York City placed the school under its auspices and began emphasizing domestic science for girls and industrial training for boys. The school opened with Miss Mattie J. Brydie as principal. When she resigned in 1896, Mr. J.C. McAdams from Kentucky took her place, to be succeeded two years later by Mr. Joseph Wiley of Nashville, Tennessee. Before Mr. Fessenden died in 1899, he requested that his body be buried on the grounds of the school he had helped build and which changed its name from Union School to Fessenden Academy to honor him.

The first class of five young ladies graduated in 1903. In 1916, Rev. H.S. Barnwell became principal for five years, to be succeeded by Mr. W.H. Kindle of New York City. Later, Mr. John M. Moore of Mississippi became principal for six years, during which time officials raised the school curriculum to junior college level and organized a band. In 1928, Mr. A.S. Scott of Mississippi became principal for one year, to be followed by Rev. Leonard F. Morse of Mobile, Alabama, who served from 1929 to 1932. Mr. Ripley Simms, a graduate of Alabama's Talladega College, served as principal from 1933 to 1938 and was succeeded by Mrs. Josie B. Sellers (1938-1941) and Mr. John A. Buggs (1941-1951). The school is on N.W. 90th Street west of Highway 25A and just north of Highway 326, which has an exit on I-75 to the west.

Further Reading:

Judy Hill, "Successfully challenged" [about Fessenden Academy], *The Tampa Tribune*, August 2, 1991, Baylife 1-2.

J. Irving E. Scott. *The Education of Black People in Florida*. Philadelphia: Dorrance & Company, 1974, p. 43+.

About nine miles west of Fessenden School is the tiny settlement of **Blichton**, the place where Jesse J. McCrary, Jr., was born in 1937. When Governor Reuben Askew appointed him Secretary of the State of Florida in 1978, McCrary became the second black to serve in the Florida cabinet (the first was Jonathan Gibbs, who served during Reconstruction—see St. Petersburg below). McCrary's father, a Baptist minister, had hoped his son would also become a minister, but instead Jesse Jr. went to law school after graduating from Florida A&M University in 1960. He then worked in Miami as assistant attorney general, in which position he became the first black to represent Florida before the U.S. Supreme Court. In 1971, he headed a commission to study the causes of riots in Opa-locka's black community before resuming his law practice. (For the story of another Ocala black who did well in the court system see Lawson E. Thomas in the Miami section above.)

Further Reading:

James Cramer, "FAMU Grad Gains Seat on Cabinet," *Tallahassee Democrat*, July 20, 1978, p. 1+.

Maxine D. Jones and Kevin M. McCarthy. *African Americans in Florida.* Sarasota: Pineapple Press, 1993, pp. 130-131.

John McDermott, "First Black Since Reconstruction Is Named to the Florida Cabinet," *The Miami Herald*, July 20, 1978, p. 1A+.

Chapter 48

Olustee

A site to the east of Lake City on U.S. 90 is **Olustee**, where the most important land battle of the Civil War in the state took place. Around 5,000 Union troops coming from Jacksonville in February 1864 met a similar size Confederate force at Ocean Pond in what came to be called the Battle of Olustee. Serving on the Union side were black soldiers in units like the 8th U.S. Colored, the First North Carolina, and the 54th Massachusetts. The latter unit had Sergeant William H. Carney, who later became the first black to win the prestigious Medal of Honor for his bravery at the Battle of Fort Wagner, South Carolina.

The blacks fighting for the Union side at Olustee faced a terrible situation. If they were wounded during the battle and left behind on the battlefield, southern soldiers might injure them further, send them to awful prisons like the one at Andersonville, Georgia, or kill them. The battle raged on for hours and saw the wounding and death of many soldiers on both sides. In the end, the Confederates claimed victory as the Union troops retreated to Jacksonville.

A doctor who served with one of the black units, the 8th U.S. Colored Troops, later praised the great courage of those soldiers:

Black units fought well on this battlefield. Credit: Florida State Archives

> Here they stood for two hours and a half, under one of the most terrible fires I ever witnessed; and here, on the field of Olustee, was decided whether the colored man had the courage to stand without shelter, and risk the dangers of the battlefield; and when I tell you that they stood with a fire in front, on their flank, and in their rear, for two hours and a half, without flinching, and when I tell you the number of dead and wounded, I have no doubt as to the verdict of every man who has gratitude for the defenders of his country, white or black.

Directions:

Olustee Battlefield is located 2.5 miles east of Olustee on U.S. 90, 15 miles east of Lake City. The battlefield is open daily, 8-5; the museum is open Thursday - Monday, 8-5. A nominal donation is expected of visitors. Phone: (904) 752-3866. Each February around the anniversary of the battle, men dressed in the military uniforms of both sides show visitors how the battle was fought.

Chapter 49

Opa-locka

This Dade County site, which has a name that comes from an Indian phrase meaning "big swamp," has a population of 15,283, of whom 10,654 (70%) are black. One of its residents, Helen Miller, served as a city commissioner and became the first black woman elected mayor in Florida. The settlement began when Glenn H. Curtiss, an early aviation pioneer, joined with James H. Bright to develop it in the 1920s land boom. They designed the place to resemble a city from the *Tales From the Arabian Nights,* and thus it has minarets and domes on some of its buildings and street names like Oriental, Arabia, Sultan, Sahara, Sesame, and Aladdin. Some 65 of the original 100 buildings in a Moorish Revival architectural style remain in what is called the **Opa-Locka Thematic Development**, a predominantly black community. The city might have had more buildings in this Middle Eastern style, but the Depression of the late 1920s and the devastating 1926 hurricane that hit the area curtailed many of the plans that Curtiss had made.

Several buildings deserve mention here. The **Harry Hurt Building** with a central dome and minarets at 490 Alibaba Avenue was built in 1926 and served as a shopping center with offices, apartments, and a social hall on the second floor. After World War II it became the Opa-locka Hotel. The

Opa-Locka City Hall at 777 Sharazad Boulevard has domes, minarets, and watchtowers that resemble Middle Eastern architecture, and the **Opa-Locka Railroad Station** has a multi-colored glazed tile that is quite remarkable.

Further Reading:

Beth Dunlop, "Opa-locka Was Araby In Mrs. Higgins' Day," *The Miami Herald*, May 4, 1977, p. 1D.

Frank S. FitzGerald-Bush. *A Dream of Araby: Glenn H. Curtiss and the Founding of Opa-locka*. Opa-Locka: South Florida Archaeological Museum, 1976.

From Wilderness to Metropolis: The History and Architecture of Dade County, Florida, 1825-1940. Miami: Metropolitan Dade County, 1982, pp. 108-109.

Florida Memorial College at 15800 N.W. 42 Avenue is one of the oldest institutions of higher learning for blacks in the state. This school is a private, coeducational, four-year college that can trace its history back to the Florida Baptist Institute in Live Oak, Florida, and the Florida Baptist Academy, founded in 1892 in Jacksonville. The two schools merged in 1941 to become the Florida Normal and Industrial Memorial Institute in St. Augustine, Florida (see St. Augustine below). Four years later it became a four-year college. After several name changes, the school became Florida Memorial College in 1963, five years before it moved to its present location. Its early presidents included Rev. M.W. Gilbert (1892-1894), Rev. J.T. Brown (1894-1896), N.W. Collier (1896-1941), Dr. William H. Gray (1941-1944), and Dr. John L. Tilley (1944-1949). Dr. Albert E. Smith became the tenth president in 1994.

Further Reading:

J. Irving E. Scott. *The Education of Black People in Florida*. Philadelphia: Dorrance & Company, 1974, pp. 53-54.

Among the other places in the town that honor blacks are

the **Nathan B. Young Elementary School**, named after the man who served as president of Florida A&M University (1901-1923), then later as president of Lincoln University in Jefferson City, Missouri, and Inspector of Schools for the state of Missouri; and the **Willie Logan Recreation Center Park**, named after the man from Opa-locka who was the first black mayor of the city (1980-1982) and subsequent member of the Florida House of Representatives (1982-). The present mayor, Robert B. Ingram, was elected in 1994 president of the National Conference of Black Mayors. Serving his fourth term as Opa-locka's mayor, Ingram is also an A.M.E. elder with a doctorate in applied behavioral science and is chairman of the Extension and Continuing Education Division at Florida Memorial College.

Chapter 50

Orlando

This city may have been named after a character in Shakespeare's *As You Like It* or from a soldier, Orlando Reeves, who died in the area while saving his companions in 1835. Now the county seat of Orange County, Orlando was sparsely settled until after the Civil War, at which time the Homestead Act of 1866 brought many into the area, including former slaves who joined a growing number of cotton and citrus farmers and cattle ranchers. From the 1870s, the city and central Florida experienced several population booms, but segregation policies in Orlando tended to isolate the blacks, many of whom lived in a segregated part called Jonestown, west of present-day Greenwood Cemetery. Today, Orlando has a population of 164,693, of whom 44,342 (27%) are black.

Further Reading:

Orlando, A Century Plus. Orlando: Sentinel Star Company, 1976.
Orlando: History in Architecture. Orlando: Orlando Historic Preservation Board, 1984.
Jerrell H. Shofner. *Orlando: The City Beautiful.* Tulsa: Continental Heritage Press, 1984.

The **Callahan Neighborhood**, bordered by Colonial

Drive, Orange Blossom Trail, Central Boulevard, and Division Street, started in 1886, when a white builder, Rev. Andrew Hooper, built the first homes in the area. City officials renamed the area, one of the oldest continuing black communities in Orlando, to honor Dr. Jerry B. Callahan, a leading black citizen of the city, after he died in 1947 at the age of 63. He was the first black physician to practice at the Orange General Hospital and a man honored in the naming of Callahan Elementary School and Callahan Park. Officials changed the name of Collins Street to Callahan Street in 1940 to honor this man who helped establish Goodfellows in Orlando and who practiced medicine in the city for 40 years.

Further Reading:

Eve Bacon. *Orlando: A Centennial History*. Chuluota, Fl.: The Mickler House, 1977, vol. 2, pp. 145-146.

The **Callahan Neighborhood Center**, formerly Jones High School, at 101 N. Parramore Avenue is the site of one of the earliest educational facilities for blacks in the city. As Jerrell Shofner describes in his *Orlando: The City Beautiful* (p. 162):

> Education for Orlando's black schoolchildren formally was established in November 1882, when the Orange County School Board approved a petition to open the Orlando Colored School. Located in a frame building at Garland and Church streets, the school first was headed by principal I.S. Hankins. Before 1900, the school moved to Jefferson and Chatham streets and was renamed Johnson Academy, in honor of its second principal, L.C. Johnson. Johnson Academy's third principal, L.C. Jones, came to the school in 1912 and helped build what is now known as Callahan School. Jones' family donated land at Parramore and Washington for the school, which opened in 1921 as Jones High School, with grades six through ten. Elementary students re-

The Callahan Neighborhood Center was formerly the old Jones High School. Credit: Kevin M. McCarthy

mained at Johnson Academy until additional wings were built at Jones. The first high-school commencement was held for graduating seniors in 1931. For years, Jones High School and Hungerford Normal and Industrial School in Eatonville offered the only formal education to blacks in central Florida.

Today the Callahan Neighborhood Center serves the community's needs for meeting facilities, after-school programs, and cultural festivals. Among the school's graduates was Wesley Snipes, star of the movie entitled "New Jack City."

Among other buildings of note in the area is the **Gabriel Jones House** at 50 N. Terry Street. Built in 1907 by black businessman Gabriel Jones, this building has been used as a rooming house for immigrants from Africa and the Caribbean. The **Hill-Tillinghast House** at 626 W. Washington Street was built in the early 1920s by black builder James Murrell for Viola Tillinghast Hill, wife of pastor Rev. H.K.

Hill of Mt. Zion Missionary Baptist Church. The house has served as a meeting place for such famous people as educator Dr. Mary McLeod Bethune and aviator Bessie Coleman. In the 1940s, young women in a sewing program used it, but today it is a private residence. Another important house in the neighborhood is the **Crooms House** at 504 W. Washington St., where the Crooms family, early black pioneers in Orlando, lived. Moses Crooms, Sr., and his wife, Daphane, built this house, today a private residence, after moving here from north Florida in 1905. The **J.A. Colyer Building** at 27-29 Church Street in downtown Orlando was the site of early black businesses. Built by Colyer in 1911, this building housed the Colyer and Williams tailor shop and later a pharmacy and today is an Irish pub.

Chapter 51

Palatka

The name of this town goes back to the Indian word "Pilotaikata," which meant "crossing" and referred to a place for crossing the St. Johns River. After the Seminole Indian wars, settlers began moving into the area to harvest and cut the cypress that grew in the area and to grow citrus, at least until the devastating freezes of the 1890s ended that venture. The town attracted many visitors and fishermen in the early 20th century as people discovered the beauty of this "Gem City on the St. Johns." Today Palatka has a population of 10,201, of whom 4,783 (47%) are black.

Further Reading:

June D. Bell, "A Wealth of History," *The Florida Times-Union* [Jacksonville], March 15, 1994, p. A-1+ [about a black dentist, Napoleon Ben Hester, who lived in Palatka from 1914 until the 1970s].

Susan Clark. *A Historic Tour Guide of Palatka and Putnam County, Florida.* Palatka: Putnam County Historical Society, 1992.

Brian E. Michaels. *The River Flows North: A History of Putnam County.* Palatka: The Putnam County Archives and History Commission, 1976.

The **Bethel A.M.E. Church** at 719 Reid Street is a large church in the Romanesque Revival style that members of the

The Finley Homestead was the home of a man whose son became a well-known protozoologist. Credit: Kevin M. McCarthy

congregation built between 1908 and 1912 to serve the residents of the black community of Newtown. The congregation was organized around 1866, right after the Civil War, and built the first church in 1875 at the corner of Hotel and Emmett streets. Members bought the present property around 1904-1905.

The **Finley Homestead** at 522 Main Street was the home of Adam Finley, a free black who worked as a barber in Palatka. His son, Eugene Finley, owned Finley's Barber Shop on Lemon Street and became involved in civic activities and even formed a band at the high school. His son, Dr. Harold E. Finley, became a well-known protozoologist, researcher, and head of the Department of Zoology at Howard University in Washington, D.C.

Central Academy High School at 1207 Washington Street began in 1892, when Putnam County's board of public instruction built two buildings on Orange Street (now Reid Street): one for the white students and one for the black students. Before that time, schooling for the black students took place in various halls of the city. The school for blacks was called Central Academy, and its colors were purple and gold. During the administration of Prof. A.J. Polk in 1936, when fire destroyed that first school, the children once again had to have their lessons in various churches and halls. Officials built a new school building on the corner of Washington and 12th streets and opened it for classes in 1937. Between 300 and 400 students enrolled in the school. In the mid-1920s, Central Academy was accredited, possibly the first black high school in Florida to be accredited. The school board of Putnam County now uses the building as a service center.

The principals of the school have been W.M. Berry, J.W. Holley, E.H. Flipper, E.S. Holmes, C.B. White (who resigned to become the first black mail carrier in Palatka), B.F. Hartwell, T.E. Debose (the pastor of Leete Chapel M.E. Church and the one who added the ninth and tenth grades to the school), J.A. Lockett (who introduced football and basketball), Clarence C. Walker (who helped the school become accredited), H.M. Richards, K.C. Lynon, C.W. Banks, and A.J. Polk (who had to find places for the students when fire destroyed the school). By the late 1930s the school had 869 students, 26 teachers, and 350+ graduates that included ministers, physicians, businessmen, and nurses.

One of the school's more famous students, Robert H. Jenkins, Jr. (1948-1969), was born in Interlachen, Florida, and attended Oak Grove Elementary School (1955-1963) and Palatka's Central Academy High School (1963-1967). He joined the U.S. Marines in 1968 and was assigned to Vietnam late that year. On March 5, 1969, he was killed in action when he threw himself onto a fellow marine to protect that man from an exploding hand grenade. For his bravery in saving the life of that other Marine at the risk of his own life, the U.S. government awarded Jenkins the Medal of Honor, the highest honor our nation can give a soldier. He is buried in Sister Spring Cemetery in Interlachen, Florida, and the former segregated school he attended in Palatka has been renamed Robert Jenkins Middle School in his honor. The Medal of Honor Park near Sebring, Florida, honors Jenkins and another black, Clifford Chester Sims. (See Sebring below.)

Further Reading:

Maxine D. Jones and Kevin M. McCarthy. *African Americans in Florida.* Sarasota: Pineapple Press, 1993, pp. 116-117: "Two African American War Heroes, 1968-1969."

Palatka is also important for having given to baseball one of its more famous black players, John Henry "Pop" Lloyd, who was born there in 1884. Playing baseball in the Negro Leagues long before Jackie Robinson broke the color line in the modern major leagues was very hard for such players as Lloyd. The players spent much of their time traveling from town to town in order to play the games, earned little or no money, and had to stay in segregated hotels.

Lloyd's father died when the boy was still an infant; when John Henry's mother remarried, his grandmother took over the job of raising him. He quit school before finishing the elementary grades and became a delivery boy in a store. His baseball skills became apparent at an early age, and he began playing semi-professional baseball with the Jacksonville Young Receivers before he went north in 1906 to play for the Cuban X Giants. Unlike many ballplayers, Lloyd set a good example by never drinking alcohol, never cussing, and seldom if ever smoking.

Lloyd played and managed for such black teams as the Acmes of Macon (Georgia), the New York Lincoln Stars, the New York Lincoln Giants, the Chicago Leland Giants, the Chicago American Giants, the Brooklyn Royal Giants, the Columbus Buckeyes, the Atlantic City Bacharach Giants, the Philadelphia Hilldale Club, and the New York Black Yankees. He also played for Henry Flagler's hotel teams in Palm Beach (see Palm Beach below). When some fans compared Lloyd to the great white shortstop, Honus Wagner (1874-1955), Wagner was honored: "They called John Henry Lloyd

'The Black Wagner,' and I was anxious to see him play. Well, one day I had an opportunity to go see him play, and after I saw him I felt honored that they would name such a great player after me." Lloyd, who sometimes played baseball in Cuba, where the Cubans called him "Cuchara" or "shovel" because his big hands were able to scoop up any ball hit near him, was voted into the Baseball Hall of Fame in 1977, 12 years after he died.

When asked if he had been born too soon, he replied, "No, I don't feel that I was born at the wrong time. I feel it was the right time. I had a chance to prove the ability of our race in this sport, and because many of us did our best for the game, we've given the Negro a greater opportunity now to be accepted into the major leagues with other Americans."

Further Reading:

Black Diamonds: Life in the Negro Leagues from the Men Who Lived It. Westport, Conn.: Meckler, 1989.

John B. Holway. *Blackball Stars: Negro League Pioneers*. Westport, Conn.: Meckler, 1988.

Rayford W. Logan and Michael R. Winston, editors. *Dictionary of American Negro Biography*. New York: Norton, 1982, p. 397+.

Robert Peterson, *Only the Ball Was White: A History of Legendary Black Players and All-black Professional Teams*. New York: McGraw-Hill, 1984.

David L. Porter, editor. *Biographical Dictionary of American Sports: Baseball*. Westport, Conn.: Greenwood Press, 1987, p. 333+.

Collier-Blocker Junior College, which was established in 1960, was one of 12 black junior colleges in Florida (see St. Petersburg below). Unlike the other 11 black junior colleges, which shared the facilities of a local black high school, Collier-Blocker used a former Baptist church for its classrooms. Its first president was Mr. Albert B. Williams, and it enrolled 105 students in its best year before merging with St. Johns River Junior College. The enrollment figures for the junior college were as follows:

1960-1961: 59 students **1961-1962: 78 students**
1962-1963: 105 students **1963-1964: 72 students**

Chapter 52

Palm Beach

The history of this exclusive resort on the Atlantic Ocean has involved blacks in an important way, although the 52 who officially live there today make up less than 1% of the 9,814 residents. Before the wealthy winter visitors discovered Palm Beach and made it into one of America's prized addresses, blacks were living along what later became Sunrise Avenue. Some of them, like Joseph Bethell, came from the Bahamas, whereas others were escaped slaves from north Florida plantations who found a home with the Seminoles living in the area.

After developer Henry Flagler had visited Palm Beach in the 1890s, he decided to develop the little town, especially after he extended his railroad to the area and constructed a railroad bridge over Lake Worth to link the resort with the mainland. In 1894, he built the Royal Poinciana Hotel, the world's largest resort hotel with its ability to accommodate 2,000 people, and two years later the Palm Beach Inn, later known as the Breakers. Five years later he built the luxurious Whitehall mansion for his third wife.

Flagler also built two baseball diamonds, one at the Royal Poinciana Hotel and the other at the Breakers Hotel. The players who played for the Poincianas and Breakers were blacks who also worked as bellhops and waiters at Flagler's hotels. Hotel owners in Long Island had discovered how popular baseball teams were that were made up of waiters and other employees of expensive hotels. The Cuban Giants, for example, began at Long Island's Argyle Hotel in 1885 to entertain the wealthy white guests. When Flagler built his hotels in Florida sites like St. Augustine and Palm Beach to go along with his railroad, he also established black baseball teams for his guests' entertainment. To run his programs, Flagler hired a former center fielder for the Philadelphia Phillies named Ed Andrews, who is honored today by Andrews Avenue in Fort Lauderdale. Historian Stuart McIver quotes from an early spectator who wrote the following in 1907:

> ...I went over to the baseball game and such sport I never had in my life. Both teams are colored and composed of employees of the Breakers and Poinciana hotels, who are hired because of their baseball ability and then incidentally given employment as waiters or porters. Many of them play on the Cuban Giants team during the summer so that the quality of baseball ranked with professional white teams.
>
> The greatest sport was in listening to the coaching and watching the antics of a full grandstand back of first base. Their sympathies were pretty evenly divided between the two teams, so accordingly, whenever either team would make a hit, then was the time to watch the bleachers. The crowd would yell themselves hoarse, stand up in their seats, bang each other over the head, and even the girls would go into a perfect frenzy as if they were in a Methodist camp meeting.
>
> The third baseman on the Poinciana team was a wonderful ballplayer and kept the whole crowd roaring with his horseplay and cakewalks up and down the sidelines.

Andrews recruited the black players from such teams as the Cuban Giants, the Cuban X Giants, the Royal Giants, and the Leland Giants (all of whose team names showed the popularity of the New York Giants in those days). Among the players who entertained the wealthy hotel guests was John Henry "Pop" Lloyd, an excellent shortstop from Palatka, Florida (see above). Also playing on those black teams were such standouts as pitcher Smoky Joe Williams and home-run hitters Oscar Charleston and Louis Santop. When a huge hurricane destroyed the Royal Poinciana in 1928, it also wrecked the baseball bleachers there, signalling the beginning of the end to black baseball at the resort.

Further Reading:

Stuart McIver, "Cooks to Catchers, Bellhops to Batters," *Sunshine* [*News/Sun-Sentinel*, Fort Lauderdale], August 22, 1993, p. 23+.

Many of the workers who built Flagler's railroad and his large sumptuous hotels were blacks from Jamaica, the Bahamas, and Haiti. Once the buildings were completed, many of the blacks stayed on to work in the hotels; one job many of them did was to pedal tourists around in rickshaw-like vehicles called afromobiles (or aframobiles). Some 400 of these blacks lived in a shantytown on the north end of Palm Beach on Sunrise Avenue in a place they called the Styx, a name coming from Greek mythology referring to the river encircling Hades. The black doctor who served the blacks in the Styx was Dr. Thomas Leroy Jefferson (1867-1939), a generous man who devoted his life to his patients.

Once the workers were no longer needed to build Flagler's hotels and he decided to develop the land they were on, he wanted to remove the Styx to the western shore of Lake Worth, but the squatters refused to move. On November 5, 1906, many of the black families were on the mainland, possibly celebrating Guy Fawkes Day, a British holiday that the blacks had learned of in Jamaica or the Bahamas. Late that night a fire broke out that completely destroyed the Styx. Some accused Flagler of perpetrating the arson, but no one could prove it. In any case, the next day the blacks salvaged what they could from the charred remains and went to the mainland to settle. That fire effectively ended the black presence in Palm Beach. Flagler then developed the area, which today is the land along Sunrise Avenue at North County Road. (For more about West Palm Beach, see below.)

In the mid-1920s, the local government passed an ordinance that prohibited whites from setting up businesses across the railroad tracks where the blacks were living. That official segregation, which lasted until the early-1960s, enabled black businesses to operate in the black area without fear of competition from larger white businesses.

Further Reading:

Bill McGoun, "Dr. Thomas Leroy Jefferson," *The Palm Beach Post*, June 20, 1977, pp. B1-2.

James McJunkins and Brenda Lane, "Up From the Styx—The Black Experience," *The Palm Beach Post-Times*, September 9, 1973, C1+. Continued September 10, 1973, p. A7+; September 11, 1973, p. A7+; September 12, 1973, p. B1+; September 13, 1973, p. B1+; September 14, 1973, p. B1+; September 15, 1973, p. A4+.

Dan Moffett, "Charred History: Styx' Burning Was the End of Palm Beach's Black Community," *The Post* [Palm Beach] June 13, 1982, p. B1, 3.

Theodore Pratt. *That Was Palm Beach*. St. Petersburg: Great Outdoors, 1968.

Vivian Reissland Rouson-Gossett, editor. *Like a Mighty Banyan: Contributions of Black People to the History of Palm Beach County*. Palm Beach County: Palm Beach Junior College, 1982.

J. Wadsworth Travers. *History of Beautiful Palm Beach*. West Palm Beach, no publ., 1931, esp. pp. 37-38: "Colored Folks."

Chapter 53

Panama City

As in so many Florida sites, the first settlers here were the Indians, who were eventually succeeded by the English, who came after the American Revolutionary War. Development began in the 1830s and increased after the Civil War, as more and more people discovered the beaches and fishing grounds and isolation of the area. The Panama City area, which had only 987 people in 1830, attracted more and more residents in the 19th century; the place took its name from the fact that it lies on a direct line between Chicago and Panama City in the Canal Zone. Today the city has 7,232 blacks (21%) out of a total population of 34,378.

Further Reading:

John Paul Jones, "Panama City, Queen City of the Gulf," *North Florida Living*, vol. 4, no. 4 (April 1984), p. 5+.

Panama City was the home of **Rosenwald Junior College,** which began in 1958 as one of 12 black junior colleges in Florida (see St. Petersburg below). Its first president was Mr. Calvin Washington, principal of Rosenwald High School. Its first-year enrollment of 35 total students, including those in the vocational program, was so much lower than the 125 expected that the junior college had to meet in a wing of the black school, but little by little it added students until it had 177 students in the 1964-65 school year, before merging with Gulf Coast Community College in 1966. The enrollment figures, which included college parallel courses and vocational courses, for Rosenwald Junior College were as follows:

1958-1959: 35 students **1959-1960: 65 students**
1960-1961: 96 students **1961-1962: 84 students**
1962-1963: 147 students **1963-1964: 151 students**
1964-1965: 177 students **1965-1966: 143 students**

Chapter 54

Pensacola

One of the oldest settlements in Florida, Pensacola traces its European background to Don Tristan de Luna y Arellano, who was appointed Governor General of Florida. He established a small settlement in the area in 1559, but a hurricane, famine, and poor leadership caused the settlement to give up and leave the area. Eventually the Spanish returned to establish a stronghold there, and the English also settled there in the late 1700s.

The first blacks to live in the Pensacola area probably came with the Tristan de Luna expedition in 1559. Over the next few centuries blacks settled in the area to work as soldiers or as farmers, fishermen, and workers. During Spanish rule in west Florida, those blacks who were free owned property, operated businesses, worked at different trades, and experienced less discrimination than did slaves. Many blacks worked in the lumber industry, building Spanish fortifications and later, when the United States took over Florida, the buildings and houses of the Americans. Life was hard for blacks and much discrimination existed. (See Key West above for the Jonathan Walker incident and "The Branded Hand.") Blacks also worked in the bricklaying industry, building structures like Fort Pickens, and eventually as physicians, attorneys, and journalists. By 1900, 43% of the total work force in Pensacola was black. The city had two private black schools, black barbers who served both races, and many black professionals. The races seemed to be getting along well.

Further Reading:

Charles Boyd, "S.W. Boyd, Sr., D.D.S." [about a black dentist in Pensacola], *Pensacola History Illustrated*, vol. 1, no. 1 (summer 1983), pp. 21-22.

John W. Cole. *Pictorial History of Pensacola.* Pensacola: Fiesta of The Five Flags Association, 1952.

Lucius and Linda Ellsworth. *Pensacola: The Deep Water City.* Tulsa, Okla.: Continental Heritage Press, Inc., 1982.

Virginia Parks. *Pensacola: Spaniards to Space Age.* Pensacola: Pensacola Historical Society, 1986.

Leora Sutton. *Blacks and Slavery in Pensacola, 1780-1880.* Pensacola: Leora Sutton, 1992.

One of the city's best-known blacks was Matthew M. Lewey, the owner and publisher of *The Florida Sentinel*, the South's largest black newspaper. He had established the *Gainesville Sentinel* with Josiah Walls in 1887, changed its name to the *Florida Sentinel* when he moved to Pensacola in 1894, moved to Jacksonville in 1914, and sold the *Sentinel* to W.W. Andrews in 1919. The newspaper, which eventually became the Tampa *Sentinel-Bulletin*, is the oldest black paper published continuously in the state. Lewey also served as the first president of the Florida Business League, an association that was geared to help blacks in business.

The association invited Dr. Booker T. Washington to Pensacola in 1913, and he was so impressed by the city that he wrote in his book, *The Negro in Business*, that the city was a "typical Negro business community" with its many opportunities for blacks. Among the black businessmen were Sam Charles, who owned a shoe store on Palafox Street; D.J. Cunningham, who owned the Excelsior grocery; and G.B. Green, who operated a furniture store.

Further Reading:

Leedell W. Neyland. *Twelve Black Floridians*. Tallahassee: Florida Agricultural and Mechanical Foundation, 1970, pp. 7-14.

Karen Smith, "For Black Businesses, The Old Days Were Good," *The Pensacola News*, January 25, 1984, p. 1+.

Around that time, however, when the city's economic slump and a doubling of the white population forced workers to compete for a dwindling number of jobs, a bitterness between the races rose up to destroy any good feeling that existed before. The city council passed a Jim Crow ordinance for street cars, restaurants and railroad cars that enforced segregation, and downtown merchants forced black businesses to relocate in the Belmont-DeVilliers area. Blacks had many restrictions placed on them in Pensacola. Historian James McGovern wrote that "In a city where people associated primarily on the basis of similarities of wealth, status, residence, ethnic make up and color, blacks became Pensacola's most restricted and publicly ghettoized group.... Local businessmen, who hoped to put politics on a more efficient basis, preferred to minimize political participation by Negroes." (p. 63)

Further Reading:

James McGovern. *The Emergence of a City in the Modern South: Pensacola 1900-1945*. DeLeon Springs, Fl.: Painter, 1976.

Only in the 1970s and 1980s, with the passage of federal civil rights laws and the efforts of public officials have relations between the two races improved. In 1991, for example, the Society for the Preservation of Pensacola Black History helped sponsor the first annual Enshrinement Ceremonies for Pensacola's Black Americans. The African American Heritage Society, Inc., has exhibits and programs throughout the year dealing with African Americans. Today Pensacola has a population of 58,165, of whom 18,506 (32%) are black.

Further Reading:

"Story of Black Business Unfolds," *News Journal* [Pensacola], February 28, 1988, pp. 1-2D.

The **Julee Cottage Museum** at 210 E. Zaragoza Street in the heart of the Historic Pensacola Village was the home of a free black woman, Julee Panton, who used the money she earned from land speculations to help other blacks obtain their freedom. Local historians have moved the cottage, one of the city's oldest surviving wooden buildings, from its original location on West Zaragoża Street and turned it into the Center for Black Heritage, complete with exhibits, documents, and photographs, to tell the little-known story of blacks in Pensacola. The cottage is part of the Preservation Board's "living village" in the Seville Square Historical District, which mixes businesses, residences, and museums in the heart of old Pensacola. Julee bought the cypress house, which was probably built between 1790 and 1800, in 1808, in the last Spanish period and 13 years before the United States acquired Florida from Spain. Blacks continuously owned the house until the Civil War and then after the war until the 1970s, at which time the Preservation Society acquired it. Displays in the museum-cottage show how Pensacola blacks differed from plantation blacks, how the former were craftsmen, tailors, ironworkers, and bricklayers. Hours of operation are 10 a.m.-3:30 p.m., Monday through Saturday; (904) 444-8586.

Further Reading:

"Black Heritage Center Opening at Symbolic Site," *News Journal* [Pensacola], February 26, 1988, p. 16A.

Frances Coleman, "Pensacola History Buffs Turn Julee's House into Museum," *Mobile Press Register*, March 6, 1988.

Bill Kaczor, "LegenDary Cottage Dedicated to Black History," *The Tampa Tribune*, February 11, 1991, Florida section, p. 4.

Saint Michael's Creole Benevolent Association Hall at 416

Saint Michael's Creole Benevolent Association was a social and cultural center for a racially mixed group that felt isolated from the black and white communities. Credit: Kevin M. McCarthy

East Government Street is an 1896 building that housed a benevolent association established by Creoles in 1878. The term "Creole" since the mid-19th century designated one of a racially mixed background, usually black with French or Spanish. The association, which lasted until 1971, gave members financial help during sickness, paid doctor bills and expenses for medicines, and gave death benefits to the family members of one of the members. Members dissolved the association in 1971 when their numbers were dwindling. Workers restored the building in 1972, but it is a private residence today that is not open to the public.

Daniel "Chappie" James Jr.'s Birthplace at 1606 North Alcaniz Street is the place where the country's first black four-star general in the Armed Services was born. In this house his mother also ran a school for black children. Daniel "Chappie" James, Jr., (1920-1978) grew up in Pensacola, the naval aviation capital of the United States, and dreamed of flying in one of those airplanes he saw every day. After graduating from high school, he attended Tuskegee Institute in Alabama, where he played football and basketball. While there, he joined a Civilian Pilot Training Program and eventually the Army Air Corps. He flew as a fighter pilot in the Korean War and the Vietnam War and became the Commander of the North American Air Defense Command. In 1975, he became the first black four-star general in our history.

Today all that remains of that house are three concrete steps with the words "Chappies First Steps" painted on them. Those steps led to the house where his mother raised him and where she taught him and many other black children of the area from the 1930s until the late 1950s. Among those who attended the school were doctors Ralph Boyd, S.W. Boyd, E.S. Cobb, and Thomas James; Mrs. Lillie Frazier, Mrs. Pansey Harris, Mrs. Mamie Hixson, Mrs. Glorida Hunter, Mr. Lawrence Scott, and Dr. Robert Walker; and countless other teachers and business leaders, all of whom heard Mrs. James repeat over and over again: "Never let anyone your size beat you doing anything." Alcaniz Street is one of the major streets in the city, is west of 9th Avenue, and runs parallel to Davis and Palafox streets. The site of "Chappies First Steps" is on the east side of Alcaniz Street between Mallory and Moreno streets, eight blocks north of Cervantes Street (U.S. 90).

Further Reading:

Mamie Webb Hixon, "Miss Lillie's School," in *When Black Folks Was Colored: A Collection of Memoirs and Poems by Black Americans*. Pensacola: African-American Heritage Society, Inc., 1993, pp. 35-40.

James R. McGovern. *Black Eagle: General Daniel "Chappie" James, Jr.* Tuscaloosa: University of Alabama Press, 1985.

J. Alfred Phelps. *Chappie: The Life and Times of Daniel James, Jr.* Novato, Cal.: Presidio Press, 1991.

The **Mount Zion Baptist Church** was organized in 1880 at Number Two Hall on Tarragona Street, Pensacola. After

Rev. Joseph Cook conducted services for about a year, Rev. Daniel Washington became pastor. As the congregation grew in number, the members raised enough funds to buy from the St. Luke Society a lot on Alcaniz Street, west side, between Gregory and Wright. Under the guidance of pastors James Banks, C.J. Hardy, G.W. Raiford, and others, the congregation increased to 600+ and built a fine building. The church is located at the northeast corner of the intersection of West Jackson Street and Coyle Street, two blocks below Cervantes Street (U.S. 90), and six blocks west of Palafox Street.

Further Reading:

Robt. T. Thomas. *History of The Mount Zion Baptist Church, Pensacola, Florida.* No publ. No date.

Washington Junior College began in 1949 as the first black junior college in Florida when the Escambia County School Board added a thirteenth grade to Booker T. Washington High School at 1421 E. Cross Street. The School Board combined the junior college and the senior high school under one administrator and called it the Washington School Center to serve the black students in the community and on the naval base. The founding president was Dr. G.T. Wiggins, formerly dean of the graduate school at Texas State University. The junior college had six teachers and 95 students, most of them there under the G.I. Bill. Most (75%) of the students enrolling chose the college parallel program rather than the vocational program, which included homemaking and business courses.

Just before the school merged with Pensacola Junior College in 1965, Washington had 361 students. One of the black men who helped inspire this school was Dr. Simon W. Boyd, the first dentist in the city to use gas for oral surgery and one who had a biracial practice. The enrollment figures, which included college parallel courses and vocational courses, for Washington Junior College were as follows:

An adult education class at Pensacola's Washington School in the 1930s provided opportunities for those who wanted to do well in their professions. Credit: Florida State Archives

1957-1958: 232 students	**1958-1959: 205 students**
1959-1960: 208 students	**1960-1961: 212 students**
1961-1962: 235 students	**1962-1963: 233 students**
1963-1964: 272 students	**1964-1965: 361 students**

When the school merged with Pensacola Junior College (PJC) in the mid-1960s, the seven faculty of Washington Junior College joined the integrated college staff or the local public school system, and the president of Washington became the director of research at PJC. While the faculty were able to find places of employment, the black students at Washington, as at other newly integrated junior colleges in Florida, declined in numbers. In 1968, state officials became so alarmed at the falling numbers of black college students that they sent a memo to all junior college presidents urging them to recruit more black students. In many cases the integrated colleges had not had an effective recruiting office or programs geared to minority students.

Part of that decline in numbers may have been due to a reluctance on the part of the black students to enter the white college world or a poor academic preparation in their own high schools or financial difficulties in affording the new school. Those integrated junior colleges that took a personal interest in minority students, who placed them in part-time jobs, who instituted a wide student financial program did well in attracting minority students, but it took a concerted effort on the part of the colleges to begin such programs.

Other sites of importance to blacks are the **Ella Jordan City Wide Women's Club Building** on the corner of C and La Rua streets, a building founded by Mrs. Ella Jordan in 1930 and used as a safe haven for homeless girls in the area and also a meeting place for the many black women clubs in the Federated Club; the **Belmont-Devilliers Neighborhood** where black businesses flourished during the time of Jim Crow laws; **St. Joseph's Catholic Church**, established for blacks and creoles; the **Corrine Jones Recreation Center**, which honors a woman who inspired many local black youth.

The first members inducted into the Northwest Florida Afro-American Hall of Fame in 1989 were a distinguished group: Zebulon Elijah, the first black member of the Florida House of Representatives (1871-1873) and the first black Pensacola postmaster (1874); former Florida A&M University football coach, A.S. "Jake" Gaither; General Daniel "Chappie" James, Jr.; civil rights activist H.K. Matthews; retired educator Dr. Vernon McDaniel, who sought equal pay for black teachers; John Sunday, a wealthy community leader who had served as a first sergeant in the Union Army, Escambia legislator (1874), and city alderman (1878-1880); and Thomas deSaille Tucker, an attorney appointed by the governor in 1887 to serve as superintendent of the Normal School for Colored Students, the forerunner of Florida A&M University. More recent black Pensacolians who have done well on the national scene are athletes Emmitt Smith of the Dallas Cowboys football team and Roy Jones, Jr., a boxer;

and pianist Ida Goodson and saxophonist Wally "The Cat" Mercer.

Further Reading:

Earle Bowden, "Honoring Our Black Heritage a Vital Part of Preserving Pensacola History," *Pensacola News-Journal,* November 12, 1989, p. 19A.

Chapter 55

Punta Gorda

This town on the south side of the Peace River in southwest Florida traces its beginnings back to 1883, when Col. Isaac Trabue arrived from Kentucky and made plans to establish a settlement, called Trabue. Florida Southern Railway extended its line to the site and thus helped assure the steady growth of the place. Local townspeople voted to change the name to Punta Gorda, meaning "wide point," and it later became the county seat of Charlotte County, although the town grew very slowly in comparison to Tampa to the north. Punta Gorda, which had a population of only 1,883 by 1930, today has 10,878 residents, of whom 651 (6%) are black.

One of the most important businessmen in the early history of Charlotte County was George Brown, who operated a shipyard in nearby Cleveland. (See Cleveland above for more about Brown.) In 1921, he donated land for the all-black Masonic Tuscan Lodge 92 in Punta Gorda at the southwest corner of Marion and Nesbit streets. He also sold the land in the downtown area that would be used in 1924 for the new county's courthouse.

Albert Gilchrist, a white civil engineer and important land speculator from Punta Gorda who went on to serve as governor of Florida from 1909 until 1913, hired black foremen and surveyors to help the Florida Southern Railroad reach Punta Gorda in 1886, after which several of the blacks settled in the town. One of those men, Sam Kenedy, bought some property in town and, because he was a property owner, signed the articles of incorporation for Punta Gorda on December 27, 1887.

In 1903, when Gilchrist was elected state representative, he appointed the first black man, Dan T. Smith, whom he had once hired as a surveyor, to the DeSoto County Board of Education. When Smith went to an educators' conference in New Orleans to recruit a black teacher, he persuaded Benjamin Joshua Baker (1872-1942), the son of Suwannee County slaves and a 31-year-old man with 12 years' experience in Live Oak, Florida, to come to Punta Gorda to become the first principal-teacher for the county's first black school. Baker was a quiet man known for his strict discipline and high moral standards. Twice widowed, he never had children of his own, but was much loved by the students and parents associated with his school. In order not to show any favoritism for either of the two black churches in town, St. Mark Baptist and Bethel African Methodist Episcopal, he attended one on one Sunday and the other on the next Sunday.

Workers first built for blacks a two-room school on E. Marion Avenue at the foot of Cooper Street. When enrollment outgrew that school, a four-room school was built at the southeast corner of Mary and Showalter streets (now the playground of the Cooper Street Recreation Center) to serve black students; people began referring to it as "Baker's Academy" in honor of Benjamin Baker. Three other black teachers taught grades 1-8, while the older children were bused to Dunbar High School in Fort Myers (see above) until integration took effect in Charlotte County in 1964. The Academy was eventually torn down to make room for the Cooper Street Recreation Center, but the Baker Academy Alumni Association meets twice a year to keep alive the memory of Charlotte County's first black educator.

In 1940, after 49 years in education in Live Oak and Punta

Gorda, Baker retired, becoming the first person to benefit from the 1939 Teachers' Retirement Act. He died two years later and was buried in Live Oak, Florida, the town he was born in just seven years after the Civil War. Soon after he died, a large school for black children was built near his Punta Gorda home and named for him. Today **Baker Elementary School** at 311 E. Charlotte Avenue is used in the Head Start and pre-school development classes.

Another black from Punta Gorda, Charles P. Bailey, became a fighter pilot with the all-black 99th Fighter Squadron and won the Distinguished Flying Cross after flying 133 combat missions over Europe and shooting down three enemy airplanes. He later moved to DeLand, Florida, to establish the Charles P. Bailey Funeral Home. We should also mention here one of the great black leaders of the Reconstruction period in Florida, Robert Meacham (1835-1902), who served as postmaster in Punta Gorda; he also helped establish the African Methodist Episcopal Church in the state, as well as Florida's public education system.

Further Reading:

Canter Brown, Jr. *Florida's Peace River Frontier*. Orlando: University of Central Florida Press, 1991.

Fred Farris. *Once Upon a Time in Southwest Florida*. Venice, Fl.: Gondolier Publishing Co., 1982, pp. 103-105: "Black Teacher Became a Legend" [about Benjamin Joshua Baker].

Louise Frisbie. *Peace River Pioneers*. Miami: Seemann, 1974.

Maxine D. Jones and Kevin M. McCarthy. *African Americans in Florida*. Sarasota: Pineapple Press, 1993, pp. 37-39.

Vernon Peeples. *Punta Gorda and the Charlotte Harbor Area*. Norfolk, Va.: Donning Company, 1986.

Chapter 56

Quincy

The town of Quincy, which today has a population of 7,444, of whom 4,565 (61%) are black, is the county seat of Gadsden County northwest of Tallahassee. Gadsden was Florida's fifth county, having been formed in 1823, two years after the United States acquired Florida from Spain. The county was named after Captain James Gadsden (1788-1858), an Army engineer who served as General Andrew Jackson's aide-de-camp, built a fort on the nearby Apalachicola River, and was later responsible for the Gadsden Purchase, which expanded the boundaries of the continental United States. Quincy was named after John Quincy Adams, who was secretary of state of the United States when the town was founded in 1825.

Slaveholders established the county in the 19th century and used slaves to cultivate tobacco, cotton, sugar cane, and corn. The first census of the county, which was taken in 1825, showed that slaves made up 41% of the total population. Thirteen years later that figure rose to 57% as more and more slaves were brought in to work the fields. Tobacco became so important that it earned $400,000 for the area just before the Civil War began. After the Civil War freed the slaves, many of them stayed in the area to raise their families on their farms. The percentage of blacks has remained consistently high over the years. For example, the 1990 census

Arnett Chapel is the county's oldest black church that still exists today. Credit: Kevin M. McCarthy

showed that blacks made up 58% of the county population of 41,105.

Among the more famous local blacks was one of the state's most renowned attorneys, Simuel Decatur McGill, who was born in Quincy in 1878; in 1942, he secured the release of four innocent men, the so-called "Pompano Boys," who had been arrested without a warrant, were tortured, and then forced to confess to a crime they had not committed. They spent nine years on death row before McGill was able to prove they were innocent.

Further Reading:

Maxine D. Jones and Kevin M. McCarthy. *African Americans in Florida.* Sarasota: Pineapple Press, 1993, pp. 101-102.

Arnett Chapel A.M.E. Church at 209 South Duval Street represents an important step in the religious history of local blacks. Before the American Civil War, slave owners used religion as a means of controlling their slaves and teaching them the values of western civilization. The overseers discouraged slaves from practicing African religions, especially in the African languages the slaves had brought with them, on the theory that those religions were pagan and the slaves might be fomenting rebellion in languages unknown to the overseers. In order to keep the slaves in view, even during their religious worship, and therefore less liable to conspire among themselves to revolt, overseers insisted that the slaves attend the churches that whites established in each township. Because slaves were not allowed to sit with the white parishioners, architects built separate slave galleries in the churches. The records of plantations around Quincy sometimes noted each slave with the letter "B" for believer or "S" for sinner, presumably based on whether the slave went to church or not.

Once the Emancipation Proclamation and the end of the Civil War freed the slaves, they began establishing their own churches. The African Methodist Episcopal (A.M.E.) church and the African Methodist Episcopal Zion (A.M.E. Zion) church began in the North, in Philadelphia and New York City respectively, in the late 18th century and expanded throughout the South after the Civil War. Ministers, missionaries, and freedmen worked in Florida and established many parishes among the former slaves. In Quincy, local blacks established the Arnett Chapel A.M.E. Church, which at first met in members' homes or even outdoors. In 1867, two years after the Civil War ended, members spent $100 for a plot of land about one-fourth of an acre in size. This church is the county's oldest black church that still exists today. The second structure was built on the southeast corner of DuVal and Clark streets in 1898-1899 and named in honor of Reverend Benjamin W. Arnett, the Presiding Bishop in Florida from 1888 to 1892. The congregation met in that structure until 1938-1939, at which time another building was begun. The first services were held in the new building in 1940.

In the **Hardon Building** at 16 W. Washington Street, William Hardon, a black from Quincy, owned one of the town's earliest ice and electric plants. Ice would have been very important for a product closely associated with Quincy: Coca-Cola. In 1922, local farmers invested some money in a relatively new company in Atlanta, the Coca-Cola Company. Eventually The Quincy State Bank had shares worth more than $15 million, money that has greatly helped the town, although many of the blacks have remained in poverty to the present day. The Hardon Building, which was built around 1900, now houses an office-supply business.

The **Masonic Lodge** at 122 South Duval Street has served as the meeting hall for black Masons since 1907. The Masonic order, which is the oldest such group in the Western world, stresses friendship, morality, truth, charity, and prudence. Because Freemasonry does not allow members to discuss religion or politics within its temples, the organization was able to survive during such divisive times as the American Civil War. In many states the Masons operate homes for orphans, the aged, and the infirm and specialize in treating crippled children and burn victims. The Masonic Lodge in Quincy where black Masons have met is a simple, two-story building with an open hall on the first floor. Unlike some masonic lodges in large cities, which are often elaborate and adorned with large columns, this Quincy lodge, which was moved from its original site in 1976 and remodeled, is simple and practical.

The **William S. Stevens Hospital** on the corner of Roberts and Crawford streets was where Dr. William S. Stevens practiced medicine in Quincy for more than 50 years. The hospital treated patients through both the yellow fever outbreak of 1906 and the influenza epidemic of 1918. Dr. Stevens, who also had a clinic and a drug store, used this two-story building, which is now a private residence, to treat many of the local black people.

Further Reading:

Elizabeth Roberts, "Putting the Kick Back In Quincy's Old Coke Economy," *Florida Trend*, March 1986, pp. 56-60.

Julia Floyd Smith. *Slavery and Plantation Growth in Antebellum Florida, 1821-1860.* Gainesville: University of Florida Press, 1973.

Miles Kenan Womack, Jr. *Gadsden: A Florida County in Word and Picture.* [Quincy]: Gadsden County Historical Commission, 1976.

One of the leaders that came from Quincy was Richard Moore, who was born in Quincy, attended school there, and eventually became the third president of Bethune-Cookman College in Daytona Beach in 1947. He held that position for 28 years until his retirement in 1975. In his career he was an instructor of social studies and athletics coach at Pinellas High School in Clearwater (1932-1934), principal of Union Academy in Tarpon Springs (1934-1937), principal of Rosenwald High School in Panama City (1937-1944), principal of Booker T. Washington High School in Pensacola (1944-1945), and State Supervisor of Black Secondary Schools (1945-1947). He died in 1994 at age 87 after a distinguished life spent in education.

Further Reading:

"Services Saturday in Daytona Beach for Former BCC President Richard Moore," *The Miami Times*, January 13, 1994, pp. 1-2A.

Chapter 57

Rosewood

This small town, which is ten miles east of Cedar Key and about 40 miles west of Gainesville, in the early 1920s was home to 150-200 people, many of whom were blacks who worked for the railroad or in the turpentine industry or at a sawmill. On Monday, January 1, 1923, a white woman in nearby Sumner claimed that a black man had attacked her, a charge that led to one of the worst tragedies associated with blacks in Florida. Some local blacks believed that the woman was lying to cover up the fact that she had quarreled with a white lover who beat her and that she was trying to protect herself. Nevertheless, word of the alleged attack by the black man quickly spread among the local whites, and a mob of angry whites gathered to seek revenge. The blacks fled into the nearby swamp of Gulf Hammock, trying to escape a mob that was out of control. The mob then went through the Rosewood-Sumner area searching for any blacks, killing at least six of them from the area, and destroying their homes, churches, and meeting hall, effectively driving away forever those blacks who had been living there.

All that remains today are scattered bricks from destroyed buildings and the house of John Wright, one of the few white residents in the community and a man who had tried to help the blacks defend themselves against the mob. Although

An angry mob set fire to the cabins of innocent blacks in Rosewood. Credit: Florida State Archives

other communities in Florida and the Deep South experienced such bloodbaths against blacks, Rosewood was the only community that mob violence completely destroyed. In the spring of 1994, the Florida Legislature passed and Governor Chiles signed a bill to compensate the survivors and descendants of that massacre.

Further Reading:

David Colburn, "Rosewood," *The Gainesville Sun*, January 14, 1994, p. 15A.

Maxine D. Jones and Kevin M. McCarthy. *African Americans in Florida.* Sarasota: Pineapple Press, 1993, pp. 83-84.

Gary Moore, "Rosewood," *The Floridian*," July 25, 1982, pp. 6-19.

"Nothing Left But to Fight to Be Heard," *The Florida Times-Union* [Jacksonville], January 3, 1993, p. A-1+. Also the article on p. A-6: "Survivor Recalls Terror of Day Rosewood Died."

Karen Voyles, "Survivors Dredge up Painful Memories," *The Gainesville Sun*, February 26, 1994, p. 1B+.

That killing of blacks and the torching of their town was

not the only such incident in Florida history. In November 1920, whites in Ocoee near Orlando went on a rampage after some black people had gone to the polls to vote in an election. The whites destroyed 25 houses and two churches of black people and killed several dozen blacks. The whites lynched one black man, July Perry, and left him hanging from a telephone pole after he angered them for defending his property. Many if not most of the blacks of the town who were alive after the attack left town as quickly as they could.

Further Reading:

Lester Dabbs, "A Report of the Circumstances and Events of the Race Riot on November 2, 1920, in Ocoee Florida," M.A. Thesis, Stetson University, 1969.

Chapter 58

St. Augustine

*D*uring the Spanish control of Florida in the 17th and 18th centuries, a number of escaping slaves from the Carolinas and Georgia made their way south, determined to flee the oppressive conditions on plantations owned by the British or Americans. The Spanish had long used black slaves, beginning in 1565, to labor in Florida in both menial jobs and as servants to the wealthy Spanish. Two miles north of St. Augustine, the Spanish established in 1738 a fort they called Gracia Real de Santa Teresa de Mose, what we call today **Fort Mose** (pronounced "Moh-say"), the first free community of ex-slaves in North America.

The Spanish allowed the blacks to settle there if they became Catholics. About 100 free black men, women, and children lived in the fort and helped the Spanish defend St. Augustine from the British, who wanted to recapture the runaway slaves and take them back to plantations. Fort Mose was destroyed in 1740 during the invasion led by General Oglethorpe of Georgia, but rebuilt several years later. When England took control of Florida in 1763, residents of Fort Mose left with the Spaniards for Cuba, where they established a similar community in the province of Matanzas.

Directions:

Fort Mose is not open to the public at this time, but the state may establish a museum there in the near future.

Further Reading:

Kathleen A. Deagan, "Fort Mose: America's First Free Black Community," in *Spanish Pathways in Florida*, edited by Ann L. Henderson and Gary Mormino. Sarasota: Pineapple Press, 1991.

Maxine D. Jones and Kevin M. McCarthy. *African Americans in Florida*. Sarasota: Pineapple Press, 1993, pp. 13-14.

Jane Landers, "Blacks in Spanish Florida," *Forum* [the magazine of the Florida Humanities Council], vol. 12, no. 1 (spring 1989), pp. 9-12.

Jane Landers. *Fort Mose*. St. Augustine: St. Augustine Historical Society, 1992. This is a reprint of an article that appeared in *The American Historical Review*, vol. 95, no. 1.

Suzie Siegel, "Exiled to Cuba," *The Tampa Tribune*, February 16, 1993, BayLife, pp. 1, 6.

Jorge Biassou, a black general in St. Augustine in colonial times, led a black militia out of Fort Matanzas south of St. Augustine. (One can visit this fort, which is located on Rattlesnake Island and is now operated by the National Park Service.) General Biassou, who had been one of the leaders of the slave uprising in Haiti and had as one of his subordinates Toussaint L'Ouverture, died in St. Augustine in 1801 and is buried in Tolomato Cemetery on Cordova Street.

Further Reading:

Jane Landers, "Jorge Biassou, Black Chieftain," in *Clash Between Cultures*, edited by Jacqueline K. Fretwell and Susan R. Parker. St. Augustine: St. Augustine Historical Society, 1988.

After the United States gained control of Florida from the Spanish in 1821, St. Augustine continued to have a large black population. In fact, the 1830 census indicated that blacks, who constituted almost half of the city's population, were for the most part slaves. Of the 4,000 slaves, 6% (240)

were free blacks who were descendants of the city's early colonists and of runaway slaves from Georgia. Their condition was only slightly above those of the slaves; the free blacks, for example, could not have meetings without the permission of the white authorities, could hold only certain jobs, and had to live in one section of the city, where whites could keep an eye on their activities.

The situation of the slaves was somewhat different from that of other Florida locales because the St. Augustine whites permitted slaves to hire themselves out to fishermen, lumbermen, and railroad builders. The slave owners kept most of the money the slaves earned from this practice, but allowed the slaves to keep a small amount of the money, which they used to support their own churches and clubs. The owners also allowed some of the slaves to live outside the master's residence in a separate part of St. Augustine; there the slaves had a freedom that encouraged them to express themselves.

In the two decades before the Civil War, local white slave holders, fearful of the increasing freedom of the blacks, enacted more slave codes and sold their superfluous slaves to rural residents. St. Augustine, which came under Union control in 1862, was one of the few places where Abraham Lincoln's Emancipation Proclamation actually took effect. The vacant lot across from St. Joseph's Convent (just south of 234 St. George Street), where the slaves gathered and were told of their freedom, has come to be known as "Liberation Lot." When the Union army occupied the city in the Civil War, slaves from outlying areas began flocking into the city looking for freedom and protection. Union troops hired free blacks and former slaves to build defenses for the city and to help fill the ranks of the all-black regiments being formed throughout the South.

Further Reading:

Karen G. Harvey, "Antonio Proctor: A Piece of the Mosaic." *El Escribano*, vol. 17 (1980), pp. 47-57 [about an important black family in early St. Augustine].

Kenneth W. Porter. *The Negro on the American Frontier*. New York: Arno Press, 1971.

Daniel L. Schafer, "Freedom Was as Close as the River: The Blacks of Northeast Florida and the Civil War," *El Escribano*, vol. 23 (1986), pp. 91-116.

Lee Warner. *Free Men in an Age of Servitude*. Lexington, Ky.: University Press of Kentucky, 1992.

The **Lincolnville Historic District** was the center of black business and residential activity in the city in the early part of this century. The 140-acre area of the southwest peninsula is southwest of the downtown area and consists of about 50 blocks and streets bounded on the north by DeSoto Place and Cedar Street, Riberia Street on the west, Cerro Street on the south, and Washington Street on the east. About one-third of the 650 buildings in the district date from the 19th century, and many of them represent Victorian architecture. Two antebellum plantation houses are Yallaha at 115 Bridge Street and a wing of Buena Esperanza at 55 Keith Street. A garage at 88 South Street is the last surviving slave cabin in the city. Most of the structures in the district are single-family residences. Beginning in 1980, the Lincoln Restoration and Development Commission sponsored a Lincolnville Festival with music, food, rides, tours, and other activities.

When the area attracted former black slaves right after the Civil War, they first called the area "Africa," but soon changed it to "Lincolnville." The first settlers built homes, churches, and some businesses, and after 1877, when a "Peoples Ticket" led by political reformers including black Republican leader D.M. Pappy won the city elections, officials began building streets and making other improvements in the area. However, the segregation that followed Reconstruction and the passage of laws meant to allow only whites to vote between 1890 and 1910 greatly limited blacks in their efforts to improve their conditions. In 1902, black councilman John Papino was shot at a meeting of the city council by the white town marshall. Papino survived his wounds, but the terror reflected by the shooting, and the failure to indict the marshall, marked the beginning of the end of black office holders until the 1970s.

Lincolnville lies between two bodies of water, the Matanzas and San Sebastian rivers, and is therefore subject to flooding during heavy rainstorms, especially because of the district's low elevation. The district also suffers from inharmonious zoning and the bulldozing of many buildings to create parking lots. On the positive side, a Lincolnville Housing Project in the 1980s restored a number of old houses, and the Lincolnville Improvement Association was formed in the 1990s. Lincolnville is now listed on the National Register of Historic Places and the Florida Black Heritage Trail.

The vacant lot at 107 Kings Ferry Way was the site of the home of Richard Aloysius Twine (1896-1974), the city's first known black photographer, who took many photographs of Lincolnville in the 1920s. Workers demolishing the house in 1988 found his camera and many of his glass negatives in the attic of the house, where Twine lived with his mother and two sisters in the 1920s. Twine was born and grew up in St. Augustine and later started a photography business, which he conducted out of his studio at 62 Washington Street. In the late-1920s, he moved to Miami to join his brother in the restaurant business and later died there.

When the St. Augustine Historical Society's photo curator, Ken Barrett, Jr., organized an exhibition of Twine's photographs in 1990, Dr. Patricia C. Griffin and Diana S. Edwards interviewed many members of the city's black community with the help of city commissioner Henry A. Twine, a distant relative of the photographer. The interviewers identified people in the photographs and recorded life stories of what it was like to live in the city's black section in the 1920s.

Further Reading:

Patricia C. Griffin and Diana S. Edwards, "Results and Future Directions"

Part of the civil rights demonstrations of the 1960s was a sit-in at a segregated lunch counter in St. Augustine. Credit: Florida State Archives

[about the black community photographed by Twine], *The East-Florida Gazette* [newspaper of the St. Augustine Historical Society], February 1990. The same issue has articles about Richard Twine, his photographs, and Lincolnville.

Ann Hyman, "Photos of Lincolnville at Edward Waters," *The Florida Times-Union* [Jacksonville], October 28, 1990, p. D-6.

"Lincolnville Festival All-Day Fun July 5," *The Independent Traveler*, June 18-24, 1980, p. 15.

Dana Treen, "Lincolnville Fighting to Regain Heritage," *The Florida Times-Union* [Jacksonville], December 1, 1991, p. B-1+.

Joseph White, "Lincolnville: The Historic St. Augustine Visitors May Never See," *Folio Weekly*, Sept. 15, 1992, pp. 16-23.

During the 1964 civil rights demonstrations in the city, Dr. Martin Luther King, Jr., led many people in their attempts to gain better conditions. Police arrested him at the **Monson Motel**, 32 Avenida Menéndez, at the bayfront; that was the motel where the manager poured acid into the swimming pool to scare away a group of swimmers trying to integrate the facility. Officials later renamed Central Avenue to honor King, despite the objections of some white residents. Because of the danger of violence, Dr. King was moved around frequently when in St. Augustine. Places where he stayed include 81 and 83 Bridge Street and 156 M.L. King Avenue.

Among the other sites associated with those demonstrations are **Trinity United Methodist Church** at 84 Bridge Street; **St. Paul's A.M.E. Church** at 85 M.L. King Avenue; **St. Mary's Missionary Baptist Church** at 69 Washington Street; and **First Baptist Church** at 81 St. Francis Street. Of these churches St. Mary's Missionary Baptist Church resembles the late-medieval churches of Italy and has both Gothic and Romanesque styles in its architecture. This and the other black churches, with their distinctive beauty and careful workmanship, represent the important place that religion has played in the religious and social life of the blacks of the town and of the state. In the mid-1960s, the churches played a major role in the political demonstrations that eventually led to the enactment of landmark civil rights legislation.

St. Paul's, a 1904 church in the Gothic Revival style, was where many local blacks met in 1964 to celebrate the recent passage of the 1964 civil rights bill passed by the U.S. Senate. Like so many churches in the South, St. Paul's was the place where blacks met to pray and also to discuss the means of attaining civil rights. Whereas whites might have met in schools or places like the Masonic lodge, blacks came to rely on their churches for communication purposes. On that day in June, Dr. Martin Luther King, Jr., addressed the crowd; at that moment in his life, the 35-year-old King was the chief spokesman for this country's civil rights movement, the winner of awards for his efforts, *Time* magazine's "Man of the Year," and the future winner of the Nobel Peace Prize.

The **Slave Market** in the plaza near the Cathedral also became a focus point of the marches; despite the efforts of chamber-of-commerce types to deny it, the plaza had been a place where merchants sold slaves. The **Ponce de Leon Motor Lodge** at 4000 U.S. 1 North was the place where authorities arrested 72-year-old Mrs. Malcolm Peabody, mother of the governor of Massachusetts, when she tried to be served a meal while a member of an integrated group. Since those days, St. Augustine has made strides towards interracial harmony and has worked to better the lives of its 2,303 blacks, who represent 20% of the total population of 11,692.

Further Reading:

David R. Colburn. *Racial Change and Community Crisis: St. Augustine, Florida, 1877-1980.* Gainesville: University of Florida Press, 1991.

David J. Garrow. *Bearing the Cross.* New York: William Morrow and Company, 1986, esp. pp. 316-341.

David J. Garrow, editor. *St. Augustine, Florida, 1963-1964: Mass Protest and Racial Violence.* Brooklyn, N.Y.: Carlson, 1989.

Paul Good. *Once to Every Man.* New York: Putnam, 1970. This is a novel about the demonstrations.

Paul Good. *The Trouble I've Seen.* Washington, D.C.: Howard University Press, 1975.

William Kunstler. *Deep in My Heart.* New York: Morrow, 1966.

Randolph Pendleton, "A Racial Wrinkle for the Oldest City," *The Florida Times-Union,* January 20, 1991, p. C-1+.

James Salzer, "Civil Rights Fight Shattered 'Quaint' Town," *The Florida Times-Union,* January 18, 1988, p. B-3.

The **Willie Galimore Community Center** at 399 South Riberia Street is a recreational center that honors Willie "The Wisp" Galimore, a star athlete who had played basketball and football at St. Augustine's Excelsior High School. When he attended Florida A&M University in Tallahassee, he was a three-time All American in football. He then went on to play for the Chicago Bears in the National Football League, during which time he led the Bears in scoring (1958) and in rushing (1961), averaged 4.45 yards per carry over six seasons, and tied a Bears record by scoring four touchdowns in one game in 1957. He was killed in a car accident in 1964 at the age of 29. The Galimore Center that honors him was the site of a 1992 Freedom Fighters Appreciation Banquet held by the Black Heritage Commission, which local residents had organized in 1983. Men and women who had participated in the marches and sit-ins of the civil rights movement of the 1960s were honored.

Further Reading:

Kim Bradley, "City's Civil Rights Struggle Recalled," *The St. Augustine Record,* March 29, 1992, p. 4A. That page also contains a list of those who were honored for participating in the city's civil rights movement of the 1960s.

"'Spot-Shot' Galimore," *Ebony,* vol. 14, no. 3 (January 1959), pp. 72-76.

Time, August 7, 1964, p. 88 [Galimore's obituary].

The **Florida School for the Deaf and the Blind** at 207 San Marco Avenue served the needs of many Floridians since 1885. Its most famous alumnus is musician Ray Charles (1930-), who spent his early years in Greenville, Florida; when at the age of seven he began to go blind, his family sent him to the St. Augustine School for the Deaf and the Blind, where he learned to play the piano and prepare for a successful professional career. Another prominent black musician who attended the school is Marcus Roberts.

Further Reading:

Ray Charles and David Ritz. *Brother Ray, Ray Charles' Own Story.* New York: Dial, 1978.

Cary White, Sr., (1900-1983) became the first black deaf graduate of the school when he finished his course of studies in 1922, after which he went to work for the school. After 46 years of faithful service there as a carpenter, mason, electrician, and vocational teacher, he retired in 1968. In 1991, officials dedicated the **Cary A. White, Sr., Complex** in honor of him. The plaque there gives his years as a student (1907-1922) and member of the staff (1922-1968) and the words: "Graduate, teacher and friend of FSDB. His entire life was dedicated to helping others." Tours can be arranged by calling 904-823-4023.

Another black school that has since moved south is **Florida Memorial College**, which was located two miles west of the city and originally called the Florida Normal and Industrial Institute. It was founded in Jacksonville in 1892 by N.W. Collier, a college classmate of James Weldon Johnson. In later years it combined with the Florida Baptist Institute, which had been established in Live Oak, Florida, in 1879. Workers built the St. Augustine campus in 1918 on the site of the Old Hanson Plantation, once operated by slave labor. When famed author Zora Neale Hurston taught at the school in 1942, she lived upstairs in a two-story house at 791 West King Street just east of the campus. The school finally closed its doors in St. Augustine and moved to a new campus in Dade County in 1968. One can see what is left of the campus and its dilapidated buildings on West King Street at Holmes Boulevard.

Further Reading:

R. Michael Anderson, "Old College Campus May Shine Anew if Plans Pan Out," *The Florida Times-Union* [Jacksonville], September 14, 1987, p. B3.

Among the important black entrepreneurs and civic leaders in Lincolnville was Frank B. Butler (1885-1973), the man who developed **Butler's Beach** on Anastasia Island southeast of St. Augustine, for many years the only beach that blacks could use in the area. Butler began his meat-grocery store, The Palace Market, in 1914 near the place where he lived a good part of his life: 87 Washington Street. In the next decade he bought real estate west of the city in what became the College Park Subdivision, where many blacks built homes. In 1925, he helped establish the College Park Realty Company. Two years later he bought enough land between the ocean and the Matanzas River to establish the only beach for blacks south of American Beach on Amelia Island (see

Butler's Beach provided recreational activities for many blacks. Credit: Florida State Archives

American Beach above) and north of Daytona Beach. Near the ocean several blacks bought lots, built houses, and set up businesses. Butler himself had a cafe with 14 rooms to rent and a nearby motel where Dr. Martin Luther King, Jr., and his associates stayed during his widely publicized visit to St. Augustine in 1964. 5718 Rudolph Avenue is the current address of the place where Dr. King stayed.

The street names in the area honored Butler's family: Mary Street (for his mother), Minnie Street (for his wife and daughter), Mae Street (for his daughter, Minnie Mae), Rudolph Street (for his grandson), and Gloria Street (for his granddaughter). In 1958, the state bought some of the land for a state park, and five years later Butler's company gave land near the Matanzas River for a children's recreation area. In 1980, the park was changed from state to local operation and became the "Frank B. Butler County Park" in honor of this distinguished man.

Further Reading:

Barbara Walch. *Frank B. Butler: Lincolnville Businessman and Founder of St. Augustine, Florida's Historic Black Beach*. St. Augustine: Rudolph B. Hadley, Sr., 1992.

Chapter 59

St. Petersburg

This city, like many in Florida, is barely 100 years old, but burial mounds and ceramic remains indicate that Indians lived there for hundreds of years before white men arrived. Those Indians, whom historians call the Tocobaga, came into contact with European explorers like the Spanish Panfilo de Narváez and Hernando de Soto in the 16th century. The Pinellas Peninsula remained relatively unsettled by Europeans until the 18th century, but runaway slaves began joining Creek Indians and formed a branch of the Seminole Indians. The 19th century saw a number of what historian Arsenault calls "Spanish Indians" (p. 29), some of whom were fugitive black slaves. After the U.S. took control of Florida from Spain in 1821, thousands of settlers poured into the territory, including the adventurer Odet Philippe, who used some slaves to till his plantation.

After the Seminole Indian wars and the Civil War, more whites moved to the area, as well as a few ex-slaves like John Donaldson, the first black man to move to the lower Pinellas Peninsula after the Civil War. Russian-born railroad builder Peter Demens, who was responsible for the naming of Florida's St. Petersburg after the Russian city, used several hundred black workers along with his own work force to bring the Orange Belt Railroad to the area in 1888. What followed were more settlers and tourists and a steady building of the city. The black workers who settled down in the town after the completion of the railroad lived on Fourth Avenue South in what was called Pepper Town. Another black community on Ninth Street was called Cooper's Quarters after the local white merchant who owned their shacks, Leon B. Cooper.

Further Reading:

Raymond Arsenault. *St. Petersburg and the Florida Dream, 1888-1950*. Norfolk, Va.: Donning Company, 1988.
Hampton Dunn. *Yesterday's St. Petersburg*. Miami: Seemann, 1973.
Karl H. Grismer. *The Story of St. Petersburg*. St. Petersburg: P.K. Smith, 1948.
Del Marth. *St. Petersburg: Once Upon a Time*. St. Petersburg: The City of St. Petersburg Bicentennial Committee, 1976.

In the early part of the 1900s, blacks made up a sizable part of the 3,000 residents and worked in the menial jobs (laborers, fishermen, domestics) that built the local economy. Many blacks lived and worked along the city's so-called "Black Belt," which stretched along 22nd and 16th streets South. For entertainment they attended the Harlem Theater and the Manhattan Casino, where entertainers like Cab Calloway and Dizzy Gillespie performed. Racial violence occurred from time to time, as for example in 1914 when an angry white mob caught and lynched a black man for allegedly killing a white man and attacking the white man's wife.

Further Reading:

Jon L. Wilson,"Days of Fear: A Lynching in St. Petersburg," *Tampa Bay History*, vol. 5, no. 2 (fall/winter 1983), pp. 4-26.

Blacks suffered the segregation that many other American cities had and attended separate but unequal facilities, but the city has not had the violence associated with integration in other American cities, partly because blacks used legal facilities to redress their wrongs. For example, in 1955, after being refused entry to the Spa Beach and Pool at the city's Municipal Pier, local blacks filed a lawsuit, which they won and which finally allowed them to use the beach. Five years later, a Boycott Committee urged blacks to avoid white-owned department stores that refused to serve them food in their restaurants; it took less than a year for the lunch counters to be open to all.

In 1966, blacks entered the St. Petersburg City Hall and ripped down a demeaning mural that depicted black musicians happily strumming their banjos on a beach. The next year saw the publication of the city's first and only black-owned newspaper, *The Weekly Challenger*. Three years later, attorney C. Bette Wimbish became the first black to sit on the City Council. More recently the city's Interdenominational Ministerial Alliance, a group of 30 black ministers, has worked hard to better relations among the races. Many residents hope that a major league baseball team in the city would bring new business to local firms, including minorities. Today, St. Petersburg has some 46,623 blacks (20%) out of a total population of 238,629.

Further Reading:

Darryl Paulson, "Stay Out, The Water's Fine: Desegregating Municipal Swimming Facilities in St. Petersburg, Florida," *Tampa Bay History*, vol. 4, no. 2 (fall/winter 1982), pp. 6-19.

Among the places of importance to blacks is the **Enoch D. Davis Center** at 1111 18th Avenue South. This 18,000-square-foot multi-purpose center houses the James Weldon Johnson Branch Library, a large hall, three meeting rooms, classroom space, and office space for human service agencies serving the community. The building, which officials dedicated in 1981, honors Rev. Dr. Enoch D. Davis, a long-time activist and civic leader. Young Enoch Douglas Davis, who was born in Waynesboro, Georgia, came to St. Petersburg as a teenager in 1925. Five years later, he began his preaching and two years after that became pastor of Bethel Community Baptist Church, a position he held for more than 50 years. He was active in the desegregation efforts of Florida schools and in the establishment of equal opportunities for all.

Further Reading:

Barbara Fitzgerald and Tracie Reddick, "The Illusion of Inclusion," *The Tampa Tribune,* May 9, 1993, Nation, p. 1+; May 10, 1993, *Nation*, p. 1+.

Gibbs High School at 850 34th Street S. honors Jonathan C. Gibbs (1827-1874), the black secretary of state (1869-1872) under Governor Harrison Reed and later the state superintendent of public instruction in charge of Florida's schools. Jonathan Gibbs improved the state's school system, adopted standard textbooks, and established many schools for blacks. Gibbs High School became the first predominantly black institution to join the Florida High School Activities Association in 1965 and then won a state championship in basketball. When court-ordered integration of schools began to take effect in 1971, local officials considered closing Gibbs High School, but blacks protested and threatened to burn down the school rather than see it closed. It remained open. A former Gibbs principal, Emanuelle Stewart, in 1988 became the first black member of the Suncoasters, the committee that ran the Festival of States Parade in St. Petersburg; he also was the parade's first black grand marshal.

Further Reading:

Leedell W. Neyland. *Twelve Black Floridians*. Tallahassee: Florida Agricultural and Mechanical University Foundation, 1970, pp. 1-5.

Darryl Paulson and Milly St. Julien, "Desegregating Public Schools in Manatee and Pinellas Counties, 1954-71," *Tampa Bay History,* vol. 7, no. 1 (spring/summer 1985), pp. 30-41.

James A. Schnur, "Desegregation of Public Schools in Pinellas County, Florida," *Tampa Bay History,* vol. 13, no. 1 (spring/summer 1991), pp. 26-43.

In 1957, the Pinellas County Board of Public Instruction established **Gibbs Junior College** as the first two-year college created after a 1957 report of the Community College Council. The 1885 version of the state Constitution stated that "white and colored children shall not be taught in the same school, but that impartial provision shall be made for both." The problem with maintaining or establishing separate schools for whites and blacks in the mid-1950s was that it was illegal. The 1954 *Brown vs. Board of Education* decision in the U.S. Supreme Court outlawed segregation in public education.

Governor LeRoy Collins, who served as Florida's governor from 1955 until 1961 and who believed that much of the state was opposed to the integration of colleges, had his Community College Council plan to establish black junior colleges on the campuses of already existing black high schools. Doing so would provide immediate facilities and administrative and academic leadership until the new colleges could stand on their own. Also, the junior colleges could more easily recruit promising students among the nearby black populations of the black high schools. Sharing facilities with a high school meant that the 12 black junior colleges had to have their course offerings from 4 p.m. until 10 p.m., when the high school buildings were not being used. Governor Collins believed that the black colleges would eventually merge with the white junior colleges, at which point the developed facilities could return to the high schools.

In the fall of 1957, the first new black two-year college opened: Gibbs Junior College in St. Petersburg on the campus of Gibbs High School at 850 34th Street S. Some local officials thought that civil rights groups, bolstered by northerners determined to integrate Florida's schools, especially St. Petersburg Junior College, might stage demonstrations protesting the opening of a black college, especially after the 1954 Supreme Court decision outlawing separate facilities for blacks, but those demonstrations did not materialize, possibly because local blacks had mixed feelings about whether the integration of higher education should take place immediately. The reputations of black colleges was high in that such institutions afforded blacks the opportunity of gaining access to four-year schools and of learning marketable trades and skills.

Dr. John W. Rembert, the only president of Gibbs, opened up the school that fall of 1957 and was pleasantly surprised when over 200 students enrolled, 100 more than expected. Sharing facilities with Gibbs High School did not discourage even more students from applying; by mid-year the college had over 400 students and 11 faculty members. When Governor Collins went to St. Petersburg in 1958 to dedicate the first permanent building of the new college, one of the students was a Korean War veteran by the name of Walter Lee Smith. That young man became the first president of the Gibbs Junior College student body, later Provost of Hillsborough Community College in Tampa, President of Roxbury Community College in Boston, Massachusetts, and President of his undergraduate university, Florida A&M University in Tallahassee.

The enrollment figures for Gibbs, which included students enrolled in the college parallel programs as well as the vocational programs, were as follows:

1957-1958: 245 students | **1958-1959: 573 students**
1959-1960: 684 students | **1960-1961: 699 students**
1961-1962: 673 students | **1962-1963: 703 students**
1963-1964: 801 students | **1964-1965: 887 students**

Gibbs Junior College and 11 other such schools provided many blacks equal access to higher educational opportunities. When the black college merged with St. Petersburg Junior College in the 1964-65 school year, officials changed the name of Gibbs to The Gibbs Campus of St. Petersburg Junior College and later to the Skyway Campus. By the time the 12 black junior colleges in Florida began to be consolidated with the nearby white junior colleges in the mid-1960s, they had an enrollment of over 9,000 students. By the mid-1960s, integration was taking place in all of Florida's universities, which allowed blacks to attend universities in addition to Florida A&M University, and by 1966, two years after the 1964 Civil Rights Act, all 12 black junior colleges were gone, having been consolidated with the white schools.

Further Reading:

Portia L. Taylor. *Community College Education for Black Students, A Case Study*. Dissertation. Gainesville: University of Florida, 1986.

Arthur O. White, "The Desegregation of Florida's Public Junior Colleges, 1954-1977," *Integrated Education*, vol. 16, no. 3 (May-June 1978), pp. 31-36.

Chapter 60

Sanford

This town on the St. Johns River began during the Indian wars as a settlement around a military encampment, Camp Monroe. The site changed its name to Fort Mellon, then Mellonville, and finally Sanford after its developer, General Henry Sanford. Long before General Sanford came to the area, the Legislative Council had established Mosquito County from St. Johns County in 1824, three years after the U.S. gained control of Florida from Spain. In those early days, several blacks lived in the area as slaves of either the white settlers or of the Indians. As federal forces defeated the Indians, more and more settlers moved into central Florida. In 1860, General Sanford visited the area and liked it so much that he made plans to return. In 1870, this former minister to Belgium laid out the town that would later honor him in its name. After laying out a 100-acre orange grove and finding that labor was scarce in the area, he brought in from Madison 60 black workers for clearing and tilling the land; local white people, incensed at his attempt to bring in blacks to what they considered "white man's country," drove them out with gunfire.

When he later brought in more black workers, he established west of Mellonville the black neighborhood of Georgetown, where his workers lived. Protected from further acts of overt violence and separated from the rest of the town by a body of water and by discrimination, Georgetown developed on its own. The devastating fire of 1887 and the freezes of 1894-1895 slowed down the growth of Sanford, but farmers began growing celery, making the town "Celery Capital of the United States" in the early 1900s. Some of the black workers who worked in the celery fields lived in a settlement called Cameron City. Today Sanford has 9,225 blacks (29%) out of a total population of 32,387.

Further Reading:

Altermese Smith Bentley. *Georgetown: The History of a Black Neighborhood.* Sanford?: Altermese Smith Bentley, 1989.

Margaret Sprout Green. *Lake Mary's Beginnings and the Roaring Twenties in Lake Mary and Sanford, Florida.* Chuluota, Fl.: Mickler House Publishers, 1986.

John Paul Jones, "City on the St. Johns: Why They All Love Sanford," *North Florida Living,* May 1986, pp. 6-13.

Peter Schaal. *Sanford As I Knew It, 1912-1935.* Orlando?: 1970.

As was true throughout Florida, Sanford's schools for blacks suffered from the deprivations of segregation. The school year for black students was shorter than that for white students, and parents had to buy books and supplies for their children. The first school for blacks in the Georgetown area, the Georgetown School, was at the northeast corner of Seventh Street and Cypress Avenue; its principal was Mr. McLester, and his assistant was Miss Hampton. Later Mr. Reed and then Mr. J.N. Crooms served as principal. Construction on the school was finished in 1887.

Two other schools in Sanford should be mentioned here. **Hopper Academy** at 1111 South Pine Avenue, was built between 1900 and 1910 on land that local white people donated. Originally an elementary school, it became Sanford High school for black students when it moved to a new site, but was later replaced by Crooms Academy. The **Bookertown School** at 4615 Gilbert Street was established in 1926 by the Sanford Development Co.; black farm workers prob-

Hopper Academy served the educational needs of many black students. Credit: Kevin M. McCarthy

ably lived in Bookertown from 1885 on and may have had children attending school in 1889. The Bookertown School is now a community center.

The **St. James African Methodist Episcopal Church** at 819 Cypress Avenue traces its beginnings to 1867, when a group of Christians began having prayer services in an old house on Mellonville Avenue. Several years later the group bought some land and moved their services to the new site. Their first pastor, Rev. S.H. Coleman, helped construct at Ninth Street and Cypress Avenue a small, frame church, St. James Mission, and the church became part of the East Florida Annual Conference in 1880. The church's next pastor, Rev. T.T. Gaines, joined the church to the newly formed South Florida Conference and built a larger church. Under the pastorate of Rev. W.H. Brown the congregation built the new, red-brick building in 1913. During the subsequent pastorates of R.E. Harton, G.J. Oates, Jr., C.E. Standifer, R.A. Thigpen, and K.D. White, Jr., the congregation grew to several hundred. Another early black church was **St. Paul Missionary Baptist Church**, founded in 1878. **Zion Hope Missionary Baptist**, organized on Mellonville Avenue in 1888, was moved from a bush arbor to Fifth Street and Locust Avenue and finally to its present site at Eighth and Orange Avenue. **Trinity Methodist Church**, which used to be Trinity Methodist Episcopal, was founded in 1880. **St. John Missionary Baptist Church** at 920 Cypress Avenue dates from 1888. Also Lawrence Williams, Terrell Johnson, and Richard McPherson founded in Georgetown a mutual-aid society, The Friendship and Union, to support members in sickness and to help families in case of death.

The **John M. Hurston House** at 621 E. 6th Street, which is today a private residence, was the home in the early 1900s of the father of famed writer, Zora Neale Hurston. Another private residence, at 611 Locust Avenue, was the home of Dr. George H. Starke, a black doctor who treated the sick of Sanford, both black and white, for 51 years. Shortly after he opened his practice in Sanford in 1927, Harvard University accepted him as only one of four black doctors for a residency at Massachusetts General Hospital in Boston. He returned to Sanford in 1933 and practiced medicine until he died at the age of 80. He was the first black doctor to become a member of the Florida Medical Association and the Seminole County Medical Association and the second in the American Medical Association. In 1977, city officials named a park and picnic area on Fifth Street after him.

Finally, one blemish in the town's baseball history was the poor reception given to Jackie Robinson as the first black player in major league baseball. Arthur Ashe, Jr., reported that in 1946 Branch Rickey, the president of the Brooklyn Dodgers and the man who signed Robinson to play in the majors, "moved the entire Dodger pre-season camp from Sanford, Florida, to Daytona Beach due to the oppressive conditions of Sanford." (p. 10)

Further Reading:

Arthur R. Ashe, Jr. *A Hard Road to Glory: A History of the African-American Athlete Since 1946*. New York: Warner Books, Inc., 1988.

Jackie Robinson, "Jackie Robinson's First Spring Training," in *The American Sporting Experience*, edited by Steven A. Riess. West Point, N.Y.: Leisure Press, 1984, pp. 365-370. Excerpts from *Jackie Robinson: My Own Story* by Jackie Robinson and Wendell Smith. New York: Greenberg, 1948.

Chapter 61

Sanibel Island

Sanibel, which is 12 miles long and about three miles wide at its widest point, and Captiva, which is only five miles long and about half a mile wide at its widest, are barrier islands off the southwest coast of Florida. The Calusa Indians inhabited the islands in the 16th century and resisted the Spanish explorers seeking gold and converts. After the Spanish weapons and diseases killed off the Calusas, pirates inhabited the islands as did, eventually, lighthouse keepers at the lighthouse at Point Ybel on Sanibel, farmers, fishermen, visitors, and those who liked isolation. The building of a bridge and causeway to the mainland in 1963 brought in many more settlers and thousands of visitors, effectively changing the islands forever and driving up land values. Sanibel may combine in its name the meanings of health and beauty.

A few black families settled on the islands in the early part of this century, but work was hard to come by. Men like Isaiah Gavin, part of the first black family on Sanibel, worked for a dollar a day when he could find work. The isolation meant no electricity and no running water, but many preferred the peace and quiet of the islands. The families would fish in the Gulf, farm tomatoes, squash, and eggplant, and then hunt a rabbit or pheasant for dinner.

When hurricanes like the 1926 storm disrupted the peaceful life and flooded the island with salt water and ruined much of the farmland, some of the blacks and whites moved to the mainland where they could more easily earn a living.

When the departure of many whites after the 1926 storm left their Baptist church vacant, James Johnson, a farmer and the owner of the land on which the church stood, offered it in 1927 to the remaining black families for their first school, which became **Sanibel Colored School**. Two years later, Lee County bought the building, which had been built around 1909, from the Florida Baptist Convention for $1,500. The first principal was Miss Angelita Stafford Swain George, and Miss Hazel Hammond was a teacher who taught there until 1933. Other teachers included Helen V. Goodman and Agnes Thompson (1933-1934), Ernestine Mims (1934-1935), Wardell Salters, and Lossie Pearson (1947-1948). Although closed from 1940 until 1946 for World War II, when the black children may have been bused to Fort Myers, the building was used by the black children until 1963, when officials opened up Sanibel Elementary, the first integrated school in Lee County. Officials named the Sanibel Colored School a historic landmark in 1991, a designation that will protect the building from relocation or alteration without city approval. Today the Schoolhouse Gallery at 520 Tarpon Bay Road, which has housed an art gallery since 1973, occupies that site.

Directions:

To reach the old school building, turn west on Periwinkle Way just after crossing the toll bridge from the mainland to Sanibel. Periwinkle runs into Tarpon Bay Road, and the school is just to the left of the intersection, north of W. Gulf Drive, and south of Sanibel Captiva Road.

Further Reading:

Donald O. Stone and Beth W. Carter. *The First 100 Years: Lee County Public Schools, 1887-1987*. Fort Myers: School Board of Lee County, 1987.

Today Sanibel has only 60 blacks (1%) out of a total population of 5,468. The high cost of living, especially as high-rises and condominiums spread over the island, has kept many away. Among the blacks are the Gavins, the Jordans, the Prestons, and the Walkers, many of whom are descended from the original pioneer black families.

Further Reading:

Elinore Mayer Dormer. *The Sea Shell Islands: A History of Sanibel and Captiva.* Tallahassee: Rose Printing Company, 1979.

Linda Firestone & Whit Morse. *Sanibel & Captiva: A Visitor's Guide to Florida's Enchanting Islands.* Richmond, Va.: Good Life Publications, 1976.

Florence Fritz. *The Unknown Story of Sanibel and Captiva (Ybel y Cautivo).* Parsons, West Va.: no publ., 1974.

Mary Ann Husty, "Saving Sanibel's Sights," *News-Press* [Fort Myers], South Lee Sun edition, July 24, 1991, pp. 1-2.

Ray Weiss, "One Man Considers His Island Paradise" [about the Gavin family, the first black family on Sanibel], *Fort Myers News Press,* December 2, 1980.

Chapter 62

Sarasota

For many centuries before the white man came to Sarasota, Indian tribes like the Timucuans and Calusas lived there. White men did not come into the area to settle until around 1842. After the Civil War ended in 1865, more and more people moved there, including colonists from Scotland. The name of Sarasota may go back to the Spanish for "a place for dancing" or to the name of de Soto's daughter or to some other unknown origin. The railroad, which black workers helped build, was completed in 1903, after which more people came to stay. John Ringling arrived in 1911 and later brought the circus and built a beautiful museum of art, which opened in 1931. The city grew rapidly and has continued to attract new residents because of its setting, cultural attractions, and mild climate. Today Sarasota has 8,167 blacks (16%) out of a total population of 50,978.

The first black settler in the area was Lewis (or Louis) Colson, who helped in surveying the town of Sarasota in the late 1800s and who worked as a fisherman, land owner, and minister. More black families followed, and in 1899 Lewis and Irene Colson organized the Bethlehem Baptist Church, in which Reverend Lewis Colson ministered to the people until around 1918. Later other residents, including F.H.

Haynes, C.H. Murphy, Campbell Mitchell, and Leonard Reid, organized the A.M.E. Church.

Among the Colson children who grew up in Sarasota and prospered were John H. (or J. Hamilton or Hamp), who was a drayman and laborer; James, a waiter and laborer; David, a cement worker; Ida, a domestic worker; and Toney (or Tony), a fish dealer who owned and operated Colson Fish Market at 423 North Lemon. Colson Avenue between U.S. 301 and Tuttle Avenue east of Sarasota honors Lewis Colson; he and his wife, Irene, are buried in Rosemary Cemetery at 833 Central Avenue.

In the first quarter of this century, more and more black workers came to Sarasota from the Carolinas and Georgia to work in the booming construction business and on Charles Ringling's causeway and ten-story hotel. A historical marker on Central Avenue at 6th Street commemorates the first black community in Sarasota that once included Black Bottom (later known as **Overtown**), which had been bounded roughly on the north and south by Tenth and Fifth streets and on the west and east by U.S. 41 and Orange Avenue. That black community, which gradually expanded into the Newtown area south of the Whitfield Estates subdivision, had many small shops, social facilities, and religious centers such as its first house of worship — Bethlehem Baptist Church. Among the early black residents were John and Sally Mays, Willis and Sophia (or Sophie) Washington, Thomas Henry "Mott" and Josie Washington (who operated the Josie Grocery Store at 236 12th Street), Leonard and Eddye Reid (both of whom helped found the city's second oldest black church: Payne Chapel A.M.E. Methodist; Leonard Reid Avenue one block east of U.S. 301 and north of 27th Street honors him), Wright and Emma Bush (both of whom lived at 1723 27th Street), and Edward and Rose Carmichael (both of whom owned and operated the Royal Palm Pressing Club on 12th Street; Carmichael Avenue east of U.S. 301 and south of 27th Street honors the family).

Further Reading:

Bernice Brooks Bergen. *Sarasota Times Past.* Miami: Valiant Press, 1993, esp. p. 24 [about the A.M.E. Payne Chapel on the corner of Fifth and Central Avenue] and 29 [about turpentine camps].

Karl H. Grismer. *The Story of Sarasota.* Sarasota: M.E. Russell, 1946.

Del Marth. *Yesterday's Sarasota, Including Sarasota County.* Miami: Seemann, 1973.

Janet Snyder Matthews. *Edge of Wilderness: A Settlement History of Manatee River and Sarasota Bay, 1528-1885.* Tulsa, Okla.: Caprine Press, 1983.

Before residents could establish a black school, Josie Washington taught students in her home, but then in 1912 Wright Bush, Henry Clark, Elbert Clark, J.P. Carter, Campbell Mitchell, John Mays, John Woods, Ed Carmichael, and J.H. Glover established a public school, where Emma Booker later served as principal for many years. Ms. Booker had begun teaching blacks in Sarasota public schools in 1910, and eight years later became principal of Sarasota Grammar School, which held its classes in rented halls. For 20 years she attended college during the summers and finally earned her bachelor's degree in 1937.

Meanwhile the Julius Rosenwald Fund provided money for the building of a school, which opened in 1924-1925 with eight grades, at present-day Seventh Street and Lemon Avenue; many referred to it as the Rosenwald School, but officials later renamed it **Booker Grammar School** in honor of Sarasota's early black educator. Later under the guidance of principal J.R. Dixon, the school added more grades, and the first senior class of **Booker High School** graduated in 1935. In 1939, Booker High School and the Rosenwald building were relocated to a site near the present school and adjoining an elementary school. By the late 1940s, under the guidance of principal Roland Rogers, the Booker Grammar School was moved to its present site and the School Board of Sarasota County consolidated schools on the Newtown campus. The school received official accreditation and new buildings were constructed. In 1988, to commemorate Emma

Booker High School has modern facilities today. Credit: Kevin M. McCarthy

Booker the Sarasota County Historical Commission erected a plaque in her honor outside the Booker School on Orange Avenue at 35th Street north of Dr. Martin Luther King, Jr., Way and east of Indian Beach.

One of the school's teachers who went on to do much for black education in several Florida sites was Gilbert Porter. He later served as teaching principal at Tivoli High School in DeFuniak Springs, as the principal of Tallahassee's Lincoln High, as the executive secretary of the Florida State Teachers Association (FSTA, a black teachers' organization), and as special assistant to the deputy superintendent in Dade County. **Gilbert Porter Elementary School** at 15851 S.W. 112 Street in Miami honors him. (For more about him see Tallahassee below.) While he worked for $50 a month as a science teacher and coach at Booker High School in Sarasota, the school lasted only five-and-a-half months a year and then had to close because it had no money. As was true of other schools for black children in Florida, the Sarasota schools usually had inadequate supplies, a school term lasting less than the nine months of the white schools, and teacher salaries that lagged behind those of white teachers. The dedication of the teachers to further the education of their pupils despite the poor facilities did much to encourage youngsters to do well in school. Porter was one of the first blacks in the state to earn a Ph.D. and to receive a Rockefeller Foundation Fellowship as a public school administrator. He is also the author with Leedell W. Neyland of *The History of the Florida State Teachers Association* (Washington: National Education Association, 1977).

Further Reading:

Annie M. McElroy. *But Your World and My World: The Struggle For Survival: A Partial History of Blacks in Sarasota County, 1884-1986.* Sarasota: Black South Press, 1986.

Chapter 63

Sebastian

Although Indians lived in the area for hundreds of years, whites did not settle there until the 19th century, especially after federal forces had defeated the Indians in a series of battles throughout Florida. The settlement became an important fishing and trading center that used the river steamers to take products to and from other towns. A cut through the barrier island on the Indian River to the ocean increased the prosperity of the area, but workers had to dredge it several times to keep it open. The town was called New Haven in 1882, but changed to Sebastian in 1884 because it was near the St. Sebastian River, which itself was named by Spanish explorers in honor of St. Sebastian.

Black people moved to the area in the 19th century, although census records seemed to ignore many of them. The 1885 Florida State Census, for example, showed only one black in the area, R. Hamilton, a laborer. When Henry Flagler's Florida East Coast Railroad came to the Roseland-Sebastian area in 1893, many black men arrived to lay the tracks and stayed behind to maintain the line. They brought their wives, who worked as domestics and launderers for white families and as vegetable pickers.

When more and more black people settled in the area, they established the **Macedonia Baptist Church**, which stood for many years on Bob Circle off Main Street behind today's post office west of U.S. 1. Murray E. and Sarah Braddock Hall, a white family, donated the land for the church in 1907; Mose M. Hill, Sebrose P. Norris, and Syd Norris served as trustees of what was first called the Colored Baptist Church of Sebastian, which was built in 1908. The Sebastian Methodist Church donated to the new church benches and also a bell which had once called slaves in from the fields in Louisiana. The congregation, which grew so large that its members often had to stand outside the little church and lean into the open windows to take part in the service, named the church the Macedonia Baptist Church. The pastors of the church included reverends Thomas, Jones, Stagles, Sheddick, and Matthis. This historical church was moved to Gifford in 1994 to be preserved as a museum and educational building serving as a memorial to Dr. Martin Luther King, Jr.

Further Reading:

Adam Chrzan, "Woman Claims Church," *Vero Beach Press Journal*, January 9, 1994, p. 4.

Some of the local blacks are buried in the **Fellsmere Brookside Cemetery**, which is off Fellsmere Road (S.R. 512) and S.R. 510 just east of I-95. This cemetery, which some people incorrectly refer to as Old Sebastian Cemetery, has the black gravestones at the back over a small bridge at the western edge.

Further Reading:

Walter R. Hellier. *Indian River, Florida's Treasure Coast*. Coconut Grove: Hurricane House Publishers, 1965.

Charlotte Lockwood. *Florida's Historic Indian River County*. Vero Beach: MediaTronics, 1975.

More Tales of Sebastian. Sebastian: Sebastian River Area Historical Society, 1992.

Anna Pearl Leonard Newman, compiler. *Stories of Early Life Along Beautiful Indian River*. Stuart: Printed by Stuart Daily News, 1953.

Sebastian

Arline Westfahl, "Our Black Residents," in *Tales of Sebastian*. Sebastian: Sebastian River Area Historical Society, 1990, pp. 111-118.

Chapter 64

Sebring

This town in south Florida is mentioned here because southwest of Sebring on U.S. 27 and 2.5 miles south of U.S. 17 is the **Medal of Honor Park**, which commemorates each Florida winner of the Congressional Medal of Honor with a tree and a plaque listing his birth and death dates. Two of the men so honored with the Medal, the highest honor our nation can award a soldier, are black: Clifford Chester Sims and Robert H. Jenkins, Jr.

Sims (1942-1968) was born in Port St. Joe, Florida, graduated from Washington High School, joined the U.S. Army, and went to fight in Vietnam in 1967. In February 1968, he was leading his squad of soldiers when they encountered a booby trap that was about to explode. When he realized the danger they were in, Sims called out a warning to his men and threw himself onto the bomb in order to protect the others. By taking the full force of the exploding bomb, Sims gave up his life that the others might be saved. He is buried in Barrancas National Cemetery in Pensacola, Florida.

Jenkins (1948-1969) was born in Interlachen, Florida, graduated from Palatka Central Academy, joined the U.S. Marines, and was assigned to Vietnam. In March 1969, while he was serving as a machine gunner in that war, an enemy soldier threw a hand grenade into the bunker where he and his fellow Marines were stationed. At that moment, Jenkins took hold of another Marine, pushed him to the ground, and threw himself on top of the man to protect him from the exploding hand grenade. The tremendous force of the explosion wounded Jenkins so badly that he died soon after. He is buried in Sister Spring Cemetery in Interlachen, Florida. (For more about him see Palatka above.)

Further Reading:

Maxine D. Jones and Kevin M. McCarthy. *African Americans in Florida.* Sarasota: Pineapple Press, 1993, pp. 116-117.

Chapter 65

Sumatra

Six miles southwest of Sumatra and 15 miles from the Gulf of Mexico on the Apalachicola River is **Fort Gadsden State Park**. The first fort on this site dates back to 1814, when the British built a fortification on the east bank of the Apalachicola River at a place called Prospect Bluff to encourage the Seminole Indians to ally themselves with England against the United States in the War of 1812. Part of the force that the British raised for an attack on New Orleans consisted of about 170 blacks recruited from runaway slaves and those whom the British had freed in Pensacola.

After the defeat of the British and their withdrawal from the fort, a large group of blacks and their Choctaw allies remained behind in the facility, which came to be known as "The Negro Fort." Under the leadership of a man named Garcon or Garcia, the blacks established farms along the river and raised corn. Located on the Apalachicola River, the fort assumed a strategic importance as the natural highway into southern Alabama and Georgia, especially because so few good roads existed in the region at that time. **The Negro Fort**, situated high on a steep hill overlooking the river and protected from a land attack by a swamp at its back and fortified with artillery the British left behind, effectively controlled commerce up and down the river at that point.

Because of its threat to commerce on the river, General Andrew Jackson ordered his troops to destroy it.

When residents of the Indian villages along the river heard of the approaching soldiers, they took refuge in the fort. Lieutenant Colonel Duncan Clinch led a group of 116 soldiers and 150 friendly Creek Indians down the river where he rendezvoused with two gunboats sent up from Apalachicola and made plans to attack the fort and force its black commandant and his 300 men, women, and children to surrender. In late July 1816, the boats moved into position, and one of them fired a cannon ball which landed directly in the fort's powder magazine. The ensuing blast destroyed the fort, killing 207 of the 334 men, women, and children and maiming the rest.

Two years later, General Jackson led a band of soldiers down the Apalachicola and had Lieutenant James Gadsden of the Engineer Corps build a new fort on Prospect Bluff as a supply depot or base. The fort, which Jackson named Fort Gadsden in honor of the engineer, later played a minor role in the Civil War and faded into obscurity until the Florida Park Service developed Fort Gadsden State Park in 1961.

Further Reading:

Joseph Becton, "Old Hickory and the Negro Fort," *Pensacola History Illustrated*, vol. 2, no. 2 (fall 1986), pp. 25-32.

Mark F. Boyd, "Events at Prospect Bluff on the Apalachicola River, 1808-1818," *Florida Historical Quarterly*, vol. 16 (October 1937), pp. 55-96.

James W. Covington, "The Negro Fort," *Gulf Coast Historical Review*, vol. 5, no. 2 (spring 1990), pp. 78-91.

Robert B. Roberts. *Encyclopedia of Historic Forts*. New York: Macmillan, 1988, pp. 168-169.

Chapter 66

Tallahassee

The name of Tallahassee goes back to an Apalachee Indian word meaning "old fields" or "abandoned villages." Spanish adventurers like Panfilo de Narváez and Hernando de Soto explored the area in the 16th century, but white settlers, for example Catholic missionaries, did not move there to live until the next century. Farmers began establishing farms in the early 18th century, but the real impetus to establish a town in the vicinity came with the decree of the Legislative Council to locate the capital of the territory midway between Pensacola and St. Augustine in the 1820s. The town and surrounding Leon County grew steadily over the next century despite an outbreak of yellow fever in 1841 and a disastrous fire two years later.

During the Civil War, units from Tallahassee took part in the nearby Battle of Natural Bridge and successfully defended the city from the Union soldiers, many of whom were black. The war ended for the city in 1865 when Union troops raised the stars and stripes on May 20th, a day that local blacks celebrated as their day of emancipation for years to come. The hopes that blacks had during the Reconstruction period dissipated as white legislators slowly eroded the rights of the blacks and effectively disenfranchised them. Many blacks had to become tenant farmers on cotton and corn plantations, a situation that kept them in poverty for decades. From 1840 through 1940, blacks outnumbered whites in the area, but today blacks make up 29% of the total population of 124,773, numbering 36,276. Blacks have slowly achieved economic and political gains this century, although it took a black boycott in 1956-1957 against the city's segregated transit system, as well as sit-ins in the 1960s to integrate local stores.

Further Reading:

Fenton Garnett Davis Avant. *My Tallahassee,* edited by David A. Avant, Jr. Tallahassee: L'Avant Studios, 1983.

Hampton Dunn. *Yesterday's Tallahassee.* Miami: Seemann, 1974.

Mary Louise Ellis and William Warren Rogers. *Favored Land: Tallahassee. A History of Tallahassee and Leon County.* Norfolk, Va.: Donning, 1988.

Mary Louise Ellis and William Warren Rogers. *Tallahassee & Leon County: A History and Bibliography.* Tallahassee: Historic Tallahassee Preservation Board, Florida Dept. of State, 1986.

Bertram H. Groene. *Ante-Bellum Tallahassee.* Tallahassee: Florida Heritage Foundation, 1971.

Joan Perry Morris and Lee H. Warner, editors. *The Photographs of Alvan S. Harper, Tallahassee, 1885-1910.* Tallahassee: University Presses of Florida, 1983.

Glenda A. Rabby, "Out of the Past: The Civil Rights Movement in Tallahassee, Florida," Ph.D. dissertation, The Florida State University, 1984.

Before the Civil War, black Methodists in the South worshipped at white churches, but after the war the black members either formed Colored (later renamed Christian) Methodist churches under the guidance of the old white organizations or followed the African Methodist Episcopal or African Methodist Episcopal Zion movements. The latter movement began in the North apart from any white sponsorship. An example of a church in this movement in Tallahassee is **Bethel A.M.E. Church** at 206 West Virginia Street; Rev. William G. Stewart organized this church in 1865.

The **St. James Christian Methodist Episcopal Church** at 104 N. Bronough Street, at the corner of Bronough Street and

Park Avenue, is the oldest black church still standing in Tallahassee. The black members of the Methodist Episcopal Church bought the present-day site from Trinity Methodist Church in 1853, but did not gain title to the property until they formed a separate organization, St. James C.M.E., in 1868. White bishops at Jackson, Tennessee, consecrated the first black bishops of the Colored Methodist Episcopal Church in 1870. Three years later St. James C.M.E. Church hosted the first session of the Florida Conference of the C.M.E. Church in America, followed by another state conference there four years later; Rev. James Smith was the minister during that time.

St. James may also have been the first public school for black children of the city; Robert Meacham and Henry Matthews taught many blacks there, as did Mrs. Lydia Smith much later. The congregation built the present building in 1899 on a site that had two earlier structures. During the Civil War the church served as a hospital for soldiers wounded in the Battle of Olustee and during Reconstruction as a school for black children. In 1948, the congregation remodeled the 1899 structure into the present Gothic Revival design.

A prominent member of the congregation was John Gilmore Riley (1857-1954), a successful black businessman, prominent civic leader, and the long-time principal of Lincoln High School. From an early age, he chose to be an educator, a goal that culminated in his becoming principal of Lincoln Academy, the first local school for blacks. Riley lived at 419 East Jefferson Street in a house where his heirs lived until 1973, when the city bought the property and five years before officials placed it on the National Register of Historic Places.

Lincoln High School, of which John Riley was principal, was established as Lincoln Academy by the Freedmen's Bureau in 1869 as one of two schools in Florida that could provide advanced instruction to black students. The Chamber of Commerce today occupies the site of the original school. The first staff consisted of one man and one woman, both white, but after a few years, the first black teacher, John G. Riley, began teaching there. When fire destroyed the original structure in 1872, school officials moved it to a temporary site on Copeland Street, before building a permanent home on the corner of West Brevard and Macomb streets. The principals after John Riley included T.B. Dansby, W. Dabney, Noah Griffin, Cecil H. Walker, Gilbert Porter, James Abner, R. Frank Nims, and Freeman D. Lawrence. After 1967, during the initial stages of school integration, the Lincoln High School facility was not used.

One of those principals, Gilbert Porter, did much for black education in several Florida sites. Born in Kansas in 1909, he went on to become a science teacher at Booker High in Sarasota, in 1933 the teaching principal at Tivoli High School in DeFuniak Springs, in 1937 the principal of Tallahassee's Lincoln High, and in 1954 the executive secretary of the Florida State Teachers Association (FSTA), a black teachers' organization which merged with the Florida Education Association in 1966; in that role with the FSTA Porter worked hard against the racial firing of black teachers. In 1965, he went to Dade County to be special assistant to the deputy superintendent, E.L. Whigham. **Gilbert Porter Elementary School** at 15851 S.W. 112 Street in Miami honors him. (For more about him see Sarasota above.)

Further Reading:

Bea L. Hines, "Gilbert Porter: 'Tom' or Pioneer?" *The Miami Herald,* December 3, 1978, p. 11G.

The **First Presbyterian Church** at 102 North Adams is the only Tallahassee church from territorial days that is still standing and is the city's oldest building for public meetings that is still being used. The ties between Presbyterianism and Florida government go back to at least 1826, five years after the U.S. took over Florida from Spain, when Presbyterian minister Rev. Henry White became chaplain to the Legislative Council. Organized in 1832, the Presbyterian congregation began the present building in 1835 and finished it three years later. They financed the $13,371 church by the sale of 40 of the 44 pews for a total of $12,500. In the early days, the slaves, who were allowed to be members but had to sit apart from their masters, sat in the north gallery. Prominent early families that belonged to the church included the Butlers, Gambles, Perkins, Shines, Wards, and Wilsons. In 1932, during the centennial of the church, some members argued for a larger building to house the increased congregation, but fortunately they agreed to keep the old building and renovate it.

Another important black site is **Bethel Missionary Baptist Church** at 224 N. Martin Luther King Jr. Boulevard. Founded by Rev. James Paige, an ex-slave from Virginia and the first ordained black Baptist minister of Florida, it had its beginnings at Bel Aire (or Bellaire) one mile south of Tallahassee when the minister and his wife, Elizabeth, founded the Bethlehem Baptist Church. When many of those 200 members moved to Tallahassee in 1870, the new congregation called itself the Bethel Missionary Baptist Church. Because whites usually controlled the black schools, this and other churches became the meeting place for black community leaders, fraternal organizations, and civic groups. When the congregation finally outgrew its church building, they built a new one in 1976. Other pastors followed Rev. Paige: Horace C. Bailey, J.B. Hankerson, J.P. West, A.L. Pettis, C.T. Stamps, Harry Jones, Jerome B. Harris, William Burns, and Charles Kenzie Steele.

The last-mentioned pastor, Rev. Steele (1914-1980), became an important civil rights activist at a time when many people looked to him for leadership. Born in West Virginia as the son of a coal miner father, Charles decided at an early age to become a minister. After graduating in 1938 from Morehouse College in Atlanta, Georgia, he became a minister at a baptist church in Montgomery, Alabama. In 1951, he moved with his family to Tallahassee, where he became a minister at the Bethel Missionary Baptist Church. He also became president of the local chapter of the National Association for the Advancement of Colored People (NAACP), president of the Inter-Civic Council, and charter member and first vice-president of the Southern Christian Leadership Conference (SCLC).

In 1956, he helped lead a boycott, begun by students at Florida Agricultural and Mechanical University (FAMU), against the local bus company that practiced segregation. He kept the boycott nonviolent despite having his house attacked by the Ku Klux Klan. The year-long bus boycott succeeded in integrating the bus system, but Rev. Steele continued fighting for the complete integration of hotels, restaurants, and movie theaters in the city. The **C.K. Steele Bus Terminal** with a statue and marker at 111 West Tennessee Street commemorates this great leader.

Further Reading:

Gregory B. Padgett, "C.K. Steele and the Tallahassee Bus Boycott," M.A. Thesis, The Florida State University, 1977.

Charles U. Smith. *The Civil Rights Movement in Florida and the United States.* Tallahassee: Father and Son Publishing, 1989.

Charles U. Smith and Lewis M. Killian. *The Tallahassee Bus Protest.* New York: Anti-Defamation League of B'nai B'rith, 1958.

One of the important educational institutions of the city and the whole state is **Florida Agricultural & Mechanical University** (FAMU), a multiracial school that has given the state and the nation many important black leaders. This oldest historically black university in Florida, which is on South Adams Street, had its beginnings in 1887, when the Florida Legislature established in the city the State Normal College for Colored Students in order to train black teachers for schools throughout Florida. Beginning with just 15 students that first year, today it has over 9,000 students and over 450 full-time faculty. In 1909, the school became a four-year college with a new name, Florida Agricultural and Mechanical College, and, in 1953, Florida A & M University and a member of the state university system. Frederick S. Humphries, president since 1985 and the winner of many national honors, has attracted many outstanding faculty and students to the school, including more National Achievement Scholars than any other university.

Among the buildings on campus is the **Black Archives Research Center and Museum** in the Carnegie Library Building, the oldest building on campus and one that attracts over 100,000 people a year to its exhibits, which include tribal masks, African artifacts, and slave irons. Research facilities, a repository of manuscripts, and an oral history laboratory provide scholars with materials for documenting the history of blacks in the United States, especially Florida. Open weekdays, 9 a.m. - 4 p.m. The library, built in 1907 in the Neo-Classical style and now on the National Register of Historic Places, was the first Carnegie Library built at a black land-grant college. From 1908 to 1944 the building housed the offices of college presidents N.B. Young and J.R.E. Lee. The building is in the middle of campus northeast of Coleman Library and just south of Gamble Street.

Further Reading:

Catherine Stengel, "Racism on Display" [about the Black Archives Research Center and its curator, James Eaton], *The Tampa Tribune*, February 9, 1993, BayLife, pp. 1, 5.

On the campus on South Adams Street is the **Gibbs Cottage**, constructed in 1894 and used as a home by Thomas Van Renssalaer Gibbs, a member of the Florida Legislature who introduced in 1887 the bill that established what would become the university.

Further Reading:

Wyatt Blassingame. *Jake Gaither: Winning Coach*. Champaign, Ill.: Garrard Publishing Co., 1969. This is a biography of one of the school's famous football coaches.

Coleman Memorial Library at FAMU is a center of the beautiful campus. Credit: Florida State Archives

Leedell W. Neyland & John W. Riley. *The History of Florida Agricultural and Mechanical University*. Gainesville: University of Florida Press, 1963.

The **Knott House** at 301 East Park Avenue, which was built around 1843, was owned by the Thomas and Catherine Hagner family through the 1880s and is one of the few remaining structures in the city dating back to the Territorial Period (1821-1845). In 1865, the Commander of the Union troops in Tallahassee, General Edward McCook, used the house as his official headquarters and residence. On May 20 of that year, he reissued President Abraham Lincoln's Emancipation Proclamation from the house's front steps in order to inform the former slaves, many of whom did not realize that they were already free. As a result of that action by General McCook, blacks in Leon County celebrate May 20 as Proclamation Day. Today the house-museum, called "The House That Rhymes" because owner Luella Knott wrote poems about her house and possessions, belongs to the state and has exhibits that illustrate the history of Tallahassee and Leon County.

The **Union Bank Building** at the corner of Apalachee Parkway and Calhoun Street dates back to 1841, thus making it the state's oldest bank building. It originally stood on South Adams Street and served as a bank for territorial planters. In those early days the bank took slaves as collateral for loans. When the borrowers could not repay the loans, the bank sold the slaves to recover its money. When the bank, which later failed because of poor management, reopened under federal supervision as the Freedman's Bank for newly freed slaves, it also had poor management and failed, causing many blacks to lose whatever savings they had accumulated in the bank. The building later was used as a church, a beauty parlor, city offices, and a dental laboratory. A black shoemaker, Willis Jiles, Sr., rented the building in the 1920s and trained many workers to make and repair shoes. In 1970, Mrs. T. Aubrey Morse bought the building from the First Baptist Church and later donated it to the state, which moved it to its present site east of the Old Capitol in 1971. In 1984, after a complete restoration, the bank opened to the public as a museum of Florida history site. The bank is open to the public Tuesday through Friday, 10 a.m. to 1 p.m., and on weekends from 1 to 4 p.m. Phone: (904) 487-3803. Free admission.

Further Reading:

Kathryn T. Abbey, "The Union Bank of Tallahassee," *The Florida Historical Quarterly*, vol. 15, no. 4 (April 1937), pp. 207-231.

R.C. Morgan-Wilde, "They Gathered Together" [about the family reunion of the Jiles family at the former shoe store], *Tallahassee Democrat*, August 11, 1985, Local/State section, p. 1.

Chapter 67

Tampa

Long before the Spanish arrived in the Tampa Bay area in the 16th century, Indian tribes like the Calusas lived there, taking advantage of the good fishing and rich farmlands. The European exploration began in the early 1500s when Spanish adventurers like Panfilo de Narváez arrived and headed inland to see if they could find any gold or silver. The name of Tampa may come from an Indian phrase meaning "near it" or "split wood for quick fires" or from a Spanish version of an Indian name, "Tanpa." When white settlers began moving into north Florida in the early 19th century, the federal government forcibly moved many Indians and the runaway slaves who had taken refuge with them to south Florida, including reservations around Tampa Bay. In 1821, a band of Creek Indians led by men with ties to General Andrew Jackson burned and plundered a settlement of blacks near Tampa Bay and destroyed what may have been the first black colony on Florida's west coast.

Further Reading:

Canter Brown, Jr., "The 'Sarrazota, or Runaway Negro Plantations': Tampa Bay's First Black Community, 1812-1821," *Tampa Bay History*, vol. 12, no. 2 (fall/winter 1990), pp. 5-19.

Tampa can trace its origins to the establishment of Fort Brooke by federal troops in the early 1820s in preparation for the Seminole Indian War. After the wars with the Indians were over, the town developed into a port for the shipping of cattle, but still depended on slaves for domestics, carpenters, and army scouts. Unlike north Florida, which developed a cotton-growing economy dependent on slaves, Tampa had a more diversified economic base, but slaves still made up one-third of the county's population right before the Civil War and did much to build the settlement.

Tampa went into an economic decline after the Civil War and declined in population to 720 by 1880, although many ex-slaves stayed in the area to farm and homestead the land. A group of them established the community of Bealsville near the Alafia River, while many others moved into a part of Tampa called the Scrub northeast of Oaklawn Cemetery. The blacks often had to take unskilled jobs, a situation that contributed to their poverty. John Williamson opened a black school in 1871, at about the same time that the Ku Klux Klan began operating in the area. Some 20 years later, many blacks joined Cubans and Italians to establish West Tampa, a thriving area that the city of Tampa incorporated in 1925. A few blacks served in political office during this time, despite the harassment of the KKK.

Further Reading:

Leland Hawes, "More on Walker" [about Tampa's first black city council member, Joseph A. Walker, who served in 1887-1888], *The Tampa Tribune,* May 16, 1993, BayLife, p. 4.

Leland Hawes, "One Official's Untold Story" [about Joseph N. Clinton, a black who served almost 15 years as head of the Tampa office of the U.S. Internal Revenue office], *The Tampa Tribune,* February 13, 1994, BayLife, p. 4.

In time, Tampa became a cigar-making center, especially in Ybor City, and a stronghold of the Cuban independence movement. (Ybor City is in downtown Tampa southeast of the intersection of I-4 and I-275.) Those black Cubans who went to Tampa for the cigar-making business felt excluded from other ethnic groups in the city, for example the Spaniards, the Italians, and even the American blacks. Black and white cigarmakers had been part of the same mutual aid society, but Florida law against integrated social clubs made them split in 1900, and so the black Cubans established **La Unión Martí-Maceo**. In 1908, they built a two-story brick building, which lasted until urban renewal demolished it in 1965. Members secured another building at 1226 E. 7th Avenue that was built in 1950 and continued their meetings at the gateway to Ybor City and just east of Nuccio Parkway. The organization did much to promote heritage preservation activities in Ybor City and served black Cubans whom other Cuban and Spanish clubs excluded. Those black Cuban cigarmakers became very involved in early Cuban independence activities in the town, especially with Jose Marti. One of the black Cubans who helped Marti was Paulina Pedroso, who is honored with a plaque at the Jose Marti Park on the corner of 13th Street and 8th Avenue in Ybor City at the site where her boardinghouse stood.

Further Reading:

Susan D. Greenbaum, "Afro-Cubans in Exile: Tampa, Florida, 1886-1984," *Tampa Bay History*, vol. 7, no. 2 (fall/winter 1985), pp. 77-93.

Susan D. Greenbaum. *Afro-Cubans in Ybor City: A Centennial History*. Tampa: Tampa Printing, 1986.

Leland Hawes, "Award Salutes Loyalty to Cuba" [about Paulina Pedroso], *The Tampa Tribune*, December 12, 1993, BayLife 1, 4. Also "Marti park linked to Pedroso," p. 4.

Developer Henry B. Plant brought his railroad to Tampa in the late 1800s and built the beautiful Tampa Bay Hotel, which today houses the University of Tampa. Tampa could also claim one of the first modern films, *The Birth of a Race*, which was filmed in Tampa in 1917-1918 and which was produced after the racist 1915 film, *The Birth of a Nation*, praised the Ku Klux Klan. Among the important blacks who did much to help other blacks in the city was Christina

Meacham (1865-1927), who taught for 40 years and became the first black woman principal of a Tampa school; the **Meacham Early Childhood Center** at 1225 India Street honors this woman, who was the daughter-in-law of Robert Meacham, post-Reconstruction black leader in Florida. (For more about Robert Meacham see Punta Gorda above.)

Further Reading:

Maxine D. Jones and Kevin M. McCarthy. *African Americans in Florida*. Sarasota: Pineapple Press, 1993, pp. 37-38.

Segregation became a way of life for Tampa blacks in this century. Even when they became sick, they had to go to segregated facilities, for example the Clara Frye Hospital, which was named after a black nurse who had begun taking in black patients to her home in Tampa Heights in the early 1900s and who ran the private 17-bed facility for 20 years. After her death, the municipally operated Clara Frye Memorial Hospital opened in West Tampa in 1938 and served thousands of blacks until the formerly all-white hospitals began treating them after the Civil Rights Act of 1964 outlawed segregation. That hospital, which was located where Tampa Presbyterian Village is today (721 West Green Street), shut down in 1967 and was demolished in 1973. In 1991, Tampa General Hospital renamed a nine-floor patient-care wing the **Clara Frye Pavilion** in honor of this great woman.

Further Reading:

Leland Hawes, "Hospital for Blacks Suffered from Neglect" and "Black Hospital Began in Nurse's Home," *The Tampa Tribune*, February 26, 1989, 6-I+.

Maxine D. Jones and Kevin M. McCarthy. *African Americans in Florida*. Sarasota: Pineapple Press, 1993, pp. 70-71.

Black soldiers stationed at Tampa's MacDill Field at the beginning of World War II found that segregation kept the races apart in the city, as it did throughout the Armed Forces at that time. Officials actually worked up a contingency plan to establish martial law in Tampa in case racial violence occurred.

Further Reading:

Leland Hawes, "Secret Plan Included Martial Law," *The Tampa Tribune,* February 27, 1994, BayLife, p. 1, 4. Also "Tampa Had Share of Clashes" [about racial flare-ups in World War II], p. 4.

What helped many blacks endure segregation was the religious faith they had and the churches established to help them. For example, **St. Paul African Methodist Episcopal Church** at 506 East Harrison Street, built between 1906 and 1917, has been important as a religious site and also a leader in the fight to integrate the city. The church traces its history back to 1870, when Rev. T.W. Long walked from Brooksville, Florida, to Tampa to establish a mission. On the first night of his arrival in Tampa, Rev. Long began preaching and received his first three members. The next day Rev. Long and his new members began building a mission, called Brush Arbor Mission, out of palmetto thatch leaves. When Rev. Long went on to south Florida to establish more missions, Rev. Thompson stayed behind to work in Tampa. When the cold of winter set in, a Mr. Jones offered the use of an old log house between Franklin Street and Florida Avenue for services.

After a yellow fever epidemic of the 1890s forced the closing of this building, members bought a lot on Marion Street between Harrison and Fortune streets and there built a church, called Mount Moriah. Storms destroyed that building and another one that replaced it, but members built a new church, called St. Paul A.M.E. In 1917, the 300-member congregation completed the building of the present Gothic Revival structure at 506 East Harrison Street. As the largest black-owned building and located on a major street and close to downtown, the church was a good meeting place for different black organizations, especially during the civil rights movement of the 1950s and 1960s. The Rev. Martin Luther King, Jr., preached there and took part in the civil rights demonstrations. Thurgood Marshall, the general counsel for the NAACP, also attended meetings there in which strategies were planned for gaining equity for black school teachers.

Further Reading:

Rev. Charles Sumner Long. *History of The A.M.E. Church in Florida.* Philadelphia: A.M.E. Book Concern, 1939, p. 77.

Another church with a long history is **Greater Bethel Missionary Baptist** at 1206 Jefferson Street North. Its stately brick building, built in 1949, towers over a walled-in cemetery. The church can trace its origins back to 1893, when its few members pitched a tent near the present building and called the church Ebenezer Missionary Baptist, to be changed later to Bethel Baptist and later Greater Bethel Missionary Baptist.

Further Reading:

Karen Haymon Long, "Black Baptist Church Celebrates 100-Year Anniversary," *The Tampa Tribune*, November 21, 1993, pp. 1-2.

St. Peter Claver School at 1401 Governor Street had its beginnings in 1883, when Wm. Tyrell, S.J., pastor of Tampa's St. Louis Catholic Church, bought the Methodist church on Morgan Street to establish a school for black children. He had workers make necessary changes, and then in 1894 two sisters of the Holy Names began classes for 16 children. Less than two weeks later, arsonists burned the school down, but Father Tyrell bought property on the corner of Governor and Scott streets and had classes resume in October of that year. By the end of the school year 80 students were attending classes. The school was so good that just seven years after its founding the first of its many graduates passed the teacher's examination and was certified by the Board of Public Instruction.

When students outgrew the old wooden building, benefactors like Mrs. Morell financed a new brick building in 1929. An annex was built in 1952, but the school eliminated the seventh and eighth grades in 1970 because a nearby Catholic school had expanded its junior high program enough to take in St. Peter Claver's junior high students. St. Peter Claver is the oldest parish school in the Diocese of St. Petersburg and the oldest black school, private or public, still operating in Hillsborough County.

Further Reading:

Leland Hawes, "Scenes From a Family Album" [about one of the school's teachers, Rowena Brady, and her forthcoming book about Tampa's blacks], *The Tampa Tribune,* March 6, 1994, BayLife, p. 4

Tampa's oldest black high school, **Middleton High School** at 4302 North 24th Street, was turned into a middle school during desegregation. Among its graduates were Hillsborough County Commissioner Sylvia Kimbell and State Representative James Hargrett. A 1940 graduate of the school, Robert W. Saunders, became field secretary for the Florida NAACP in 1952 after the murder of Harry T. Moore (see Mims above) and served during the crucial years of the civil rights movement from 1952 until 1966. His wife, Helen Saunders, became president of the Tampa Branch of the NAACP in 1976 and launched a voter registration drive that was called the most effective in the nation.

In 1946, Robert Saunders worked for the city's weekly black newspaper, the *Florida Sentinel,* the oldest black paper continuously published in the state. It had been established as the *Gainesville Sentinel* by Matthew Lewey in 1887, had its name changed to the *Florida Sentinel* when he moved to Pensacola in 1894, moved to Jacksonville in 1914, and was sold to W.W. Andrews in 1919. The Andrews family still publishes it in Tampa today as *The Sentinel-Bulletin.*

Further Reading:

David L. Chapman, "Documenting the Struggle for Civil Rights: The Papers of Robert and Helen Saunders," *Tampa Bay History*, vol. 9, no. 2 (fall/winter 1987), pp. 47-54.

Mary Ellen Murphy, "School's Alumni Hope to Resurrect Their Alma Mater," *The Tampa Tribune*, September 19, 1991, p. 1+.

For the first three decades of this century, Tampa had the dubious distinction of leading the state in lynchings. In the 1930s, conditions for blacks had improved a little, but local whites still lynched a black man, Robert Johnson, for supposedly having robbed and raped a white woman; despite having been exonerated by the police, he was still kidnapped by white vigilantes and killed.

Further Reading:

Walter Howard, "'A Blot on Tampa's History': The 1934 Lynching of Robert Johnson," *Tampa Bay History*, vol. 6, no. 2 (fall/winter 1984), pp. 5-18.

Robert P. Ingalls. *Urban Vigilantes in the New South: Tampa, 1882-1936*. Knoxville: University of Tennessee Press, 1988.

In the 1950s, tensions arose as blacks tried to desegregate restaurants and public facilities. In 1959, Mayor Julian Lane formed Tampa's Biracial Committee, the state's first such committee, consisting of blacks such as Tampa resident and president of the Florida NAACP Reverend A. Leon Lowry, pastor of Beulah Baptist Church, and Perry Harvey, Sr., the president of the International Longshoreman's Union, which employed many blacks. White leaders joining them included attorney Cody Fowler and port developer Robert Thomas. Another important black leader was C. Bythe Andrews, publisher of *The Sentinel-Bulletin*, the city's black newspaper. The following year saw a sit-in at Woolworth's by Clarence Fort and some 60 students. After seven months of negotiation, local stores agreed to eliminate their "white only" eating policy and officials agreed to desegregate movie theaters and municipal facilities.

The city's tranquility was broken in 1967 when a police

officer shot a robbery suspect, an action that triggered a race riot which destroyed much of the Central Avenue black business area. Twenty years later another race riot erupted in College Hill, one of the city's poorest housing projects, when the police killed a black man with a choke-hold. However, in 1983, Tampans elected their first black state legislator and their first black city councilman. In 1992, developers proposed a pirate museum for the city, but many blacks were angry that the museum would center around the *Whydah*, a former slave ship; the Coalition of African-American Organizations (CAAO) opposed the project, and it died. Today, Tampa, which has 69,871 blacks (25%) out of a total population of 280,015, has an ongoing dialogue between whites and blacks that has done much in the last 20 years to defuse tensions that might have erupted into open hostility.

Finally, the **Museum of African American Art** at 1308 Marion Street houses the Barnett/Aden Collection of African-American art which depicts the history, culture, and lifestyle of American blacks. With one piece dating back to 1851, this is the oldest such collection of African-American art in the United States. Open 10 a.m.-4:30 p.m., Tuesday-Saturday; 1 p.m.-4:30 p.m., Sundays (except holidays); phone: (813) 229-8074.

Further Reading:

Otis R. Anthony. *Black Tampa*. Tampa: City of Tampa Publications Dept., 1989.

Michael Bane and Mary Ellen Moore. *Tampa, Yesterday, Today & Tomorrow*. Tampa: Mishler and King, 1981.

"Civil Rights Protests in Tampa: Oral Memoirs of Conflict and Accommodation." *Tampa Bay History*, vol. 1, no. 1 (spring/summer 1979), pp. 37-54.

Hampton Dunn. *Yesterday's Tampa*. Miami: Seemann, 1972.

Barbara Fitzgerald and Tracie Reddick, "The Illusion of Inclusion," *The Tampa Tribune*, May 9, 1993, Nation, p. 1+; May 10, 1993, Nation, p. 1+.

Leland Hawes, "Tampa Had Share of Clashes," *The Tampa Tribune*, February 27, 1994, BayLife, p. 4.

Elizabeth Jacoway and David R. Colburn, editors. *Southern Businessmen*

The Museum of African American Art houses one of the country's finest collections of African American art. Credit: Kevin M. McCarthy

and Desegregation. Baton Rouge: Louisiana State University Press, 1982, pp. 257-281: Steven F. Lawson, "From Sit-in to Race Riot."

Benjamin E. Mays. *Born to Rebel*. Athens: University of Georgia Press, 1971. This is the autobiography of a man who went to Tampa in 1926 to become executive secretary of the Urban League.

Gary R. Mormino and Anthony P. Pizzo. *Tampa, The Treasure City*. Tulsa, Okla.: Continental Heritage Press, 1983.

Anthony P. Pizzo. *Tampa Town, 1824-1886: The Cracker Village With a Latin Accent*. Miami: Hurricane House Publishers, 1968.

Robert Snyder and Jack B. Moore. *Pioneer Commercial Photography: The Burgert Brothers, Tampa, Florida*. Gainesville: University Press of Florida, 1992.

A Study of Negro Life in Tampa. Tampa: no publ., 1927. This is also known as *The Raper Report*.

Chapter 68

Titusville

This area began attracting white settlers when, in 1843, a captain in the Seminole Indian wars, Douglas Dummitt, received a permit to settle on Merritt Island. He began growing citrus and did so well that many more settlers arrived to take advantage of the good soil and climate. In 1845, Florida entered the Union as a slave state and continued depending on slaves to grow the many crops that its white plantation owners grew rich on. Two years after the Civil War ended in 1865, Colonel Henry Titus arrived in the area and soon built the first hotel in the town he founded: Titusville.

The next year saw the arrival of the first black settler, Joe Warren, and by 1880, the census listed 13 blacks. In 1882, workers built the town's first jail at a cost of $500; a black resident, Andrew J. Gibson, was the first jailer and cooked the prisoners' meals in his own kitchen. Gibson was also a barber, restaurant owner, and supervisor of the only public road in Brevard County. In 1885, the Jacksonville, Tampa, and Key West Railroad reached Titusville and brought in many more settlers.

Andrew Gibson and L. Ufollow started the first black church in the town in a little 12-by-12 shack owned by Gibson. When the congregation outgrew that building, they moved into a larger one owned by Tom Smith. Later Mrs. M.E. Titus gave them a larger lot and named as trustees William Gibson, Isaiah Gory, and L. Ufollow. Other early blacks included Haywood Boumny; Ellis Cobbs; Bettie Edmonson; Ella Foster; Myrtle Gibson, the wife of Andrew; Noel Gibson; Will Gibson; William Harris; Henry Maxwell, who had been sold as a slave in 1862 and arrived in Titusville in 1880; Betsy Thomas; George Warren, who owned a restaurant; and Dick Wright, who carried the mail between Titusville and Eau Gallie. In the early part of the 20th century, segregation forced the blacks to live apart and work in menial jobs like gardening, vegetable picking, fish packing, construction, and cleaning houses.

Further Reading:

Elaine Murray Stone. *Brevard County*. Northridge, Cal.: Windsor Publications, 1988.

The first black students to attend school there, six first-graders, were taught by a white woman, Miss Annie McGraph, on Washington Avenue. In 1886, the school was moved to South Street and Dummitt Avenue and remained there until 1915. One large room contained all six elementary grades. The school then moved to Wager Avenue and had grades 1-8; the school building had formerly been the white high school before it moved to Wager Avenue in 1915. By 1935, the school had nine grades. The **Titusville Negro School** added the tenth grade in 1936, the eleventh grade in 1937, and the twelfth grade in 1938. By 1936, the first students were being transported to the junior high school from Mims and LaGrange. Before the high school was established, north Brevard County black students wishing to pursue their education, like black students throughout the South, often had to board away from their homes or live with friends or relatives in distant towns that had a high school, for example Ocala's Fessenden Academy or Jacksonville's Boylan-Haven School.

The bust of Harry Moore outside the Social Services Center honors the Civil Rights leader who was killed in nearby Mims. Credit: Kevin M. McCarthy

Harry T. Moore was the principal of the Titusville school from 1934 to 1936 and is honored with the **Harry T. Moore Social Services Center** at 725 DeLeon Street, which is one block south of South Street; the center has a small bust outside the building that honors this civil rights leader who was killed by a bomb in his Mims home in 1951. (See Mims above.) Other principals of the school were Mr. T.W. Everette, who served from 1939 to 1940, Clarence W. "Snow" Harris (1940-1943), Rev. Jones, Samuel C. Nixon, Jr., Eddie Leon Thomas (1945-1955), and Daniel W. Delagall (1955-1957), who was principal when the school—known as the Wager Street Negro School—closed in 1956. In the early years, the faculty consisted of just one person, later two. As more and more teachers were added, the administrator was one of them and simply had the extra duties of making whatever reports were necessary. Among the many dedicated teachers of the school, affectionately called "The Old Barn," were Catherine Campbell (Bouie), Sadye Gibson, Victoria Gibson (Rogers), Altamese Gilbert, Carrie Gilbert, John Gilbert, Wilhelmenia Gilbert, Prof. Lockett, Bernice McDowell, Samuel Nixon, Victoria Rogers, Mae Simms, Elsie Sloan (Tunsill), Dorena Thomas (one of two who graduated from the high school in 1938), Mr. Turner, Ella Warren, Naomi Wynn (Ford), and Walter Wynn.

Mr. Delagall was the last principal of Titusville Negro School and the first principal of Andrew J. Gibson School. The man after whom the school was named was a pioneer merchant and barber who did much for the education of black students in north Brevard County; his daughter, Victoria Gibson (Rogers), was a long-time teacher in the black school. Although the new Gibson School was segregated, it had better facilities than the previous schools, for example a library, science laboratories, music and home economics suites, an industrial arts shop, and a gymnasium. Principal Delagall was succeeded by James R. Greene (who saw the full accreditation of the school by the Southern Association), Frank E. Williams (who added more departments and activities), Walter Quick, and Willie Turner. In its final year, 1968, Gibson became an elementary school. By then Brevard County had integrated schools. Today Titusville has a black population of 4,124 (11%) of a total population of 39,394.

Further Reading:

Ric Anderson, "'...A fondness for a dear school,'" *The Star-Advocate,* July 25, 1985, p. 1B+.

Titusville Negro School Homecoming Reunion Celebration, edited by Frank E. Williams. Titusville: no publ., 1985.

Verna G. Langlais, compiler. *Cemetery Census of Brevard County, Florida.* Titusville: no publ., 1984. This booklet lists those buried in the black Davis Memorial Cemetery near Queen Street.

Chapter 69

Vernon

This small town south of Bonifay and southwest of Chipley was probably named after Mount Vernon, the home of President George Washington, after whom Vernon's county, Washington, was also named. The town, which has 157 blacks (20%) out of a total population of 778, has an old church of significance to blacks.

Moss Hill United Methodist Church, located about three miles southeast of Vernon, is a plain, unpainted church built by Lamp Powell in 1857. The austere inside of the church has seven rows of pews, a pulpit, and an altar. Nearby is a 1.5-acre cemetery that is contemporary with the church and in use since the mid-19th century. The thick growth of nearby trees, many of them covered with Spanish moss, lends a peaceful setting to the church. The 40-foot-long church on brick piers has two doors, one formerly used by women and girls, the other by men and boys. The weathered church has remained relatively unchanged for the past 125+ years. The church, the oldest unaltered building in Washington County and one that slaves helped build in 1857, has no electricity, plumbing, or heating devises, other than portable units located throughout the church. The structure is one of the nation's best examples of what is known as frontier church

The Moss Hill United Methodist Church is a weathered structure built in a style called frontier church architecture. Credit: Kevin M. McCarthy

architecture. One may be able to see the handprints or fingerprints of the workers in the planks of the building.

Directions:

The church is 3 miles southeast of Vernon on C.R. 279 (Sapp Street). Go south of Vernon on S.R. 79, turn left on C.R. 279, and drive 3 miles to the church on the right-hand side of the road.

Further Reading:

Elba Wilson Carswell. *Holmes Valley: A West Florida Cradle of Christianity.* Bonifay, Fl.: Central Press, 1969.

E.W. Carswell. *Tempestuous Triangle: The History of Washington County, Florida.* Chipley: Washington County School Board, 1974.

E.W. Carswell. *Washington: Florida's Twelfth County.* Chipley: E.W. Carswell, 1991.

Chapter 70

West Palm Beach

Long before the white or black man came to this area, Indians like the Tequestas lived around Lake Worth. Shipwrecked sailors like the Jonathan Dickinson party in the 17th century also passed through here, but only in the 19th century did non-Indians move in to settle. The first blacks there were probably runaway slaves whom the Seminole Indians welcomed into their tribes in the 1830s. Before the Civil War, local settlers most likely had slaves with them, although those slaves may have also joined the Seminole bands when the whites fled to the north to escape the Indian uprisings. During Reconstruction after the Civil War, freed slaves and settlers from the Bahamas moved in, and in the 1890s more black workers came to work on the construction of the railroad and in the pineapple fields. The blacks who worked in the tourism industry, especially those in Henry Flagler's hotels, settled in a part of Palm Beach called the "Styx." West Palm Beach was incorporated as a town in 1894, 15 years before officials created Palm Beach County out of Dade County.

When the Styx, the black area of Palm Beach, burned down at the beginning of this century, the blacks who were living there moved across Lake Worth to West Palm Beach. (See Palm Beach above, for more about the Styx.) Many blacks continued working as domestics in the homes of the wealthy white people of Palm Beach, but the city of West Palm Beach practiced segregation at many levels. The city did not hire its first black policeman until 1948, and it would be another 21 years before black policemen could patrol white neighborhoods. Blacks did not vote until 1947 and did not have their first black clerk typist until 1963. In 1978, Eva Mack and Ruby Bullock were elected to the West Palm Beach city commission, and Mrs. Mack was reelected four years later and became the first black to serve as the mayor of West Palm Beach. Today West Palm Beach has 22,050 blacks (33%) out of a total population of 67,643.

In the mid-1970s, interested individuals formed the Black Preservation Society of Palm Beach County to make people more aware of the accomplishments of blacks in the community. One of the projects of that group was to preserve two buildings on Division Street in West Palm Beach and convert them into museums. The first house, at 615 Division Street, was the **Hazel Augustus Home**, where the first black architect in Palm Beach County lived.

Further Reading:

Amy Huttunen, "Architect's Home Part of Dream," *The Post* [Palm Beach], June 20, 1982, North County edition, p. B1.

The other building to be preserved is the **Gwen Cherry House** next door to the Augustus Home. Gwendolyn Sawyer Cherry (1923-1979) was born in Miami, the daughter of the first black doctor in Dade County. After teaching science to black students in Miami for 18 years, she became the first black to attend the University of Miami Law School, although she eventually graduated from FAMU Law School in Tallahassee. After deciding to enter politics, she became the first black woman elected to the Florida state legislature in Tallahassee. As a legislator she concerned herself with the rights of women, children, and minorities, as well as prison reform. In 1971, she introduced the first laws for state-provided child care in Florida, a fact which later influenced officials to name the new Department of Education Child Development Center in Tallahassee after her. The **Gwen Cherry Park** at 2591 N.W. 71st Street in Miami honors this great woman, who died in an automobile accident in Tallahassee in 1979 at the age of 56.

Further Reading:

Maxine D. Jones and Kevin M. McCarthy. *African Americans in Florida.* Sarasota: Pineapple Press, 1993, pp. 120-121.

Another important house in West Palm Beach and one that is on the National Register of Historic Places is the two-story **Mickens House** at 801 Fourth Street on the corner of Division Avenue. Haley Mickens, who helped establish the Payne Chapel A.M.E. Church in West Palm Beach in 1893, met a young Sunday School teacher there, Alice Frederick of Bartow, and later married her. He had the house constructed in 1917 soon after his marriage. Mr. Mickens, who lived in the house until he died in 1950, worked in Palm Beach for Colonel Edward P. Bradley, who owned a gambling casino there called the Beach Club; Mickens was responsible for operating the bicycle-propelled wicker carriages known as Afromobiles that white patrons enjoyed riding around in. The Mickenses never had children of their own, but they raised many children in the house.

Alice Mickens had graduated from Spelman College in Atlanta, Georgia, and continued her education at the College of the City of New York and at A. and T. College of Greensboro, North Carolina, before returning to West Palm Beach. She later went on to found the City Association of West Palm Beach, served as president of the Florida Association of Women's Clubs, founded the Florida Association of Girls Clubs, and served as Chairman of the U.S. Treasury Department of War Bonds. The American Negro Emancipation convention in Chicago in 1963 named her "Outstanding Woman of the Century," and state officials named her an

"Outstanding Floridian" in 1970. Her interest in education, juvenile delinquency, and civic improvements brought her into contact with such leaders as Mary McLeod Bethune, Dr. Ralph Bunche, Dr. Howard Thurman, and Henrine Ward Banks. She used to have local, state, and national educators, both black and white, meet in her house and even stay there when local hotels would not allow blacks to rent rooms. Among the Florida places that honor Dr. Mickens are a cottage at Lowell Correctional Institution (because of her efforts on behalf of girls who had been imprisoned with mature criminals) and the Alice Frederick Mickens Science Lecture Hall at Bethune-Cookman College in Daytona Beach.

Further Reading:

Julie Eagle, "Alice's Place," *News/Sun-Sentinel*, Sept. 16, 1984, p. 1B+.

Tabernacle Missionary Baptist Church, formerly called Mt. Olive Baptist Church, was founded by 18 members in the Styx in 1893 under the guidance of Rev. W.B. Mills. This building housed the first school for blacks in Palm Beach County. The 74 students who attended the school in 1984 necessitated that the superintendent have two school terms of four months each.

Another important educational institution in West Palm Beach was **Roosevelt Junior College**, one of 12 black junior colleges in Florida (see St. Petersburg above). Established in 1958, this college had Mr. Britton G. Sayles, the principal of Roosevelt High School, as its first and only president. When the Palm Beach County School Board announced in September 1957 that it planned to open the black junior college, despite the 1954 U.S. Supreme Court decision that outlawed separate educational facilities, local black activists strenuously protested and called the college's black advisory board members traitors who had given in to the segregationists. The activists asked Governor LeRoy Collins to use the money, not for a black college, but for efforts to desegregate

Palm Beach Junior College. The governor refused and pointed to Gibbs Junior College in St. Petersburg and Washington Junior College in Pensacola as good examples of how such schools can help black students.

Roosevelt Junior College opened, and students began attending classes in the late afternoons and evenings in the Roosevelt High School building until workers could finish a new building for the college at 1235 15th Street in West Palm Beach. The enrollment figures for Roosevelt show that it served many students:

1958-1959: 110 students
1959-1960: 208 students
1960-1961: 230 students
1961-1962: 283 students
1962-1963: 249 students
1963-1964: 245 students
1964-1965: 218 students

In the mid-1960s, black students picketed the all-white Palm Beach Junior College for admission, and the school board agreed to integrate the school and close down Roosevelt. After the 1964-65 academic year, the school merged with Palm Beach Junior College. One of the six black teachers there out of a total of 18 at the black junior college who went on to teach at Palm Beach Junior College was Daniel Hendrix, who in 1970 became the first black member of the county school board, the first black to be elected to a county office, and the only one for many years.

Further Reading:

Donald W. Curl. *Palm Beach County: An Illustrated History*. Northridge, Cal.: Windsor Publications, Inc., 1986.

"Junior College Integrated By Negro Girl's Enrolling," *The Palm Beach Post*, September 12, 1961, pp. 1, 5.

James R. Knott. *Palm Beach Revisited: Historical Vignettes of Palm Beach County*. Palm Beach: J.R. Knott, 1987.

Stuart McIver. *Yesterday's Palm Beach, Including Palm Beach County*. Miami: Seemann, 1976.

James McJunkins and Brenda Lane, "Up From the Styx—the black experience." *The Palm Beach Post-Times*, September 9, 1973, C1+. Continued September 10, 1973, p. A7+; September 11, 1973, p. A7+; September 12, 1973, p. B1+; September 13, 1973, p. B1+; September 14, 1973, p. B1+; September 15, 1973, p. A4+.

West Palm Beach

Dan Moffett, "Charred History: Styx' Burning Was the End of Palm Beach's Black Community," *The Post* [Palm Beach], June 13, 1982, p. B1, 3.

Vivian Reissland Rouson-Gossett, editor. *Like a Mighty Banyan: Contributions of Black People to the History of Palm Beach County*. Palm Beach County: Palm Beach Junior College, 1982.

Wilma Bell Spencer. *Palm Beach: A Century of Heritage*. Washington, D.C.: Mount Vernon Publishing Co., 1975.

Index

Index

HIPPOCRENE TRAVEL BOOKS

ETHNIC TRAVEL SERIES

IRISH AMERICA
Russ Malone
Over 40 million Americans claim Irish roots—That's one in five of us! In the spirit of traditional Irish good humor, Russ Malone creates an outstanding guide that will aid Irish American travelers in need of a glimpse of their heritage or a new favorite pub anywhere across the United States.
250 pages ISBN 0-7818-0172-9 $14.95

BLACK AMERICA
Marcella Thum
"A useful acquisition for all travel collections."—*Library Journal*
"An admirable guide."—*Choice Magazine*

Organized by state, this fully indexed guide describes more than 700 historic homes, art and history museums, parks, monuments, landmarks of the civil rights movement, battlefields, colleges and churches across the U.S., all open to the public.
325 pages ISBN 0-87052-045-8 $11.95

BLACK WASHINGTON
Sandra Fitzpatrick and Maria Goodwin
"The authors provide a much-needed corrective and show how black Washingtonians affected not only this city but the nation and indeed, the world."—*The Washington Post Book World*

Explore over 200 sites in our nation's capital, central to the African-American experience. Gain insight into the heritage that had a profound impact on African-American culture and American society at large, including information about such pivotal figures as Frederick Douglas, Ralph Bunche, Anna J. Cooper, Duke Ellington, and Senator Edward Brooke. From Capitol Hill to Shaw to Lafayette Square to Georgetown, the authors systematically cover the entire city.
288 pages ISBN 0-87052-832-7 $14.95

HISTORIC BLACK SOUTH
Joann Biondi and James Haskins
"The book provides some wonderful reading and inspires tourists to go and explore a part of the south that has not been emphasized in travel." *—Library Journal*

This unique guide describes over 1,000 sites which pay tribute to the significant and often overlooked contribution of the southern African-American community. Read about, then visit, churches, art galleries and jazz clubs, beaches and barbershops, as this guide opens doors to a new appreciation of the historic Black South for all. Includes a description of attractions open to the public, listing hours, fees, directions, and phone numbers.
300 pages ISBN 0-7818-0140-0 $14.95

HISTORIC HISPANIC AMERICA
Oscar and Joy Jones
"This is an unusual guide that any serious traveler to the southwest would find informative."*—Library Journal*

This guide focuses on uncovering the living heritage in the southwestern U.S. for historians and travelers alike. Both Spanish and Indian presence is still felt in the language, religion, customs, and attitudes that reflect a deep respect for a passionate heritage in the United States. Landmarks and historic sites are listed with hours of operation and directions.
300 pages ISBN 0-7818-0141-9 $14.95

(All prices subject to change.)

TO PURCHASE HIPPOCRENE BOOKS contact your local bookstore, or write to: HIPPOCRENE BOOKS, 171 Madison Avenue, New York, NY 10016. Please enclose check or money order, adding $4.00 shipping (UPS) for the first book and $.50 for each additional book.

U.S.A. TRAVEL

MIDWESTERN TRAVEL

AMERICA'S HEARTLAND: A Travel Guide to the Backroads of Illinois, Indiana, Iowa, Kansas and Missouri, *2nd Edition*, by Tom Weil
$14.95 • 528 pages • maps • 0-7818-0044-7

CHICAGOLAND & BEYOND, by Gerald and Patricia Gutek
$14.95 • 288 pages • maps, b/w photos • 0-87052-036-9

SOUTHERN TRAVEL

AMERICA'S SOUTH: The Atlantic States, by Tom Weil
Includes Florida, Georgia, North and South Carolina, and Virginia
$14.95 • 400 pages • maps and photos • 0-7818-0139-7

AMERICA'S SOUTH: The Mississippi and Gulf States, by Tom Weil
The companion which completes award winning author Tom Weil's tour of the entire South includes Mississippi, Louisiana, Kentucky, Arkansas, Tennessee and Alabama.
$14.95 • 400 pages • maps and photos • 0-7818-0171-0

WESTERN TRAVEL

THE ROCKY MOUNTAIN STATES, by Henry Weisser
$14.95 • 366 pages • b/wphotos • 0-7818-0043-9

THE SOUTHWEST: A Family Adventure, by Tish Minear and Janet Limon
$16.95 • 440 pages • b/w photos, illust. • 0-87052-640-5

(Prices subject to change.)

TO PURCHASE HIPPOCRENE BOOKS, contact your local bookstore, or write to: HIPPOCRENE BOOKS, 171 Madison Avenue, New York, NY 10016. Please enclose check or money order, adding $4.00 shipping (UPS) for the first book and .50 for each additional book.

Hippocrene U.S.A. Guide to Black New York

Joann Biondi and James Haskins

Covering sites scattered over the five boroughs of New York, the ***Guide to Black New York*** directs the reader to famous and infamous legends, jazz joints, soul food diners, media—radio and newspapers. It leads you to the museums, historic sites and festivals that honor the past and present work of African-Americans who have contributed their minds, their labor, their music, and their art to make the city what it is today.

From the pre-Revolutionary War period to the Civil War to the Civil Rights Movement to the monumental election of Mayor David Dinkins as the first black mayor of the city, this guide highlights sights and sounds of a culture that has been long overlooked in history.

Jim Haskins is professor of English at the University of Florida in Gainesville. He is the author of over 80 books about black culture in America including *The Psychology of Black Language* with Hugh Butts and *The Cotton Club.* He lives in Florida and New York City. **Joann Biondi** is a freelance writer and the author of five travel books. Her articles have appeared in the New York *Times* and numerous national travel magazines. She lives in Miami where she teaches tourism and geography at Miami-Dade Community College. Both authors have also co-written the *Hippocrene U.S.A. Guide to the Historic Black South.*

250 pages 5 1/2 x 8 1/2 $14.95paper ISBN 0-7818-0172-9